Becky Wicks was born in 1979 in England and has since lived and worked in New York, Dubai, Bali and Sydney. She's the author of *Burqalicious: The Dubai Diaries*, a true account of the madness in the Middle East, and *Balilicious: The Bali Diaries*. Becky is currently working on *Latinalicious: The South American Diaries* between learning the tango and testing various bottles of Malbec for research purposes.

Subscribe to Becky Wicks on Facebook,
bex_wicks on Twitter and get the latest news at
www.beckywicks.com

Balilicious

THE BALI DIARIES

A true story of magic, mystery
and not quite mastering yoga

Becky Wicks

HarperCollins*Publishers*

HarperCollins*Publishers*

First published in Australia in 2012
by HarperCollins*Publishers* Australia Pty Limited
ABN 36 009 913 517
harpercollins.com.au

Copyright © Rebecca Wicks 2012

The right of Rebecca Wicks to be identified as the author of this
work has been asserted by her under the *Copyright Amendment
(Moral Rights) Act 2000.*

HarperCollins*Publishers*
Level 13, 201 Elizabeth Street, Sydney NSW 2000, Australia
31 View Road, Glenfield, Auckland 0627, New Zealand
A 53, Sector 57, Noida, UP, India
77–85 Fulham Palace Road, London W6 8JB, United Kingdom
2 Bloor Street East, 20th floor, Toronto, Ontario M4W 1A8, Canada
10 East 53rd Street, New York NY 10022, USA

National Library of Australia Cataloguing-in-Publication entry

Wicks, Rebecca.
  Balilicious : the Bali diaries / Becky Wicks.
  ISBN: 978 0 7322 9515 8 (pbk.)
  Wicks, Rebecca – Anecdotes.
  Women travelers – Indonesia – Bali (Province) – Diaries.
  Bali (Indonesia : Province) – Description and travel.
910.4

Photographs courtesy of Rebecca Wicks
Cover and internal design by Natalie Winter
Typeset in 11.5/17pt Minion by Kirby Jones
Printed and bound in Australia by Griffin Press
The papers used by HarperCollins in the manufacture of this book are a natural, recyclable
product made from wood grown in sustainable plantation forests. The fibre source and
manufacturing processes meet recognised international environmental standards, and carry
certification.

5 4 3 2 1   12 13 14 15

For Ubud,
and everyone who stepped into
my world on this journey.

'Out in the Dutch East Indies, a week east of Singapore, a night east of Java, and just south of the equator lies the little island of Bali.'

— Hickman Powell, 1930

'Out in Indonesia, two-and-a-half hours east of Singapore on AirAsia, six hours and 25 minutes from Sydney on JetStar, lies the largest tourist destination in the country. Bali.'

— Becky Wicks, 2012

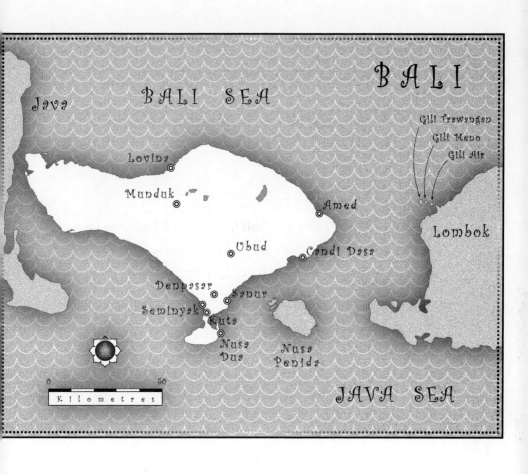

A little note ...

Six months in Bali doesn't sound like a long time in which to write a book, but I guess when you plant yourself in one of the most mystical islands on Earth you never know what might pop up! I never dreamed I'd be shaking on an ashram, lugging guitars and books up a mountain, hanging with the Bali Nine, hunting witches, diving shipwrecks, watching teens be possessed by wild animals, getting my unmentionables steamed in an ancient pre-wedding ritual ... let alone appreciating a linen-filled wardrobe.

Obviously there are a million more things still left to explore and uncover. Bali is a complex island of luscious layers and I've only skimmed the surface. But what follows is a taste of an experience that will stay with me all my life.

As well as talking to hundreds of people, I've also spent many hours in the Ubud Pondok Pekak library (libraries still exist!) and our global library, Google, so all cultural facts have been checked and are correct to the very best of my knowledge. Sorry for any errors!

There are too many people to thank, as Bali's unquestionable magic has worked on many occasions to bring the most helpful, insightful, knowledgable and bloody brilliant people into my path throughout the writing of this book. But I'll start with my friends: Bob Supernant, Paul Barker, Jen Baxter, Susan Berg, Trevor, Cat Wheeler/Ibu Kat, Wayan (Number 9), Putu, Sumeena and Sandesh Gupta, Elizabeth Henzell, Chara Love, Joanna Witt, Budhi, Siddhartha Hewison, Made Surya and Bar Luna. And yes, you can be friends with a bar (thanks for the coconut killers).

Thanks also to Margaret Gee, Jeanne Ryckmans and to my friends from afar who either came to experience part of this journey with me or have supported me from their various corners: Mum, Dad, Tracy, Dacey, Gaby, Pip, Russ and River.

And thanks of course and with all my heart to Bali, for the magic.

I hope you like my story.

Becky x

Coming unstuck...

I just had a cry. I feel so silly because it was one of those 'huff-n-puff, stand in the middle of the room, put your head in your hands and let it all out' kind of breakdowns, which are always embarrassing. I embarrassed myself and I was the only one who witnessed it. I still made it to the mirror though.

Sometimes when I cry I like to look in the mirror because I don't really cry all that often and I like to see what I look like when I do. Is that weird? I think it might be weird ... but in a way I like to remember life's mini tragedies as turning points, visible only in the private tears on my face and the spit on my lips, rivers of mascara landing on a quivering chin. I think it's the real me, somehow; the bare bones of me, the part I never show. It's like reminding myself who I am.

Anyway, I have a good reason to be a bit emotional I suppose. I'm back in Ubud, finally, after three full months of travelling. It's the end of the line but it's also the beginning of something I can't describe because obviously it hasn't happened yet — and this is scary.

What I was thinking prior to the breakdown, as I folded yet another measly Cambodian T-shirt into my new drawer, was how I feel as if I'm standing on the threshold of the rest of my life. It's a turning point that most people would embrace, but everyone I guess would look at it differently. I'm thirty-one years old. I should probably be scouring another big city, looking to join the masses of people I know updating their Facebook profiles every day with new prams and scans and excited plans to extend their bubbly little families. But I've sort of run away from all that.

As I wheeled my trusty Winnie-the-Pooh suitcase out of sight — a ceremonious occasion after him being a part of my life for so long — I also thought how everyone can say the same thing about standing on a threshold, at every single minute of every single day.

'Oh look at me, I'm on a threshold, oh tell me do, which way should I turn?'

'What do you mean?'

'A THRESHOLD, can't you see it? I'm so lost.'

'Er, you're really not. You're standing on the floor in your bedroom.'

'But it's a *threshold* to the rest of my life. I just don't know which way to ...'

'Look. You're quite near a spa. How about you think about it tomorrow and go for a nice massage?'

It's how you deal with these threshold situations, I suppose, that determines how you live your life. Me, I've been working hard for years to hone my skills in avoidance and denial. I'm never stuck and rarely do I come unstuck. Like so many people today, I'm quite good at conveniently forgetting what it is I'm supposed to be doing and doing instead what I like. This is probably why

I've wound up here in Bali, doing a Liz Gilbert. Not to find myself *per se*, but to lose myself all over again in something else.

I told my friend Gaby last month of my plans to move here and explore as we drank from coconuts on the streets of Bangkok.

'Bali?' she said, frowning. 'If you start smelling of hemp or saying *namasté* I'm going to smack your face.'

Gaby is a fellow traveller from England. We met when we lived in Dubai and neither of us have lived in the UK ever since. I have to say I'm a bit scared of going home. I mean, just last week there were riots; people were stealing shoes from shops and running down the streets with 42-inch televisions that didn't belong to them, setting fire to dustbins along the way. Watching the news was like watching the apocalypse from afar. I see it all as a sign that I shouldn't go home. I bought so many cheap synthetic clothes while travelling I wouldn't be flameproof enough to live there anyway these days.

Back to the crying. I might as well own up now that this sudden burst of emotion is because of a man. Of course it is. Feel free to sigh, and go on then, roll your eyes:

'Weren't you just saying how you never come unstuck?'

Well, yes I was. And trust me, I feel like an idiot admitting this because I've only really known CK for three days (I know, I know), but it feels like I've been waiting ages to feel with someone what I felt with him on that beach, on my very first day in Bali.

I guess in spite of all this denial, jumping from threshold to threshold like a character in a bad Nintendo game with no real meaning, laughing in the face of prams and scans, lugging my life around in a Disney suitcase, secretly I *have* been hoping that pretty soon I'll find the thing that'll make me want to stop moving.

I knew I'd be living in Bali for a while ... six months if all goes to plan, so when I got CK's invitation (I'll call him CK as he wears sexy glasses like Clark Kent) to join him and a friend at Balangan Beach before heading to Ubud, I thought it would be a great excuse to see another part of the island. It didn't seem to matter that I'd only met him once before, in Sydney. CK is a very nice man.

Balangan Beach is not like Nusa Dua or Kuta, where vast hotel developments cling to the lip of the ocean like ugly ulcers. So far, development is pretty slow and unobtrusive here and it's relatively untouched by tourism. There are just a few damp beach shacks to host overnight visitors. It's a bit too rough and rocky to swim much, but the way the waves rise and crash like giant galloping horses against spectacular sunsets is reason enough to stick around … oh, and the surfers of course.

Anyway, there it was that the coming unstuck-ness started. Oh, the clichéd talks about dreams, global treks and ambitions, the holding hands across sun-lounges, the fevered kisses overlooked by lizards in a thin, rickety cabin. The falling was fast on my part and the conversation flowed to the point of tears over an ex who broke him into pieces. Ugh.

In the space of just three days, I went from thinking, 'Woah, this could be it!' to 'Oh shit! This so is not it.'

I can't fix him, obviously, but now I've let him get to me. The thought of him is buzzing around my every move like an obnoxious mosquito, stinging me as I try to do the simplest things … brush my hair, clean my teeth, hang my cheap, flimsy selection of Thai sundresses in the wardrobe. I see him everywhere, but even when our heads were side by side on the same mouldy pillow I couldn't really reach him. There's only one thing for it, I think; to play Adele's *Someone Like You* on repeat and have another cry.

Oh, mirror mirror on the Bali wall, is this place as magical as they say it is? If I can't fix him, maybe you can fix me? I am currently a pathetic person. All I want is to taste his sweat again in that filthy beach shack; to merge his beautiful, tortured soul with mine. All I want is to know him, really … and maybe watch another apricot sunset with his hands in my sandy hair. I never even got to know him. If only we'd had a few more days. If only he wasn't so sad. If only.

What a woebegone beginning to my new life in Bali, I hear you cry. How terribly awful. Well, yeah, but I'm sure it won't all be like this. At least I hope not … I hate being a misery-guts. I just miss what we never had.

From where I'm now writing I can smell the frangipani flowers sprinkled on my brand new bed and a pristine coat of paint on the spotless walls of a very nice villa I'm sharing with a lady called Diana from Copenhagen. Who knows how long I'll be here, or what's in store, but Adele is singing reassuringly about the future. *Never mind, I'll find someone like you …*

I read a poem once that I'll always remember. The basic gist of it is that you have to learn that kisses aren't contracts and presents aren't promises. You have to accept defeat with your head up and your eyes open with the grace of an adult, not the grief of a child. It says you should plant your own garden and decorate your own soul instead of waiting for someone else to bring you flowers. I used to love this poem.

I've been planting my own garden for a long time now, so to speak, and I know what I can do on my own. I can blaze across the greatest thresholds, do astounding things all by myself with no-one else to hold my hand. I can move to Bali! It's taken me a long, long time to grow this strong and there's no way on Earth I should be unravelling now, *especially* not over a man I've only just met.

The thing is, though … hmm … perhaps I'm being overly emotional, but yes, I think I do want someone else these days, to blaze all these thresholds along with me. And if it's not CK who busts the door down, grabs my hand and says:

'OK, you know what you said about merging my beautiful, tortured soul with yours? Wanna start now?' then it has to be someone else. Someone who makes me feel like that. *Someone Like Him.*

And it's with this knowledge that I now unpack my few worldly belongings in a place where hardly anyone knows or cares who the hell I am.

No-one but the mirror, at least.

03/09

Eat, Pray, LIES ...

With hopes of getting a certain man out of my head and perhaps enjoying a surprise encounter with my very own Javier Bardem or Billy Crudup (who I'd bump into quite unexpectedly on the street in a flattering ray of afternoon Bali sunlight), I set off in search of something new this morning, starting with an all-important touristy trip to the Monkey Forest. *Lonely Planet* said it was essential I see it and you don't argue with the greats.

In the movie *Eat, Pray, Love*, Julia Roberts is shown cycling through a leafy jungle, smiling as the furry little monkeys sit quietly on the sidelines, looking cute. It's a very short scene but you can see she is clearly having a lovely time. I hate to be the one to break the news but now that I've done it, I know for sure that Hollywood has lied to us.

I was probably only in the forest for about ten minutes before a baby monkey had jumped on my shoulders and tried to steal my ponytail. Its mother danced on the perimetres, shrieking like it was *me* jumping all over *her* family and before long I had about nine of them circling me, baring their teeth in a way that I'm still not sure was supposed to exhibit excitement or seething hatred. Monkeys are weird.

Perhaps it was because it was quite early and there weren't too many other people about that they all focused on me, but either way there was no quiet sitting and observing in my own 'Eat, Pray, Love-the-monkeys' experience. And they were loving each other, too, I should add. There was humping happening all over the jungle, plenty of frolicking and even the odd bit of swinging. I definitely saw a few amorous threesomes about to begin in the trees, but when it came to me, well, to be frank, they were quite disrespectful.

Maybe I should have taken them some fruit, but a little man outside had warned me not to. And if they were so enthralled with my hairstyle that they were scrambling onto my very person to touch it, I can't imagine what they would have done for a banana.

Julia could never have taken a bicycle in there, either. The monkeys would have nicked it faster than she could've whipped that Oscar-winning smile off her face. If she'd really cycled around that forest, her bike would still be hanging in the trees covered in abandoned banana skins and bird poo. Every now and then, someone would make the news for being attacked with a wheel, or a handlebar, or a pedal. I'm telling you, that place is scary.

I fought my way out, dehydrated, sweaty and cursing both *Lonely Planet* and Julia for luring me into a false sense of security. Once safe, I crossed the street to buy myself a refreshing and rewarding 'I'm a Survivor' ice-cream.

Feeling relief flood through me, I clutched the icy packaging and tore it off, but in the space between discarding the wrapper and raising the treat to my mouth, another group of monkeys had raced out of the forest and formed a threatening circle around me. As they stared at me their lips curled back *en-masse* to reveal more razor sharp teeth. We stood there in a standoff, like extras from *Planet of the Apes*.

'Give us your ice-cream.'

'Sod off, it's mine!'

'Give it to us!'

'No!'

'KILL HER!!!'

As they moved in for the attack I had no choice but to throw my uneaten ice-cream down the street as hard as I could, sending them hurtling after it like a fuzzy tsunami. The man who'd told me not to tempt them with fruit was grinning from across the street. He'd said nothing about ice-cream. *Swine.*

I don't think I'll be visiting the Ubud Monkey Forest again. They're plotting to take over the town, I can tell. They're hanging out, biding their time, stealing more and more pony tails and technology from stupid tourists until it's time to use it all against us. In a few years' time, Ubud will be fenced off, accessible only by helicopter. Hotels will crumble and the tourist dollar will be spent only on lowering fruit inside at the demands of the monkey chief, a big grey beast who wears a crown made from ice-block sticks and screeches orders from the saddle of a stolen bicycle.

It doesn't take a disastrous encounter with the resident wildlife to realise that many of the things in the Hollywood version of Liz Gilbert's travel memoir have been embellished to romanticise Bali. I've only been here a few days but I've already met people who came here specifically to see the medicine man featured in *Eat, Pray, Love*, Ketut Liyer. They all told me he says the same thing to everyone. There aren't any hot Brazilian expats anywhere.

Move aside Julia Roberts

It appears that an influx of disappointed thirty- and forty-something women still intent on finding themselves no matter who tries to stop them, are now sitting about in overpriced, internationally owned cafes, earnestly dissecting their existential attitudes and waiting for inspiration to strike. Let's just say the Julia Roberts Syndrome is rife.

Speaking of which, I've discovered that our shared villa is actually on the very same street that hosted some of the filming for *Eat, Pray, Love*. I did not move here because of this movie, in case you were wondering. I moved here because I'm a freelance writer who can't justify spending $800 a month in rent and $800 a month in coffee in the western world right now (and also because I'm running out of working-visa options).

Anyway, in the movie, Julia was shown cycling down this street in Ubud with verdant fields of green on either side. She also got to hang out lots in a nearby beach bar — an impressive feat when you consider Ubud is actually closer to the mountains than the sea.

Padang Padang Beach, the pretty sun-drenched spot where Julia storms from Javier Bardem for wanting to take her out on a boat (how dare he, that heartless bastard!) is in fact in the south of the island on the Bukit Peninsula, on the way to Uluwatu. If she'd cycled there, as we were led to believe in the movie, it would have taken her all day, maybe even two. I guess that would explain her mood swings.

I don't think there were quite so many houses on my street when the movie was filmed, either. I took a ride out and just one kilometre further up the road is a different kind of Bali altogether; one where waddling ducks still quack their way through the leftover rice stalks without bumping into villas on their path. At my end of things, lots of the paddies have now given way to concrete and bamboo developments. In some parts of town it's like a mini Seminyak sprouting up. I think I've counted about five Polo stores so far. Why would anyone come to Southeast Asia and buy 'real' Polo shirts?

Anyway, how much of this sudden growth spurt is a result of one book and movie is something we'll probably never know for sure. Tourism slowed after the bombings in 2002 and 2005, so you could also argue that the influx of travellers is due to the general assumption that Bali is safe again, almost a decade since the explosions killed 255 people in Kuta.

In spite of it feeling slightly over-developed these days, Ubud feels like a pretty good base from which to explore. There's an interesting vibe here. I can't really explain it at the moment. Still, I should probably make the most of it, before the monkeys take over.

Are you there, goddess? It's me, Becky ...

Even without the constant fear of stepping on an unsuspecting snake, it's hard to walk through a rice field. There are passages of grass between the fields which are typically used as mini walkways by the farmers. But the ground can be uneven and can give way at any moment, meaning a stroll often involves hopping skilfully over several perilous gaps, or failing and losing a thong in a swampy puddle.

I had reason to continue, however. I had some things to discuss with a goddess called Dewi Sri (*Dewi* literally means goddess) and I was not giving in to nature before I reached her. Nature kept me up last night. I thought there was a baby elephant with a bad cold living in my bedroom, but it turns out that the native geckos make a noise like an elephant sneezing, and one of them is living a very comfortable life behind one of my paintings.

It's quite a nice, intricate painting, so obviously this gecko has an artistic eye. I've called him Monet. Monet is a good-looking guy; a decent ten-inches long, blue–green with orange spots and a captivating disregard for gravity. When he calls in the dead of night, it's ridiculously loud and he can perform this sound on loop for minutes at a time. It always ends with a weird, throaty croak too, like an old man wheezing after too many Marlboros. Sometimes I tut in his direction when he ups the volume, but he just smiles down at me, maybe drops a little poo on my bed sheets and says:

'Yeah, yeah, you might think I'm annoying, but you just thank your lucky stars it's me you're sharing with and not all those mosquitoes I'm eating for you.'

Here's Monet contemplating when to poo on my bed

He knows he's got me under his webby little thumb. We're pretty good roommates, I suppose. Monet lets me live free from insect bites and I let him snack on all the other bits of nature I don't like as much as him. But there are things in Bali that have the potential to terrify even a tough guy like Monet. The other day I moved my shampoo bottle in the shower to find the hugest spider I've ever seen.

'Hello! How are you?' he said politely, as I screamed in his face and jumped up and down in the nude. I had to get Ayu, our awesome *pembantu* (housekeeper) to come in and sweep him up and deposit him outside, where he scuttled off into a bush, no doubt offended that I showed such opposition to him living behind my Pantene Pro-Vitamin.

I've never seen such beasts as I'm seeing here. The dragonflies are beautiful but they're the size of *actual* dragons. The romantic in me would quite like to see one perch on the end of my nose as I sit on a bench in a sun-lit garden with a notebook, but the realist in me knows that if that happened, my nose would probably break from the weight of it and the flames from its mouth would issue third-degree burns to my entire face.

The insects here all appear to be the result of some morbid science experiment in mutation. Just the other day I was leaving the villa and I swear I was chased down the path to the front gate by a hovering UFO. I turned around and realised it was a giant bee. I screamed again. That thing was an anaphylactic shock waiting to happen. It was carrying enough ammunition to pollen-bomb the entire town in one shot. Luckily, a humiliating flappy run down the street on my part was enough to escape it but had it been having a bad day …

Anyway, back to the rice fields. There are, indeed, snakes aplenty living in the rice fields, but thankfully I haven't seen any yet. I stuck to the fields around my villa for my mission.

'You're prob'ly gonna think I'm crazy for saying this,' my Australian friend Paul whispered the other day, leaning closer to me over the table, 'but the rice fields here are magic. The other day I went out there for a walk, asked them for what I wanted and the next day, I got it.'

He must have seen my eyes widen. I love all this stuff. The more people I talk to here, the more people I find who actually believe that Ubud itself has a special kind of power. My flatmate Diana told me today that she's done the same and got some speedy results.

Paul is a retiree on the search for some land on which to build a villa. We met back in June when I was here on holiday and I stumbled across a spot called Bar Luna. It's basically expat central and hosts a literary night every Thursday. Paul has come so, so close to finding the perfect patch of land on many occasions, but something always seems to go wrong at the last minute … as it did after the last time he talked to the rice fields, or more specifically, a very well-respected goddess who resides among them.

Paul now sees this as the way it's supposed to be. He trusts Bali to let him know what's right and wrong, so every time another deal falls through, he sees it as a signal that the perfect place for him just hasn't been discovered yet.

To the Balinese, I'm learning, life is an eternal exchange between humans and the gods. The gods are worshipped, because without them working hard on our behalf, our families, friends, our bodies, the environment … it would all just wither and die. People here live at the mercy of the gods and the terraced, fertile plains we visitors walk across (and lose our thongs to). The rice fields are the result of generations of thanks to Dewi Sri.

The Balinese worship Dewi Sri both as a motherly figure and as the goddess of rice, prosperity and fertility. Dotted throughout paddies across the whole of Bali are pretty little shrines erected just to please her.

Taking one final, last-minute snake-check, I stopped and looked at the emerald blankets stretching out in front of me all the way to the river. I thought about CK: how much he'd love it. I really, really want him to come to Ubud. I want to show him a different side to Bali, something a world away from Balangan and Seminyak, something special. I know he'd love it here … not just because he'd find the time and space to relax and clear his head, but because I'm here too, and I like him. And I'm pretty sure he likes me, even though he hasn't been in touch once since we parted. Hmm …

I always like to help where I can

Summoning all the power of the paddies I possibly could, I breathed in deeply.

'Are you there goddess?' I asked.

'I know we've never spoken before, but I've heard you're really nice and I was hoping you could give me a sign on something. Tell me, is this man I'm still thinking about worth fighting for, or is he not?'

The breeze ruffled my hair. The crickets roared like miniature circus lions and before the moment could pass me by and Dewi Sri could turn her attention to someone with an issue far worthier of her concern, I sent CK a text message.

'Come to Ubud before you go back to Sydney. You'd love it here, I promise. x'

Surely he'd feel it when he read it; the power, the magic, the emotion. Perhaps he'd even see me in the back of his mind as the message flashed onto his screen, standing in a field, reaching out, invoking the spirits, at one with nature, swathed in a golden light as welcoming and providing as Dewi Sri herself.

It took extra confidence to do it. But Bali would help me, like it helped Paul and Diana. Surely, that was a nice enough text message? It was honest, from the heart. It said I'm thinking about him, without being desperate or needy, right?

It could have gone one of two ways, of course. He could have replied and said no, which would've crushed me, but at least then I'd know he didn't really want to see me and I could ask Dewi Sri for something else … something less selfish, like an economy for America or freedom for the dolphins of Japan.

Or, he could reply and say 'OK, I'm coming,' which would make my day and confirm once and for all the true power of Dewi Sri and the rice paddies.

I didn't even contemplate the third outcome, however, which was that I'd receive no reply whatsoever. Nothing. *Nada*. It's now three hours later and I still haven't had a response. Maybe the magic just doesn't work for me.

Or maybe this is just the sign I was asking for?

06/09

A series of unfortunate encounters …

What they don't tell you before you set up camp in Bali is that even if you've previously prided yourself on your grace and agility, you're now going to spend a hell of a lot of your time falling on your butt.

The pavements in Ubud in particular are a maze of broken slabs that in any western country would only be found, say, on the site of a demolished building. While extremely charming and adding to the character, they're so perilous and often set so high above what seems in places like an underground water system, that you'd be forgiven for wanting to take a helmet, flashlight and rope ladder with you when attempting to pop out for lunch.

There must be thousands of tourists stuck in holes all over Bali. There's probably an entire underground movement going on, literally beneath our feet, of lost Chinese and Americans who all thought they'd go for a nice little walk to the Monkey Forest but never made it back to the tour bus. Bali may well know this, which is why, to save grace and keep us flocking in, they play the *gamelan* so loudly, all day and all night, to cover the screams.

You're also going to step on a lot of flowers. The Balinese make daily offerings to positive (high) and destructive (low) forces that must each be appeased in order to coexist in harmony. The offerings to the low spirits are the ones left on the ground, which is great if you're a demon or a stray dog looking for a little snack, but not so great if you're a tourist on your way for a *latte* and you accidentally skid on a marigold or burn your ankle on some incense.

Taking a walk while sending a text message is dicing with death in these parts, and forget looking at the street-life through a lens as you potter along with your new camera. If you don't wind up destroying someone's carefully placed offering to a force unseen, you're going to wind up unseen yourself, stuck in a hole with the Chinese. You've been warned.

In spite of all these pitfalls, walking the streets of Ubud has become my new passion. In fact, right now, if anyone asked me what my passion was I would no longer say writing, or downloading musical soundtracks and singing the ballads into my bathroom mirror while pretending I'm a tormented war widow. Nope, I would say my passion is now walking. It's a passion that's been born mainly from my fear of getting a motorbike.

Today, while indulging in my passion (keeping my eyes to the ground, of course) I found myself walking past a bar with a very happy Buddha on its sign, which sent me into even more of a sweat. I sped up, hoping to get past as fast as possible but a dog raced out in front of me. I was forced to stop and an excited voice called my name. *Shit.*

Nyoman was hurrying towards me from inside. *He's grown his hair,* I thought. *It looks good. Dammit.*

'Hey! Where have you been, Becky?' he asked, grinning and holding up his hand for me to high-five.

'Um … Thailand,' I said as I slapped his palm awkwardly. *And hiding, from you.*

I could tell my face was beetroot red, but bless Nyoman, he just looked happy to see me, and cute in a way that only a carefree, super sexy, twenty-three year old Balinese bartender can look.

I should explain. Back in June, on the night I met Paul at the literary event at Bar Luna, I also met a fabulous lady called Cat Wheeler, known in Bali as Ibu Kat. She's lived here for years and writes for the *Bali Advertiser*. She's also written a brilliant book about her experiences here called *Bali Daze*. Anyway, we got chatting and she introduced me to *arak*.

Arak is a drink that God made by mistake and promptly threw down the sink, only to have it collected underground in a goblet by Satan who snickered evilly to himself and distributed it all over Bali. They quite like it here, and I quite enjoyed my first one, and my second as I chatted to Ibu Kat about her adventures. Like any sane person would do, Ibu Kat went home at the end of the night, after just one drink. Me, however … well, I ended up in the happy, smiley Buddha bar talking broken Indonesian to Nyoman who continued the theme by whipping me up a few of his special 'Arak Obamas.' Once he'd finished his shift, I also got him to take me to a club on the back of his motorbike.

Somehow (and only Satan knows how) I woke up on my own in my hotel room the next day, covered in mud, sprawled on the bed and needing four hours' worth of stomach-emptying time with the toilet. Flashbacks of snogging Nyoman in a rice field haunted me all week, as did the taste of *arak*. And then I left for Thailand.

'I'm so glad you're back!' he said, beaming as I shuffled uncomfortably in his doorway.

'Oh, me too, I've been meaning to come and say hi,' I lied. *Fuck, fuck, fuuuuck, what can you remember that I can't?*

We exchanged small talk for a few minutes with me promising to come in and see him for a drink some time. He really was very nice and unlike a bunch of guys I can think of who might have mocked my shameful, drunken behaviour, the lovely Nyoman never found the need to bring our embarrassing encounter into the conversation. The *arak* night was never discussed and thankfully I was able to leave with a restored ability to walk past his bar without feeling like a knob.

If all Balinese guys are as nice as Nyoman, I'm going to like it here a lot. But I'm also never going to drink *arak* ever again.

Continuing my walk, I discovered a popular cafe called Bali Buddha (and no, not every venue in Ubud has a Buddha in it). This one serves up healthy food and drinks and is a cute little purple building with steps up from the ground that make it look as though it might be on stilts. It's next door to a ludicrously expensive shop, clearly targeted at wealthy expats. (Top Tip: if you've been missing your spaghetti Bolognese you can get a recognisable western brand of pasta sauce here for $7; enough to feed a typical Balinese family for a week, or yourself, once, in your posh villa).

I scanned the outside wall of Bali Buddha, which also acts as a community message board and was bombarded with opportunities for spiritual enlightenment. Just looking at them made my head spin: devotional singing, yoga, *reiki*, tarot readings, past-life regression, crystal healing, craniosacral therapy, an introduction to your spirit guides, Native American healing, how to eat raw and make more friends …

These invitations presented themselves like the petals of a beautiful flower, drawing me in as I scribbled it all down for future reference. I knew Ubud was a haven of wholesome intent and goodness, but one could get quite carried away here. The sheer number of advertisements suggested it would be pretty difficult *not* to 'find yourself' here, if yourself is what you were looking for. With so many people desperate to help you and all of these different avenues, the only way you could possibly get lost would be to fall through one of those gaps in the pavement.

Heading upstairs for a smoothie, I picked up the local paper to read Ibu Kat's latest column. The *Bali Advertiser* is basically your regular community newspaper, only I'm pleased to say that this one is positively bursting at the seams with life-affirming specials and good advice. In fact, the *Bali Advertiser* is how I imagine newspapers all over the world must have been before cynicism and depression (and copy editors) took over and people started craving stories on rape, pillage and murder. Good news abounds here. Everything has a misspelled positive edge.

Let's take, for example, an article written by an expat (not Ibu Kat) from Australia about asbestos. Apparently, some concerned-sounding visitors were throwing the word asbestos around her local coffee shop and when the writer looked up, she noticed it on the ceiling. In the UK, she writes, asbestos was banned in 1999. Australia banned it in 2003, but in Bali … no-one's banned it at all. It gives ten useful tips on *How to Identify Materials That Contain Asbestos in Ubud* and then goes on to talk about how it can cause lung cancer. This could be a seriously depressing article.

In the UK the headline would scream: 'COFFEE SHOP KILLS CUSTOMERS SLOWLY WITH ASBESTOS'.

But here in Bali, where life is viewed in a more balanced way, the headline reads 'Paradise … In sickness and in health.'

I don't know about you, but to me, this headline implies feeling great while you fester; maybe taking a holiday somewhere even more exotic to make your last few months on Earth remotely bearable. Maybe living life to the fullest as your lungs collapse and your equally exposed family perish slowly and unknowingly in your very home, as you all sip mint tea and talk about things like how the geckos get louder when it's about to rain.

I'm inspired by all this positivism. I've lived in misery-inducing cities my whole life and they all end up bringing you down, one way or another. From now on I think I'll take a leaf out of Ubud's book and look for a positive spin on absolutely everything. Except *arak* of course, and falling to my early demise through a gaping hole in the street.

08/09

Those who can't do teaching …

'Sing us a song!' one girl cried, clapping her hands together and nodding, encouraging me with huge beguiling eyes. I faltered. I wanted nothing more than to break out into a bit of Katy Perry right there, thrusting my hips and waving my arms in the air and batting my eyelashes in a full copy-cat routine complete with glitter. The crowd would have loved it.

In the cold light of day, however, I realised that a musical pop-star performance just wouldn't have been right. I was, you see, in a classroom filled with thirty judgmental teenagers.

I'm wincing just thinking about it. In all honesty, I'm pretty sure I just experienced the most excruciating hour of my life.

I was driven this morning, along with Diana, to a school in Denpasar. She'd been approached to teach graphic design and asked if I'd like to volunteer my services too. I'd never done it before and I thought teaching English to Balinese kids might be fun. I also thought jumping head first into a challenge might stop me over-analysing stupid things like the fact that CK has still not been swayed by Dewi Sri to reply to my text message. Or my email. Or the note I sent after that on Facebook. *Hmph.*

When Diana told me that this particular school was looking for volunteers every Saturday morning, I had visions of myself sitting in a sunny field under a palm tree, reading tales aloud of ducks and tractors and policemen in funny English helmets.

All eyes would be on me, bewitched and enchanted, as I turned the pages of a giant storybook. A soft Balinese breeze would be tussling my hair and ruffling my rainbow-coloured *sari*, carrying the children's laughter across the paddies where their parents would be listening and smiling to themselves, thinking, 'Ah, that must be Becky making them laugh. She's *such* a good teacher.'

Even birds would stop mid-flight to revel in our joy. I'd be like Mary Poppins. I'd fall in love with them and they with me. And when we were done learning all about farm animals, we could bake cookies together and have a harmless food fight, peppered with giggles and fun. We might even play with some rabbits.

The thing is, the kids at this IT school (designed specifically to teach computers, hospitality and tourism, I later discovered) aren't interested in baking, or bunnies, or sitting in fields. They're not even particularly interested in tourism. They're fifteen and they want to put my photo on Facebook; preferably an embarrassing one, where I'm blinking at an inopportune moment, or crossing my legs in a way that accidentally reveals my underwear. (I've since found out that as of March 2012 Indonesia ranks third in the world of mobile Internet users after the USA and India!)

As we pulled up in the 4x4 to a frenzied teenage *paparazzi*, all with camera-phones pointing at our heads, I freaked out. And that was *before* I was separated cruelly from Diana like family entering Auschwitz, and thrust straight into a classroom. Here I was made to sit in front of them all on a tiny plastic child's chair and talk.

Can I just say that there's nothing like sitting on a child's chair with everyone looking at you to make you feel like a totally ridiculous human being. Plus, your arse feels massive.

'Tell them about hospitality,' my Bahasa Indonesia and English-speaking fellow teacher instructed before I'd even had a moment to breathe. The irony was not lost on me.

'Um …'

'Or tourism?'

'Um …'

'Tell them something.'

'Isn't there some sort of course outline for this?'

'Just speak English.'

'Is there a particular curriculum you'd like me to work to?'

'Just say some things in English, about tourism.'

'OK. Fine. Well. I like hotels. I stay in them sometimes.'

Blank faces.

The papping starts again.

I feel quite crap admitting I hated every moment of my teaching experience this morning, because I woke up with such hope and optimism, such determination to be good and really make a difference. I even put some lipstick on, like Mary Poppins.

I'm sure these things just take time though, right? It's nerve-wracking, being the keeper of valuable information, especially if you don't know how to share it properly. After all, I wasn't given any instruction, the kids were *much* older than I anticipated and I don't know any Indonesian yet, either.

Apart from the pointing and papping, not being able to understand them any better than they could understand me was the worst part, I think.

I told myself, as I writhed like Superman in a kryptonite cave, that they were probably all just admiring my fringe or something. But the part of me who was once a terrible, tactless schoolgirl with a gaggle of snickering counterparts told me otherwise. I've no doubt whatsoever that my fringe, make-up, skirt, top, shoes, bag and lipstick grimace were all being scrutinised and photographed for later group dissection. And just like I wouldn't have given a crap back in the day if Mary Poppins had walked in with a talking squirrel on her shoulder and announced that we were all going to spend a wonderful day together, none of them wanted to read a giant storybook under a tree with me, either.

For one entire hour I just sat there, coping, breathing. Occasionally I wrote things on the white board with a big black pen, because that's what teachers do. I refused several more times to sing.

Under instruction to 'teach about food for hospitality', I painstakingly spelled out all-American hotel breakfast ingredients, like bacon, eggs and tomatoes in easy-to-read capital letters, as the kids continued to take panoramic photos of my arse. Although I saw the occasional glimmer of interest, their gaze and giggles continued to burn and I'm pretty sure my slow, agonising inner-death will be more than visible when they all upload their videos to YouTube.

And to think I'm expected to do it all again next Saturday. The thought makes me want to cry. It sucks to be a quitter, but I have a sneaking suspicion I'll be finding another way of volunteering my time in Bali.

I applaud all teachers from this point onwards. I don't know how they do it.

10/09

Selamat datang ...

I've never had much luck learning languages before. I tried learning Spanish once in London, weeknights after work, but I always found I was too hungry and tired to concentrate. Plus, annoyingly, everyone in England insists on speaking English, so there was no-one to practise with.

At school in the UK I had an amazing French teacher, but my friends and I spent so long tormenting the poor woman that nothing really sank in. On one occasion we climbed out of an open window when her back was turned and walked back in through the door. She was so confused she didn't even tell us off. Another time, when we were supposed to be watching a French movie in assembly hall, we made the entire class sneak outside as she sat glued to the screen in the front row. Obviously we didn't know what to do once we got outside. We worried for a bit about getting expelled, then snuck back in again. Stupid. But I remember the prank now more than I remember that movie.

Anyway, school was school and French was something us kids in England surely didn't need to know. But I did think, seeing as I'm going to be here in Bali a while, I should definitely take Bahasa Indonesia lessons. Feeling so useless in front of those school kids the other day made me more determined than ever. There's nothing like feeling helpless in a foreign country to spur you into action. Or having pictures of your arse on YouTube.

I thought a few basics wouldn't go astray. I'd feel more comfortable at this point if I knew I could at least say 'Point that camera somewhere else, you little monster' when walking past a school.

You know what? After only one class and a few hours of study here and there I'm feeling so much better and so much more in tune with my surroundings. I'm practising every day in a breezy spot called Tutmak, and with the taxi drivers, and with our *pembantu* Ayu as she potters about the villa compound. Ayu taught me the word *cuci* the other day, which means wash. It's my favourite word. You pronounce it *chew-chee,* as all c's are pronounced as ch's in Bahasa Indonesia. I'm not entirely sure why she chose to teach me that word first. I'd rather not think about it.

My mind now feels more flexible than my body does after a yoga class. So far we've mastered the numbers one to ten, the days of the week, colours and how to tell the time. I'm the Bahasa-Indonesia equivalent of an English toddler and boy, I feel ALIVE!

After one class I'm thinking, damn, if I'd only enjoyed French this much, would I be living in Paris by now? If only I'd concentrated harder, or at all, would I be smoking those thin, minty cigarettes with my hair tied in a bun, married to my aristocratic obsession; a moustached man who spoke every word in French, except the word 'fuck', which itself would sound so elegant in his beautiful accent that it would make us both laugh as we sat sipping Bollinger on our balcony, discussing at length the dying Occitan, basking in our rare and romantic ability to converse in the language of the Troubadours?

I'll never know.

Bahasa Indonesia is a tough language to get the hang of, but I don't think it would be too bold of me to tell you that the basics are pretty easy to get your head around. If I can do it, anyone can. And I have an amazing teacher/guru too, called Fivi. She's young and super cool, engaged to a Canadian and she's lived in Japan as well as Indonesia. She knows three languages and zooms round town on a pink motorbike. Ridiculously chic. I'm in good hands and Diana and I are going to have one lesson with her every week, for ten weeks. Watch out kids, I'm coming for you. And I'm gonna be talking *back*.

Diana needn't worry that I'll lead her astray like I did my friends at school, either. I doubt I'll be climbing out of Fivi's windows when her back's turned. She's way too nice.

So many things make more sense now here in Bali. Street signs, greetings, shop talk. I can even ask for coffee. *Kopi dan susu* means coffee and milk, but you might not get the milk. The Balinese are very proud of their coffee. They slurp it straight and see no need for additives, like milk. It's more of a snack than a drink, really; a thick, gravy-like substance that sits at the bottom of your cup like slime in a murky swamp until you stir it and crunch its crispy grit between your teeth. The effect of this stuff is mind-blowing and if I wasn't a coffee addict before, I definitely am now.

I have a long way to go, but the language ship has been launched and I'm sailing. Ahoy! The foreign shores are in sight and they're welcoming me to port. *'Selamat datang* Becky, join us'!

Well *terima kasih,* Bali. I'd absolutely love to.

12/09

Special occasion essentials …

Tampax tampons in my local shop cost A$11.45 at the current exchange rate. I just discovered this today. And that's for a pack of ten 'normal flow'.

If you're a man you're probably wincing and thinking, *well, this is a little unnecessary,* and that's OK. You can skip the next bit. I won't know, so I won't mind. If you're a woman, you might well be reacting the same way I just did in a little store, in front of a very amused shop assistant called Ketut.

'WHAT THE …? What kind of a price is *that?* Surely the currency exchange thingy is wrong! It's never failed me before. Let me type that again … 100,000 rupiah comes to … NO WAY. It *still* says $11.45? For ten tampons? Are you sure? Ketut, *tidak, mahal sekali* … too expensive!'

Ketut shook his head, beaming a beautiful Balinese smile that should by all rights have invited butterflies into the store and inspired passing angels to sing. There's no smile like a Balinese smile and there's one for absolutely every occasion, even one as dire as a lady not being able to buy tampons in Circle K.

I was defeated. I placed the little blue pack back on the shelf. There were no other brands. I simply couldn't justify the purchase.

Say I needed three boxes per 'time'. That's almost $36 a

month. If I live here for six months, that's $216. That's more than two million rupiah. A typical police officer earns two million rupiah per month. The average hotel worker's wage is just $35 per month. Imagine if in the western world we had to choose between Tampax, or a roof over our heads and food for our kids? It's a stupid comparison I know, but when you have to really think about these things, trust me, you make the stupid comparisons.

Serendipitously, I came across an advert on the wall of the café where Diana, Fivi and I were taking our language class:

ORGANIC COTTON WASHABLE MENSTRUAL PADS
Pembalut kain
Plain cloth (M) 25,000 Rp
Plain cloth (L) 30,000 Rp
Holder and cloth 55,000 Rp
Leak-resistant insert 25,000 Rp

Bloody hell. Literally. They come in all sorts of different colours too. I pondered it for a moment, visions of laundry day at the communal sink flashing through my mind ... and getting worse by the second. Hmm. I might be desperate but I don't think I'll ever reach the point where I'll be hand-washing my own sanitary towels after use, thank you very much.

Diana and I discussed this and decided there are many items in Bali that seem to be seriously overpriced. This is obviously because they have to be imported, but as women, the things we've noticed the most are tampons and decent wine. We came up with the idea of setting up a shop one day called The Cork, which will sell only these two things, cheaply. I think we've found our niche.

Anyway, eventually I caved in and bought a pack of tampons where I found them the cheapest — in the vast, confusing labyrinth that is our local supermarket, Bintang (like the beer brand). Bintang is so called (one could assume) because beer is the only regular item they have in stock no matter what, as well as snow globes featuring bug-eyed Nemo fish and luminous pink coral reefs. Bintang is also an extortionate place to shop. And I'm not exaggerating. Muesli, imported from Australia, costs the equivalent of $10. I think they enjoy watching expats gasp and flap and frown and whip out our currency convertors, before thrusting whatever it is we really 'can't live without' into our trolleys in annoyance and moaning about it for the rest of the journey round the store. Silly rich white people; they are a constant source of amusement.

As far as Tampax go, I'll just have to use them sparingly. I have labelled these all-absorbing treats my 'special occasion tampons', for when I really just *can't* go without.

Suffice to say, my friend Pip, who's coming to visit me in a few weeks, has been given a shopping list of things to bring with her from Sydney.

14/09

Sacred Spice and the Yog-Off…

'Hi Ubuddies. Anyone know a place to buy cheesecloth? Would like to use for sprouting and making nut milk. thanks so muchie!! XX'

Just another little nugget from my Facebook feed for you there. I'm getting a lot like that since I joined various online Ubud community groups. Every morning there's a new line-up of treats in my inbox. Here's another:

'Is anyone coming to Bali soon? I'd love some *Saccharomyces boulardii*! X'

And there's more:

'Hi! I will be coming to Ubud for a workshop in learning how to read Akashic records next month. I would love to learn where to find cacao.'

I subscribed to these news feeds to find out what's going on in town and in the hope that I'd make some friends under the age of sixty. But I'd be a tiny bit afraid to meet these people. They know way too many healthy words. I think I'll have to carry on being a spy until I feel confident enough to interact.

I didn't even know what cacao was before I Googled it. It's a place in Puerto Rico, apparently, but I think she must be referring to the other cacao, which is the source of cocoa. I didn't know cocoa had a source, did you? I thought cocoa *was* the source ... of chocolate? So much to learn.

As for *Saccharomyces boulardii*, Wikipedia tells me it's 'a tropical strain of yeast first isolated from lychee and mangosteen fruit in 1923 by French scientist Henri Boulard'.

What would you want that for?

And why would you want to make milk from nuts?

I had a flatmate in Sydney once who used to spend days drying trays of nuts in our oven. Not hours, *days*. It got to the point where I could never use the oven. On a sticky summer's day our kitchen would be hotter than a sauna in the underworld and still these nuts would be shut behind that door, getting the moisture baked out of them in a process that cost us more in electricity than it probably would have cost to buy an entire nut plantation in central California.

My flatmate used to say these nuts offered more protein and stored less harmful fats when they'd been slow-cooked. I only just managed to get my head around that, and now the expats of Ubud want to *milk* them? Oh, come on, it's not just me is it? It's not just me who doesn't understand this? And as for worrying about locating cacao before coming to Ubud, a month in advance … well, actually, she may have a point there. It's hard enough getting tampons.

I admit, I'm just jealous that I don't fit in, and that I'd have absolutely no clue what to take to a dinner party with anyone in this place. It's a worrying thought because I have been invited to a raw food party in a few weeks' time and I've got no idea what's expected of me. My usual full-fat cheese platter with biscuits would most likely be greeted with audible gasps, removed, bound with hazard tape and thrust into the nearest pond, whereupon someone else would be forced to drag it out again for fear of jeopardising their new super-vitamin-infused home seaweed plantation.

Even the cafes here aren't really safe for ordering anything naughty. Someone you know will always see you. I bonded with an Australian girl called Susan the other day over the fact that we both overheard a worrying conversation between a father and his eight-year-old son. It took place in a fabulous place on Jl Hanoman called Clear Cafe (like most of Ubud I do a lot of my freelance work in here, because the Wi-Fi is fast and they have yummy food).

'What would you like to drink?' asked the man. 'How about a milkshake? Chocolate? Strawberry? Vanilla? Sacred Spice?'

The boy practically leapt off his seat. 'Sacred Spice!!!' he cried, as though he'd tried it before and it had launched him to another planet.

'OK. And your usual for lunch?' his dad continued, without looking up.

'Yes! Miso soup, miso soup!!!' His son was now literally bouncing on the floor with the thrill of it.

Sacred Spice and miso soup ... for an eight-year-old child. I practically choked on my tuna burger. Part of me wishes I'd had such health-conscious parents to steer me on the right track when I was that young, but the thought of consuming anything with a name like Sacred Spice never occurred to me until university, and not for the right reasons.

Out of curiosity I ordered one. It tasted like cinnamon, star anise and cloves. Not exactly sacred, but a tiny bit spicy, I suppose. It was actually delicious. Children are so wise these days.

Having become firm friends in the space of an hour while discussing our sinful lack of knowledge regarding health foods, Susan and I headed out that night to a bar called Boom Boom. And straight into the middle of a Yog-Off.

I called it a Yog-Off, because somehow we found ourselves witnessing the people of Ubud compete to perform various yoga moves, one by one, in the middle of the dance floor. The live band played and sang as normal, as several girls and a couple of guys took it in turns to see how long they could hold their One-Legged King Pigeons, Parsva Bakasanas and Revolved Half-Moons. I have to admit, it was fascinating; like scoring a free pass to some sort of underground Olympic event. I felt like Baby in *Dirty Dancing*, the first time she sees what the people at her stuffy holiday camp really get up to behind closed doors. There may have even been some alcohol fuelling these yoga moves.

It was on the dance floor that I first noticed River. He was struggling to bring the sole of his bandaged left foot onto a shelf he had cleverly created with his left upper arm. Parallel with the floor, all eyes on him, he brought his foot as high on his arm as he could and held it there as everyone gasped and applauded. I clapped too. And when he was done I sat this long-legged, curly-haired, super-toned yogic superstar down for a chat.

River is from Montana. He's a travelling web developer (who obviously dabbles in yoga) but he's recently had a motorbike accident which has stopped him heading east to do all the diving he was planning to do. Instead, he's set up camp in Ubud … like I said, it's a good place for freelancers, especially single ones.

As the Yog-Off continued behind us, River and I got to know each other (there may have been a cheeky kiss involved) and by the end of the night he, Susan and I were firm friends with plans to meet the very next day for a Sacred Spice. Hurrah!

I still might not know what to do with my *Saccharomyces boulardii*, but it when it comes to a flexible web developer from Montana, I can think of a few ideas.

17/09

An Ecstatic Movement …

Everyone in Ubud knows the Yoga Barn. It's a sort of second home for eager expats, all of whom are quite happy to spend an extraordinary amount of money for the right to bend and stretch with one of the most beautiful views in Bali. There are numerous classes every day and I'm sure I'll get to those later, but I should probably tell you that the yoga is not the best thing about the Yoga Barn. Not by a long shot. The best thing is the Ecstatic Dancing.

People here, I'm discovering, have a habit of doing the sort of things I'd normally do drunk, without an ounce of alcohol in their bodies. It's amazing. For example, in my usual surroundings I'd never dream of prancing round a room waving my limbs about like a bush in a hurricane unless I was powered by wine. But last Friday night, as my friends in faraway cities were no doubt settling down to a bottle or two of Cabernet Bordeaux, I took to the dance floor in a bikini top and flowing skirt propelled by nothing more than a beetroot and ginger smoothie.

Let me be clear about something: on wine (red or white, doesn't matter) I'm the greatest dancer in the world. My friend Gaby and I have a routine which involves taking over the entire floor of whichever bar we're in, usually under the guise of fairies taking their first fanciful flight. In that moment, in the middle of our routine, pop song pumping and neon lights flashing, everyone in that room is enamoured. Half of them want to be with us. Half of them wish they *were* us. We're beautiful, graceful and free as we spin and whirl and glide. On wine, we own the world.

On beetroot and ginger, even Gaby wouldn't come near me with a barge pole. I'm alone. Everyone's watching and they're not looking pleased. No-one wants to be me because I'm the worst dancer to ever have been born with feet. And no-one wants to be *with* me 'cause I'm sweatier than an athlete's bellybutton and I smell like vegetables.

Well, that's how I feel, anyway.

The idea behind Ecstatic Dancing is that rather than remain constipated with the things we just can't say, we *feel* them, work through them, shake them out through body movement and stamp all over them. With freedom of expression comes inner peace and harmony. We can do whatever we want to do to reach this stage of wellbeing, except drink wine. In ninety minutes of music, from hip-hop, to R&B, to Bollywood, right through to chill-out Zen, you can do exactly what your body wants to do and leave all inhibitions at the door. It's a beautiful concept. But, oh my … the smell.

As if fighting a sober battle with self-consciousness isn't enough, there's the smell of Ecstatic Dancing to contend with. I don't know why some people have such a resistance to deodorant, do you? I've thought about this before but it's always been fleeting: on a train carriage, in a supermarket queue, in line for the loo at a music festival. I've never had to swirl among the stench while trying simultaneously to clear my mind. It was like performing *La Bayadere* in a sewer.

I'm not entirely sure who the offenders were exactly; Ecstatic Dancing takes place in a darkened yoga studio with only the light of the moon and a few dim bulbs above you (think being at a disco for the blind). I've a feeling one bare-chested, dreadlocked travelling man might have been the main contributor. At one point, after bopping about for ten minutes, we had to lie on the floor and 'think about the sky'. A majestic cumulonimbus was forming in my mind when all of a sudden it got pretty wet. *Rain's on the way*, I thought, before realising that no … no … I was just lying with my left arm in a seeping pool of malevolent fluid leaking slowly across the floor from a semi-naked hippy.

The other person competing for the Stinkiest Person in Public award I'm pretty sure was the good-looking young man who appeared to be dressed as a chimney sweep from 1917. He was wearing a cream shirt tucked into baggy pants, braces and an airtight flat cap. I'd have to cover my nose of course, but I harboured hopes that *Chim Chiminey, Chim Chim Cher-oo* might come on so he could really let loose. It didn't.

I was about to leave … but then the vocal unravelling started.

This bit's good, but you need to be prepared for it. I wasn't. I was quite happy just to keep bopping quietly on the spot, you know, not attracting any attention as I worked through my issues but the petite, middle-aged lady next to me felt the sudden urge to scream at the top of her lungs. With no-one else in the room making any sound at all, she made me jump by deciding, somehow, that it was time for her to writhe on the floor at my feet, yell at my ankles and then get up and beat the walls of the yoga studio like a bloodthirsty zombie in a horror film. Seriously, she was doing things I wouldn't have even done on wine. Even the cheap wine, that's mostly chemicals. Obviously, this lady must have been very stressed.

I skipped away from her on several occasions and even attempted the fairy dance, albeit half-heartedly, across the floor, but the screaming continued. Others joined in from time to time, perhaps communicating in some lost language of freedom I have yet to learn. Some howled. I think it was a full moon.

By the time the slow songs came on, I'm pleased to report the initiator looked much better. She'd stopped banging on the walls and her screams had diminished to erratic, loud moans during moments of silence. No-one else felt the need to join her by then. They were all sufficiently free of despair. She was obviously what I have come to call an Ecstatic Try-Hard.

At the end of the class, we sat in a circle and held hands. We were encouraged to say a word that we felt in our hearts and squeeze the hands of the people on either side as we said it. I made sure my place in the circle was as far away from the stinking dreadlocked man, the chimney sweep and the zombie woman as possible. When it was my turn, I chose the word 'relieved'. Everyone smiled and nodded, relieved to be free from energy blocks and issues. In all honesty, and with all due respect to them, I was definitely more relieved to be heading out to meet River, and a glass of wine.

I found the whole thing excruciating. But ... if I'm honest ... *really* honest, perhaps part of that was due to the realisation that like most of my friends, pretty much my entire twenties was spent in a warm, fuzzy, alcohol-enhanced stupor believing things about myself and my abilities that simply weren't true. Sure, confidence carried me through, but how much did I ever really benefit from dancing like no-one was watching, when most of the time I was too pissed to care? Hmm.

As I left the studio, the Ecstatic Try-Hard was still lying on the floor moaning. I've no idea how long she stayed there, emitting little zombie sounds on her own. Perhaps the cleaners ended up sweeping around her as she begged them not to sweep what was left of her broken soul? Perhaps they wound up locking her in, heading home for the night, only to find her still there the next day? Perhaps they had to lie her gently over the seat of one of their motorbikes and take her back to her house and remind her she had an entire expat family to feed and that she probably shouldn't be *so* 'Ecstatic' for so long in the future?

I should mention there's also Sunday Dance at the Yoga Barn, which causes me similar fear because it's held in broad daylight on a Sunday morning when most people are in bed with a hangover. There's a lot of clapping in this one. Sunday Dance when combined with Ecstatic Dance is a movement that would put Hare Krishna to shame.

I think I'm actually a little bit jealous that I can't seem to dance Ecstatically. One of the things I'm slowly coming to notice, as the days go by here in Bali, is that I seem to have an almost crippling fear of letting myself go. Am I that conditioned by western society, that shallow, *that* bothered by what people think of me, that guided by my stupid ego that I simply can't do it? I guess I am …

I *can* still do an awesome drunk fairy routine, though. Ask River.

Island of the dogs ...

'How did you sleep?' I asked my visiting friend Russ as I found him crashed out by the pool at my villa this morning.

'OK,' he said, 'but the sweeping woke me up again.'

This is becoming a bit of a theme. Our *pembantu* Ayu, like many Balinese people, absolutely loves to sweep. Now, don't get me wrong — everyone appreciates a swept surface and God knows we'd be even more disturbed if she whipped out a vacuum cleaner and started threatening Monet and his mates with a suction device, but this kind of sweeping (native only to Bali) is usually conducted between the hours of 5 and 6 a.m. right outside your bedroom door.

This special style of sweeping is performed using a huge, extremely stiff brush made of large twigs. Hunched old women in storybooks use the same ones. The resulting sound of one of these strokes on a stone floor is one of an Olympic stadium filled with 80,000 people all saying 'Sssh!!!' at the same time.

On more than one occasion my dreams have been rudely interrupted by a humongous fire-breathing snake, slithering under my door and trying to squeeze itself through my ears while hissing in short, sharp bursts. There's no way in a million years you're going to sleep through the rhythmic sweeping in Bali, so I've grown to take it as an alarm-clock even more efficient than the resident roosters. These start their fussing at roughly 4.30 a.m., so unless you've got an early flight or you're planning to trek to the top of Mount Agung before sunrise, you'd be advised to wear earplugs to bed.

This sweeping isn't limited to early mornings, although that's when you'll notice it the most. It also takes place right next to you when you're trying to Skype your mum. Or when you've refused ninety-five offers of transportation on one street while trying to locate some shampoo and you've finally decided to sit back somewhere quiet with a cup of tea. Or when you've escaped one place because of the sweeping, only to discover it's actually 'sweeping hour' and someone at the *new* place has only just started.

Anyway, I was able to leave Russ by the pool to catch up on his missed sleep, while I headed off to 'work', safe in the knowledge that Ayu wouldn't be back with the broom for at least another couple of hours.

I've been volunteering for the past week or so at BAWA, which stands for the Bali Animal Welfare Association. Having failed so miserably at teaching children (all right, I suck because I quit — they were too scary), I thought I'd offer some help to the needy animals of Bali instead. I've been peddling to their office by the Monkey Forest every morning, carefully parking my borrowed bike where it won't be stolen by monkeys.

BAWA are doing some great work here and over the past week I've met some truly inspiring people. Most of them are volunteers who are doing a host of commendable things to help Bali's sick and mistreated dogs. You can't help but notice that there are a lot of dogs in Bali that could do with a bit more attention. It only takes a walk around the block to realise that while they're appreciated for their good 'security guard' qualities, most of them aren't rewarded whatsoever.

I've never really been a dog person. They always seem a bit too needy for me and if I can't stand men slobbering at my feet there's no way I'm putting up with something even hairier, with even *worse* morning-breath, doing it either. But either way, pets and animals are treated very differently here to the way they're treated in western communities. Hell, in some places, people *eat* dogs. I met a guy in Seminyak once who said he picked up some grilled satay sticks from a roadside stall while he was drunk. As he chewed the sinewy flesh he realised it was nothing like anything he'd ever chewed before. But he was really hungry so he let it slide.

While Bali's dogs are kept as guards for compounds, shops and temples, they're rarely offered anything except food in return. A lot of the time they're starved of affection. Many roam the streets covered in scabies and as a result of their limited interaction with friendly humans, loads of them have horrible personalities and can actually make you feel pretty uncomfortable when you walk past, especially at night.

There's a pack of them on my street that often chase me in the dark. During the day they're quite placid and barely raise an eyebrow when I pass, but at night it's like they're suddenly 'on duty', like someone's pressed an ON button to spur them into defence mode. Even Russ was shocked when they sprang into action behind us the other night. I think he thought I'd been exaggerating, but it's true; a dog quite content to lounge all day long on the steps of a temple can transform by the light of the moon into a grizzling, growling, razor-toothed werewolf hurtling after you at the speed of a shooting star, intent on puncturing your bicycle tyres with his teeth.

Anyway, yes, some of them are horrible and scary, but I guess there's usually a reason for it. They're not mean by nature.

Due to the rabies outbreak in late 2008, a law was put in place which stated that all dogs in Bali must be chained, caged or killed. In spite of BAWA's tireless efforts, and the vaccination of more than 275,000 dogs, there has still been a disappointing lack of effort by the Balinese community or government to educate people in animal welfare or responsible pet ownership. As a result, many animals in Bali endure long hours in cages in the hot sun with no food or water, suffering horrifying abuse and neglect.

There's an estimated 350,000 dogs in Bali. I discovered that so far, BAWA has vaccinated 75 per cent of them against rabies.

BAWA is a non-profit organisation founded by American expat and jewellery designer Janice Girardi. Janice, who rescued her first Bali dog from the streets in 1981, is still actively involved. Her official missions, as well as to eliminate rabies once and for all, are to relieve the suffering of these animals by providing twenty-four-hour medical care and to stop overpopulation. She's a pretty awesome woman.

Earlier in the week I was driven to the clinic, just a short distance out of town, to see how they go about spaying and neutering these animals. The on-site BAWA vets will treat dogs belonging to people as well as dogs they collect from the street. So as well as their staff bringing in animals they've just caught in huge nets, people are also pulling up around the clock in cars or on motorbikes with their pets. There's definitely no shortage of disadvantaged dogs in Bali.

I stood there and squeamishly watched some surgery being performed on a big black dog. He lay anaesthetised on a table in the open air as the vet went about slicing up an area around his rear. Bits were twisted, wrapped, pulled, tied, stitched back up again … I won't pretend to know exactly what went on … but within minutes it was over; another Bali dog prevented from reproducing, and hopefully from displaying aggressive behaviour, like eating someone's bicycle at night.

It really was quite fascinating to watch this production line in action. I'd like to say they're training me up as a doggy surgeon so I too can contribute first hand to this worthy cause, but I'm not sure that would be wise. Qualified volunteers fly in from all over the world to help in BAWA's medical mission. Once I'm done with learning the whos, whys and hows of the organisation, I'm going to help instead with any marketing material and appeal letters that need to be written to help spread the word about their wonderful work.

I'm pretty sure I'll be first into the office when they need me there. I have the sweeping to wake me up nice and early.

24/09

Exploring Islam Lite ...

The Imaj Villas and Spa sits on top of a hill, about ten minutes out of Senggigi, Lombok. It's a magnificent place but the way to the top involves a treacherous taxi ride on a road that threatens to rip the bottom off every car that dares to climb up or down it. In another corner of the world, the hotel my friend Russ and I chose to stay at would probably have been closed and declared unsuitable for visitors on account of this dangerous driveway. But in Lombok, arriving anywhere with bruises from your journey seems to be the norm.

'Jalan gila!' I screeched in my limited Indonesian as my head was smashed full force against the window in the back. *Crazy road!* Our driver simply smiled.

Within ten minutes of arrival, I was being whizzed back down the same road on the back of a motorbike by a young member of staff, adamant about locating me some fresh young coconuts. With the coconuts collected, he then kindly took me to his family compound where I got to meet his mum, his brother, his brother's wife, his unmarried cousin and his uncle.

Poor Russ was probably wondering whether I'd been flung from the road and had my brains splattered all over a coconut garden, but there I was, providing English entertainment to a local family. I sat on the wall in my flowery sundress, surrounded by chickens, sipping obnoxiously sweet Bali *kopi* (coffee), relishing the opportunity to practise my conversational skills. We established each other's names, the fact that I'm from England and that yes, I do like living in Bali very, very much. We also agreed that it was very hot in Lombok. It was a wonderful cultural exchange.

This kind of thing happens in Bali too — you think you're paying for a ride to the supermarket when in fact your allocated driver has a much better plan for your afternoon together. It's a lucky dip where you'll end up, and you might not get any loo roll like you planned, but it's usually fun.

Anyway, overly friendly hotel staff aside, Lombok, or what we've seen of it so far — which admittedly isn't too much — is lovely.

Our trip from Bali started by boarding a fast boat across from Padangbai, the small town that serves as the main ferry port for travel to Lombok and the three tiny outlying islands known as the Gilis. On arrival, we were swooped up in a beaten-up taxi and taken on the scenic route to Imaj. The journey to our destination just out of Senggigi wasn't too long but our driver was keen to keep stopping to let us take photos, encouraged by our oohs and aahs and obviously extremely proud of his home.

Up and down winding hillsides we drove towards Imaj, snapping panoramic views of iridescent oceans and vast, sweeping rows of palm trees waving into our windows like welcoming butlers in green. I would have happily stayed in that bumpy car for hours; it was like being in a nature documentary.

Lombok seems to have a completely different vibe to Bali, which is hardly surprising, I suppose. Here's a brief explanation, in case you're interested. A minority Balinese-Hindu culture remains in Lombok, although the local inhabitants are Sasaks, who make up 85 per cent of the population and are predominantly Muslim. Whereas Bali developed its hybrid version of Hinduism a thousand years ago (now an intriguing mix of Monotheism, Hinduism and Animism), Lombok was busy developing its own indigenous form of Islam. Although there were long periods of Hindu and Buddhist influences in Lombok (from Java), what's left is an almost relaxed version of Islam, at least compared with what I experienced living in Dubai. Islam Lite, perhaps.

In spite of its unquestionable natural beauty, Lombok doesn't seem to have the colourful flair of Bali. Perhaps this is partly because of the religious differences between the two. The pretty temples, daily floral offerings on banana leaves making rainbow carpets out of every cracked pavement ... the sights that equate (in my mind, at least) to the appreciation of nature as a presiding force in Bali, are pretty much non-existent in Lombok.

Russ and I have been exploring the vicinity, although admittedly it's been tough to leave the Imaj Villas. Our gorgeous poolside suite (Number 5) sits raised on a pretty flower-covered platform with just two more suites as neighbours. The bathroom has a gargantuan tub and when we sweep aside the curtains in the bedroom we can see the turquoise blue of the inviting swimming pool below. We even had a guitar delivered to the room after I mentioned I'd quite like to play, and the staff and I had a bit of a sing-song.

After watching an outstanding sunset over the sea from Senggigi Beach and chatting to a lovely man called Wayan with a pet civet (like a ferret crossed with a cat), Russ and I stumbled across a bar called Happy Cafe. Propping up the bar, I seized the opportunity once more to practise my Indonesian.

A few cocktails down the line, my new language 'skills' had endeared us to the bar manager who ushered us both over to his

Me and Russ in sunny Senggigi

table close to where the live band was playing and proceeded to feed Russ and me plentiful amounts of local whisky. We also learned quite a few profanities, which according to the manager will come in handy (I'm not sure when or why).

In case you ever need them, which you hopefully won't, *ngentot ko* translates as 'fuck you' but if you'd prefer something a little less severe, you could always try *kontol*, which is basically calling someone a dangling piece of a man's anatomy. Neither are very hospitable, but after several cups of whisky, listening to an old barman in a floral shirt hiss them at great volume through the gaps in his yellowing teeth was quite amusing.

The Happy Cafe is aptly named, though the strip on which it sits is kind of a seedy tourist trap set back from the beach by a good seven-minute walk. There's nothing really on it except a few similar bars and restaurants. Maybe it's low season, but there's definitely more action in Bali right now.

You can get a decent massage and a tan in Senggigi, and the locals who gather on the beach to watch the sunset every night are more than up for a conversation, so it's a nice place to spend a few relaxing days if you don't fancy heading over to the more raucous (or so I've heard) Gili islands. I like the look of them. In fact, I'm already planning a trip to Gili Trawangan, maybe when my friend Dacey visits for my birthday …

There's a lot more of Lombok to see another time, I guess. I hear great things about hot springs and waterfalls and various trails that even *Lonely Planet* have never walked or talked about. Lombok's Kuta allegedly has a stunning white beach, too. Perhaps this *is* the new Bali … a bit like the current one was thirty years ago before … well, before people like us showed up.

26/09

A bit of energy surgery …

When I whispered, very quietly I might add, to Susan that I was going to see a clairvoyant and Cherokee medicine woman called Galactica Blanco, the last thing I expected her to say was 'Me too!' It made everything OK again.

Galactica Blanco is a renowned clairvoyant mystic and pretty much everyone I come across here in Ubud has either heard of her, made an appointment to go and see her, or has already been.

As well as delving into the future with tarot cards, palmistry, astrology and tea leaves, she can also tune into the angels, summon up spirits, perform 'energy surgery' and heal people with major illnesses. Imagine having that on your CV.

The all-American Galactica Blanco has lived and worked all over the world to extraordinarily high acclaim. But she's settled quite comfortably in Ubud with her family in a nice house on the corner of a particularly prosperous rice field. This field, she says, is frequented by a soaring and colourful Dewi Sri, the goddess who ignored me when I asked for a sign ... and then delivered me River (ooh, I never thought about that before, thanks Dewi!).

When I finally got inside her mystical chamber, which is a cosy room built onto the side of her house, the first thing Galactica Blanco did was perform a song. She picked up a drum, beat it with a stick and half sang, half chanted something to invoke the Native American spirits, who show up to her in the form of animals. I was represented by a buffalo, just so you know. A fighting, headstrong, independent buffalo who protects but apparently also needs protection.

Maybe because of the song, maybe because I like buffaloes, I instantly warmed to Galactica Blanco. She's this larger-than-life character with an infectious laugh that tells you she doesn't take herself too seriously. Thank God. I hate serious psychics, don't you? I've been to loads in the past. They all inevitably end up droning on about a piece of jewellery left by a relative, and the possibility of a new career move, and the fact that you are the way you are because of your mother and 'isn't there some sort of issue with your dad that you've been meaning to address?'.

I know most 'fortune tellers' are probably full of it, but I always go and see them anyway. In spite of a healthy cynicism,

I'm unshakeably fascinated by the psychic profession. Mum and I used to watch that sexy American, John Edward, in *Crossing Over* all the time. He'd connect with the dead in front of a live audience, who'd all end up sobbing and nodding and confirming that yes, he really did just change their whole lives by stating the colour of their deceased cousin's bed sheets, and now they can move on, safe in the knowledge that everything's all right. I've read his books too. John Edward could see dead people when he was a kid and, shock, horror … people used to think he was *weird*.

Galactica Blanco told me she used to think everyone could see dead people. When she was fourteen at a friend's father's wake, she saw the dead man himself pacing the grass. That same afternoon she saw him again, standing clear as day beside his friends and family. It was only then that she realised no-one else could see him. Apparently, she never told her friend that her dead dad came right up to her that day and asked her to pass on the message that he was OK. She was too afraid of scaring her.

Tons of these people are out there faking it and I've spent enough good money on determining my future to know it inevitably includes getting scammed while trying to determine my future. Galactica Blanco, however, was not making things up.

I don't think.

Except *perhaps* the part where she saw Ganesh sitting on my head, bathing in my splendid, purple aura.

And the part where she saw me riding on a dolphin in her crystal ball.

And the part where she saw me sitting on a mountain, meditating, with white light pouring out of my heart.

I'm not writing it off, don't get me wrong. Find me a dolphin to ride and I'll be off, but still, I'm not so sure it's an imminent part of my destiny.

So what else did she tell me, after the singing and chanting and drumming and crystal-ball gazing? Well, that would be telling. But seeing as you asked, on the relationship front (which is always the most interesting) she said that there are three men around me: an ex with a great sense of humour who's always nattering in my ear in spite of having moved on (true); a tall man who thinks of me fondly but is pained and has sadness in his eyes (CK?); and another man I haven't met yet, with the initial 'S'.

Maybe we shouldn't put this in print. But on the other hand, if we didn't and it happened, how could we prove it? OK ... sod it. She said when I meet him, this guy with the initial 'S', he'll be very proud of something he's worked hard to accomplish. Apparently we're going to have a connection that's so special that I'll almost consider him a gift, and our bond will survive an initial distance until we can be in the same place. She said he's very tall and handsome and she could see us laughing together, and that he definitely isn't English. Yay. I hope he hurries up and gets here ... he sounds hot.

Galactica Blanco said there will be a woman I should look out for too, who may try to sabotage me. Apparently if this happens, I should go back to Galactica Blanco so we can do an energy-cleansing meditation together (for a small donation).

Ketut Liyar came up in our conversation, too. You know, the medicine man from the movie *Eat, Pray, Love*? She spent an afternoon with him five years ago before the book even came out and apparently the first thing he said to her was, 'You're psychic. You must tell me when I'm going to die.'

Galactica Blanco refused initially and he went about his business, conducting various rituals and making predictions. He stroked her leg at one point, chanting something that he told her would protect her from death when the time came for her to be involved in a terrible car accident!

'And *were* you in a car accident?' I asked.

'Yes, a horrible one,' she said.

These days, apparently, Ketut is pretty senile, but she has no doubt that he has, or used to have, some very impressive powers. Allegedly his family is in charge of all the money he makes from readings with tourists now, and Ketut doesn't even really know how much they're charging people for his services. He does, however, remain a very kind and caring man, who's an invaluable member of the Ubud community.

Eventually, under pressure, Galactica Blanco did tell Ketut when he was going to die. He said he needed to know so he could be sure to plan his work around it. And no, she wouldn't tell me when it's going to happen.

In her spare time, if she ever finds any, Galactica Blanco conducts tours to the places in Bali that remain important for spiritual growth and does seminars on things like astral travel that last up to four days. Astral travel! Imagine the saving on airfares.

I've got the feeling I'll be seeing Galactica Blanco again, though I do hope it's to show her my hot new handsome boyfriend with the initial 'S' and not because I've been sabotaged. Gulp.

28/09

The Yobud Pros ...

'Since I've been doing yoga my voice has gotten deeper. Like, last night I was talking and I heard myself and I was like, is that me?'

This is the sort of conversation I'm treated to these days, especially when I take a class at the Yoga Barn. Of course, I've dabbled in yoga before, stuck a little toe into the sweaty pool of Bikram, struggled with my Downward-facing Dog in Hatha. I even bought a sleeveless top with OM on it to show commitment to a class in Sydney's Bondi Junction (which I attended twice). But this is a different league entirely.

There's no fooling the Yobud Pros. Yoga in Ubud is yoga of the highest order and if you're not serious, its people will have you splayed, Twister-style, on a mat with your chakras laid bare before you can scream, 'What in the name of Shiva!?!?'.

When I'm at the Yoga Barn I am not in my element. I quite enjoy the challenge, but as with Ecstatic Dancing, I always feel like a bit of a misfit. You see, even if the men and women slavishly attending these daily classes aren't the greatest at performing yoga itself, they are pure in their intention to *become* great. Many have their own mats. Many have entire outfits of OM in all the colours of their aura. Some even have water bottles with mantras on the sides and pictures of Ganesh on the caps. When they touch their mouths with these bottles, they probably believe they are drinking down the energy of the deities and growing more spiritual with every sip because they bought them from the special yoga store, which has been blessed.

These yoga fans have flocked to Ubud because even though they didn't really understand the practice in California, or France, or when they did that retreat (*dahhhling!*) on the delta of the Lena River up in the Arctic Ocean, they're definitely going to 'feel' it here because Bali is, of course, the best place to do yoga in the whole wide world. They've eaten raw food in preparation. They've prayed and paid up front. And they're damn well going to *love* it.

In class, in an effort to not think about what a moron I must look taking three seconds longer than everyone else to do each move because I still don't really know my left from my right, I'm usually found focusing instead on the butt cheeks of my achingly gorgeous instructor. I'm aware that this may be where I'm going wrong … but he's Canadian, tall, tanned, as slick as a snake on roller skates and, like River, he has this curly, tousled hair that sort of falls in his eyes when he drops to the Child's Pose, making me want to sweep it off his face and rock him against my bosom like a baby.

The more I focus on Mr Canada, the worse is my yoga, which of course he sees as an invitation to swagger over and place his guiding hands on my sinfully uncoordinated solar plexus. I swoon. I fall. He helps me back into position and such is my exasperatingly pathetic yogic cycle. His perfect presence unnerves me. And that's before he aligns his head with my butt crack and instructs me to do a headstand.

I don't understand why I must do a headstand in a yoga class. It's not the circus. No-one can benefit from it. It fucking hurts. As far as I can see, its sole purpose in an Ubud class is to ignite a furious sense of competition between the Yobud Pros. It's a secret way of determining who's the best, who's worthy of a bit more encouragement and who's simply whimpering in the doorway of a world that will never be able to accept them. There are those who will pass the Yoga Barn headstand test and there are those who won't. I fall, quite literally, into the latter category.

Of course, you can do your headstand in front of the wall if you like; that'll stop you folding lamely onto the floor like a worn-out puppet. Maybe. Chances are you'll still fall, but instead of landing with your nose squished into your vagina through your OM leggings, you'll get stuck against the wall with your shoulders locked and your entire vertebral column stacked like a wobbly Jenga tower on top of your head. Doing your headstand against the wall already classes you as an amateur … a bad thing to be in these parts. The last thing you need is for everyone to stare at you in pity.

I don't understand the hugging thing, either. People who do yoga hug a lot, usually for minutes at a time and usually with their eyes closed, and these huggers can attack at any minute. Unfortunately, it's never the hot Canadian instructor types who want to hug *me*. The ones who want to hug me are the middle-aged, perspiring women with hairy upper lips sporting beads of sweat that threaten to dislodge and splash my face whenever they move their mouths into one of those sickly, empathetic smiles.

You can be standing by the water cooler filling up your Ganesh bottle and keeping to yourself, when all of a sudden one of these people will have appeared from nowhere and pressed you deep and hard into her armpit, like she thought you were dead. But now everything's OK because you're *not* dead, you're alive, and you're even more alive than you were before because of course, you've just done some yoga, with her. Your souls are entwined and you're open for hugs, for the simple reason that you've laid on some mats in the same room, and probably both failed at a headstand.

Because I am oh-so bad at all things yoga (and because I have a sneaking suspicion that even if I practised it for nine hours a day on a flying carpet in Shiva's own living room I would still suck at it, there is absolutely no point obsessing over my instructor. I have to get over it. It would never work for so many reasons. Aside from being far too hot for me to handle, along with a yogic lifestyle comes countless other niggling things that would, I'm sure, drive a wedge between us eventually.

I've made a list to read when those taut butt cheeks spring to mind … when the thought of his hands on my solar plexus sets my soul on fire … no Becky, DON'T go there. Look at the list.

Why I could never *realistically* date a yoga instructor:
1) He'd write stupid Facebook updates that would make me and all my friends roll our eyes, like: 'Even though we're far apart, you're always stored in my heart-drive.'
2) If I asked him how my new eyeshadow looked he'd frown and say something like, 'It doesn't matter, as long as your third eye is beautiful.'
3) He'd order silly things like a Gochi Turmeric Super Duper, or a Serving of Bee Pollen while I was in the toilet and then silently judge me when it was served at the same time as my pizza.
4) He'd get annoyed in the bedroom if I couldn't do Downward Facing Doggy-style for twenty-five minutes without switching positions.
5) If our relationship ever failed it wouldn't be because I was a total cow who didn't appreciate anything at all about his spiritual lifestyle, it would be because 'the universe decided we weren't working'.

Because I'm in Ubud and it is what is expected of me, I dare say I'll be continuing my journey into the world of yoga. It's definitely interesting and it's clear from my marginally firmer thighs that it's not really doing me any harm, except for all the abandoned headstands denting my dignity.

There are lots of different classes every day at the Yoga Barn, so I'm sure it's not too hard to find one without an angelic Canadian to urge me into an upside-down position. But whether it's possible to come through the other side without turning into a full-time OM-chanting, stranger-hugging Yobud Pro remains to be seen.

The Green School and a lesson in fruit ...

I always wanted to go to school dressed as a princess. Once I went dressed as a sailor but it was only really the dress that was blue and white; my imagination provided the hat, parrot and ship, which I parked for the day in the fishpond.

Yesterday, at Bali's Green School, I watched a little girl make my dressing-up dreams come true. Not only was she running about in a pink, floor-length princess dress complete with glittery wings, she was proudly teaching some visiting friends the benefits of having a troop of pigs on the premises. They snuffled around in the mud next to the school billy goat as she leant over the filthy fence, getting dirt all over her costume. My inner child was overcome with envy.

I'd never have been able to find Green School without my friend Sarah at the wheel. Sarah is a young-adult fiction author living in Ubud and we met randomly via Twitter. God bless technology. Her daughter Alula is lucky enough to attend the awesome Green School, for the astonishing sum of $10,000 a year (you can't put a price on a green education, people). There's also a scholarship program for local Balinese children whose families pay very little so they can attend too.

The founders, John Hardy, a Canadian art student and Cynthia, an American who would later become his wife and business partner, saw the potential for something very special way out in the Balinese rice fields back in 1989. When the school opened its doors in September 2008 it had just a hundred pupils and a tailor-made campus, and it became a massive and instant success. You should see this place. It blew my mind.

Alula and her friends get an internationally recognised academic education, but they also get to play with animals. They drink purified water pulled from a well and learn how to plant and look after their own garden. They learn the essential core subjects of English, mathematics and science and then go hang out on a gigantic pirate ship. They mix academia with the creative arts, learn yoga, wrestle for kicks in a special mud-pit, and are exposed to experiential, environmental and entrepreneurial learning activities. One such optional activity involved dancing around a huge, pink healing crystal in the garden, dazzling everyone in the process, including me.

Alula was eager to impress. She bounded up to the crystal and instructed her mother and me to stand on the stepping-stones which form a circle around it. 'Make a wish,' she said. 'The crystal will make it come true.'

I did as she requested. I'll let you know how it goes.

The aim of Green School is to 'push' the boundaries of learning. Amazingly, they're delivering a generation of global citizens who care about the planet and how they can affect it in a positive way. They're doing this so successfully that they actually offer educational tours to enlighten others as to the principles of the school. Seriously. A group of ogling Japanese rocked up on a bus while I was there, complete with iPads on which they took their squillions of photos in the colossal bamboo schoolhouse — the only one of its kind in the world.

Food is a big thing at the Green School — the kids eat veggies from the garden as part of their daily meals. I can't remember

57

learning anything about food when I was a kid. Of course, we had the Gleed School for Girls' compulsory home economics classes, during which we rather enjoyed cracking eggs down the sides of the ovens, so the bad smells would eventually see to it that we didn't have to take the lessons anymore. We were left to believe what we liked about things like fresh produce, so for ages I thought fish fingers were the fingers of a special kind of fish. I also thought pineapple was a manufactured, circular dessert that came in a can.

On my visit a little boy was running around with a pineapple in his hands looking for a place to bury it in the bushes. I'm not sure why. Do pineapples grow into trees if they're buried whole? This child clearly knows more about fruit than I do.

When I was at school, we were too busy struggling to remember the names and shady pasts of the country's dead kings to spend any time on the future. But here, sustainability is a hot topic.

At Green School, the children work in open-air classrooms, on bamboo desks, sitting in bamboo chairs. Air-conditioning is provided by a special, futuristic bubble that's inflated as and when they need it. Geology lessons are in 3D.

Green School is so ridiculously cool that it has free Wi-Fi for waiting parents to use in a special outdoor canteen near the entrance. As I waited with Sarah for Alula to finish her day I was given a fresh *kelapa muda* (young coconut) with a straw, which tasted extra special because it was slightly fizzy.

I found the toilets in this area particularly amusing too, because there are two in each cubicle, one for number ones and another for number twos. The poo toilet comes with its very own laminated sign of instructions (placed at child height), which explains how to spread the sawdust over your deposit for the ultimate in proper composting. How good is that? I was almost disappointed I didn't have to use it.

The lucky students who get to spend their days at Green School come from different corners of the globe and are mostly sons and daughters of fee-paying expats. They're encouraged to share with their friends the differences in their countries of origin. They are also instructed in puppet-making and in constructing and flying kites and paper planes. They even learn how to make ice-cream. By mixing fun with the boring stuff, this Steiner-influenced education system encourages critical and creative thinking. The school produces mini eco-warriors, who head out into the world with the confidence to do pretty much anything. They aren't even afraid to wear superhero capes (or princess frocks) in their quest for a better world.

Sarah says having a kid who goes to the Green School is a sort of fashion statement in these parts. God knows, I'd be making sure everyone knew about it if mine went here. It's so fun they'd probably have to usher me out every morning with a broom to stop me mucking about on the pirate ship. It's like a youthful Ivy League school for the esoterically aware and environmentally friendly: 'Is *your* child learning the benefits of a special poo-composting toilet this semester? Or practising the Downward-Facing Dog on her lunch break? No? Call yourselves *parents?*'

On the way home I discovered that in spite of its excellence in other areas, Green School perhaps needs to pay a bit more attention to where it buys its coconuts. Turns out a fizzy coconut isn't fresh at all, but fermenting and will actually cause your insides to reappear in your mouth. Driving home, we were forced to stop while I made a dash to decorate someone's driveway with the remains of my lunch.

Spotting the dregs of my not-so-green *kelapa muda* now crusting unbecomingly around my lips, Alula was not impressed. Did I not know the difference between a good and a bad coconut?

Hmm … Perhaps if I'd actually been a student at Bali's Green School in my youth, I'd have learned a little sooner.

Serendipity and the dolphin cartel …

Heading up to Lovina with my new friend Susan was a spontaneous decision made the night before. We were dissuaded from going to Candi Dasa, our first choice of weekend-road-trip destination, by *Lonely Planet* who warned us — in only slightly different wording — that it would be deathly dull and full of old people.

The town of Lovina sits roughly three hours to the north of Ubud, hugging a half moon of black sand sloping gently into the ocean. While pretty quiet compared with other 'touristy' areas in Bali, it promised to be a bit more exciting than Candi Dasa. The guide book also told us we would get to meet wild dolphins, which immediately piqued my interest; Galactica Blanco saw me riding a dolphin in her crystal ball! The *Lonely Planet* might occasionally lie, but Galactica Blanco … ?

Susan and I found ourselves being driven up north by Wayan Number 9, a guy I'd met the night before when he'd taken me home from Boom Boom on his motorbike. I'm making a lot of friends this way, hence the fact that he's Wayan Number 9 in my phone. Wayan Number 8 is actually a tour guide and Wayan Number 7 sells honey on the corner of the Ubud soccer field, though he too offers transport services.

This may be a good time to point out that the first-born in Bali is always called Wayan, Gede or Putu. The second is called Made (pronounced *Mah-Day*), Nengah or Kadek. The third is called Nyoman or Koman and the fourth, Ketut. Any sibling born after that is also called Wayan, Gede or Putu and so it begins again. It should make things simpler, but let me tell you, it really doesn't.

Anyway, we all got to Lovina at lunch time. It's a pretty place, but unfortunately considerably lacking in atmosphere. As Susan and I walked around in search of something/anything to do, we realised we were being stalked (very obviously) by a multitasking guy on a motorbike. Making his intentions known, he introduced himself as Eddie. Eddie was determined to help us:

a) find accommodation
b) book a snorkelling trip
c) book a dolphin-spotting tour
d) buy his friend's sarongs
e) eat at his friend's excellent restaurant.

Eddie was everywhere. All afternoon. Eddie was at the sports bar when we ordered our first pineapple juice. Eddie was at the sports bar when we finished our third vodka and Coke. Eddie was outside the restaurant when we went in and ordered tuna steaks and he was there when we left, beckoning us over for one more attempt to get us to part with some cash.

We didn't have the heart to tell Eddie we'd booked our snorkelling trip with a far less scary but just as persuasive stalker called Dokie. Dokie sat with us for an hour in another bar (ignoring Eddie waving at us from outside), pulling out maps and photos of his twenty-foot boat, promising us the finest lunch of quality Indonesian cuisine and even a bonus trek round a national park. He promised we'd see not one, but *two* different kinds of turtles and what's more, instead of the usual price of 700,000 Rp each, Dokie was giving it all to us for just 400,000 Rp each, on the condition that we didn't tell our friends.

He then got his mate to buy us a Bintang each, which was when we finally caved in and handed over the cash. We bought a two-day snorkelling and dolphin-spotting tour from Dokie, but felt slightly less special as he sidled off within seconds to start his spiel all over again with the bikini-clad English students sitting at the next table. He bought them beers, too.

With a big day of fish- and turtle-spotting ahead of us, we decided to hit the hay early in the cute little hotel we'd chosen on the main drag. But fate had other ideas. Just as we were making our way back, who did we see walking three metres ahead of us, waiting to cross the road? My bendy, stretchy, motorcycle-injured web-developer man, River.

I blushed in his arms as he swept me up in a hug and we both tried to pretend we weren't really happy to see each other. How about that? We hadn't seen each other in a few days as he'd decided to leave Ubud and brave the world of motorcycling once more. He didn't really know where he was going, and Susan and I were supposed to be in Candi Dasa. But destiny had deposited him right on my corner. Our sidewalk embrace was as serendipitous and spontaneous as a Gene Kelly movie moment. It was so romantic it almost occurred in black and white, and before we went our separate ways again I told River he could stay at my villa when he got back to Ubud, as his current place will be full thanks to the upcoming Ubud Writers' and Readers' Festival.

As promised, the next day we saw two big turtles. The snorkelling around Lovina is the best I've seen in my entire life; better than Fiji, even better than the Maldives. I'm not so

A once in a lifetime moment

sure, however, that Dokie was telling the truth about his fine 'Indonesian cuisine'. Our lunch was a tiny sandwich made with cheap, sugary bread filled with a miniscule serving of chicken and a Kraft cheese slice.

He also stretched the truth a little about his 'twenty-foot sailing vessel'. The boat was more like a twelve-foot rickety canoe. It particularly freaked Susan out because she is in Bali to write a book about her life, which tragically changed forever the day her parents and brother drowned in a boating accident in Australia when she was a teenager. She was the only survivor. It was undeniably brave of my new friend to be on any kind of boat at all, but Dokie's looked and felt like it was about to fall apart. Not ideal.

The next morning, after another sleepless night, we got up bright and early for our 6 a.m. dolphin-spotting tour. (Lovina miraculously springs to life after dark and every bar and restaurant has a live band that ups its volume to drown out the next. Take earplugs.)

Five fifty-nine rolled around. Six a.m. followed, then 6.01, 6.05, 6.10 ... uh oh. There was no sign of Dokie or a tour bus as promised. Susan was fuming. I was pretty pissed off too. Nerves were frayed through utter exhaustion. We could forgive the overselling, the broken boat and bad sandwiches but would Dokie really stand us up and deny us our dolphin experience? Galactica Blanco couldn't have been this wrong, could she? We were supposed to be swimming with Flipper by now!

Suddenly, who appeared on the horizon, a mirage on a motorbike? Our good friend and stalker Eddie.

'Oh, so Dokie never come?' he said, pulling up next to us and smiling.

We shook our heads. We'd called him several times but his phone was ringing off.

'Hmmm. Well, that's not unusual,' Eddie continued, frowning. 'I don't want to miss the dolphins,' I wailed.

Eddie looked thoughtful. 'You come with me, I'll take you,' he offered, pointing to his motorbike. 'I have friend, he can take you,' he gestured to Susan. 'Cheap price.'

I shook my head. 'But we already paid. We can't pay again.'

Well, we couldn't, could we? We'd already paid the equivalent of $40 for the two trips and yesterday's wasn't exactly what we'd been promised. Flipper was getting further and further away. I hoped no-one else was missing out because of Dokie; some poor old lady with days left on the clock who'd come all the way from Mississippi via Kathmandu just to see the dolphins ...

And then I saw the light. Those scamming swines! They were all in this sneaky cartel together!

'You know Dokie, don't you Eddie?' I said, hands on hips. 'And you knew he wouldn't come. And you both know we want to see the dolphins, so you came here to make us pay again.'

He grinned. I frowned. The dolphin cruises are supposed to run at a fixed rate across the board and these guys all work on commission. Obviously they've found a way to make a bit of extra cash between them. Quite clever really, not that we were going to tell them that.

I could tell Susan had cottoned-on. 'We should write about this on TripAdvisor!' she said defiantly.

Panic crossed Eddie's face.

'Yeah, TripAdvisor,' I said, shaking my head. 'Such a shame, but we should really warn other tourists not to book with the wrong company and miss the dolphins ...'

Eddie looked nervously at his friend, who was waiting patiently up the street on a second motorbike. 'No, no, we take you free,' he said, hurriedly. 'Quick, we miss dolphins, get on!'

I clapped my hands together. 'Really? Oh, thank you Eddie, thank you, thank you! You're so kind, such a kind, *kind* man!'

'No problem,' he said begrudgingly, as I climbed on the back and Susan got on the other waiting bike.

In the end we whizzed thirty seconds round the corner to the beach where, predictably, his mate was waiting with a beaten up *jukung* (a traditional Balinese double-outrigger canoe). Still no sign of Dokie.

The dolphins were still 'on display' when we got out there, but on reflection I think it might have been better if we'd missed them after all. As soon as they dared to poke a fin out of the water, no less than thirty-five *jukungs*, all filled with tourists like us, were hot on their tails. It was the oceanic equivalent of watching the cast of a teen movie being chased by the *paparazzi* on their way to the supermarket. There was no jumping off to swim with them (Galactica Blanco was wrong, this time) and the closest our own *jukung* got to the action was probably thirty metres. Poor things.

Later that evening we saw Eddie and Dokie hanging out together by Eddie's friend's sarong shop. They were having a nice chat but stopped to smile and wave us over. We waved back and said 'hi'. Having had no sleep for two nights running we decided we were way too tired to question Dokie about his appalling no-show. And we also decided it'd be a waste of time to mention the overselling on the snorkelling trip. We had a nice time, they made some money, we saw two turtles as promised. Whatever.

I'd go again … maybe, when I'm old. And I'd recommend checking out Lovina for something different. But if a man called Dokie offers to buy you a Bintang in a sports bar, run for the hills.

05/10

Naamastayyyy …

I've been sabotaged! Well, not so much sabotaged, more like misquoted … but I'm annoyed. A lady I know from my writers' group (which I first started attending back in June because it's really fun and also a great way of meeting nice people) has written about me in a group email to mutual acquaintances. I wasn't supposed to find out, I don't think, but a friend saw it and pinged it to my inbox.

I know I shouldn't take it personally, but apart from the fact that she's used my real name to point the finger at what I simply didn't say, it feels more hurtful because it happened here in Ubud. It feels a bit like this lady, whom I've only met a handful of times in my whole life and whom I thought was quite lovely, has just burst my little Bali bubble (sniff).

Anyway ... what did she write, what *did* she write? Well, this is what she wrote:

'Becky hates yoga. It's a vicious, toxic, spiteful malice that brewed itself up inside her unexpectedly at the Yoga Barn, anointed its gills with notes of rage, irritation, disbelief, frustration and pointed itself in a gurgling, seething, dangerous way at the teacher. She said she thought she had hidden it quite well. I said I thought I doubted it.'

Horrible right? And there's more:

'But then at the end, he (the yoga teacher) just went too far,' Becky continued, locking my gaze with her indigo lassoes. 'We made it through the hour or whatever, I was glad it was over, and then he says, in this horrible accent, in this slimy sort of way, "*namasté*". She sneered it out, in American 'naamastayyyy ...'

And that's it. Very good writing and very creative, especially as I don't have any indigo lassoes. My eyes are greeny brown. Perhaps she's referring to my eyeshadow, but that's more emerald than indigo. Or my mascara, which is black. Hmm ... I don't know — we all exaggerate sometimes, I suppose, us 'writers'. But, really, I didn't say any of that stuff. The thing about the writer's group is that you read aloud what you've written, and I wrote this:

'I've got to be honest, I really don't like the word *namasté*. When I think about why I don't like it, I realise it's not specifically the sound of the word, or the structure, but rather the knowing nodding of the head that always follows, the hands in a prayer-like position. It's almost like a secret world I'm not allowed into. Like watching other people who all know something I don't.

Yesterday I had another class at the Yoga Barn and the instructor, while very nice, used the word *namasté* and the sound of it rolling off his Canadian tongue seemed a little trite. Maybe I'm just too new at the moment, too jaded to really appreciate the peace-loving sense of harmony that seems to possess so many people here in Ubud.'

So you see, not a vicious, toxic, spiteful piece of malice in sight. No 'gurgling' or 'seething' or danger brewing itself up inside me, nor pointing itself at the very nice teacher … who actually, as I think I've said before, is one of the most beautiful specimens of manhood ever to have pulled the Warrior move in front of me.

River sent me his favourite definition of the word *namasté* for me to digest. It goes like this: 'I honour the place in you in which the entire universe dwells. I honour the place in you that is of love, peace, joy, and life. And when I am in that place in me, and you are in that place in you, we are one.'

How nice is that?

I suppose the fact is that I just don't feel like I'm in the same place as everyone else when I'm in a yoga studio … which is what I was trying to fess up to in the privacy of our writer's group. I'm always on the outside looking in. It's true, I haven't managed to feel included or enthused as far as yoga, or Ecstatic Dancing, or anything like that is concerned, yet … but I don't hate it.

It appears I have been squished while content in my comfy shell by an unseen, spiky-heeled shoe. Funnily enough though, Galactica Blanco predicted this happening. She was wrong about the dolphin swim, but bang on the mark with the sabotage … if we can call it that. If she was right about this, maybe she'll be right about my future man, the one with the initial 'S'. I hope he hurries up and gets here. I could do with a Warrior right about now.

So, what am I going to do? Well, to be honest, I don't really feel the need to accept Galactica Blanco's offer of an energy cleansing (for a small donation). I think I'll take the *namasté* approach. I shall honour the place in other creative writers that is of love, peace, joy and life. And when I am in that place in me, and they are in that place in themselves, hopefully, we will be one.

08/10

Ubud Writers' and Readers' Festival …

When I first volunteered to help out at the eighth Ubud Writers' and Readers' Festival, I had a somewhat exaggerated idea of what it would involve, especially as a member of the media team. Thanks to various media-type jobs in the past, I pictured swanning about for five days with my laminated VIP pass round my neck and a glass of champagne fixed permanently in my fingers. I pictured mingling with superstar authors and making intelligent observations on all things bookish, and being ever-so literary in really nice dresses.

None of that has happened.

As a volunteer member of the media team, I was given the title of 'Blog Coordinator' and it has been my full-time job to keep on top of all blogging matters. Among the chaos in a town that appears to have quadrupled its tourist population in the space of just five days, I've had to find the peace and quiet necessary to concentrate on coordinating a group of writers who've come from Australia, Java and elsewhere in Indonesia, who also volunteered their services for the cause. I'm pleased to report that so far they have all been covering the festival quite happily without access to any champagne, while sporting some pretty funky custom-designed Ubud Writers' and Readers' Festival T-shirts. *Go team!*

The festival itself was founded in 2004 in response to the 2002 bombings as an independent, non-profit, non-government organisation. The festival's founder and director, Australian-born Janet De Neefe, hoped to build stronger communities on the island she'd grown to call home through various arts and cultural programs. She succeeded, and this Ubud powerhouse is undoubtedly one of Bali's most successful women … not to mention a downright lovely lady. I've met Janet De Neefe several times at Bar Luna, which is another one of her ventures. She came up with the idea for the literary nights in order to keep the festival in people's minds all year 'round. (Their 'coconut killer' cocktails are a good incentive to keep attending, too!)

Having become an Indonesian citizen through her absolute devotion to the country, this switched-on entrepreneur, along with her Indonesian husband, has also opened two restaurants, a bakery, two guesthouses and a sewing room, which is responsible for making everything that's used in her guesthouses. She also runs a cooking school, which I've heard is pretty cool, though I've yet to try it.

Through Janet and her team's tireless efforts to score financial support through various sponsors, the Ubud Writers' and Readers' Festival has since been named by *Harper's Bazaar*

UK as 'among the top six literary festivals in the world' and by Australian Broadcasting Corporation's Asia-Pacific network as 'the next Edinburgh Festival of Asia'. Oh yeah. This little town is officially on the literary map and it continues to attract some of the world's most talented writers.

There's been a ton of fantastic stuff going on this week; live music from temples, comedy shows and bands in all the favourite spots, even a man called Marzuki Mohammad, who regaled his audience with stories of a recent trip to New York and other states in America alongside his *batik*-wearing rap group, the Jogja Hip-hop Foundation. Surprisingly, a number of eighteenth-century Javanese songs mixed in with a bit of modern-day hip-hop have resulted in a musical sensation. Some of these tunes were even used in the city of Jogjakarta as a rallying cry during recent conflict. Impressive stuff.

One has to wonder if *batik*-wearing hip-hoppers would have the same effect in a western political activist's march. Would they even be allowed on Downing Street with all that stuff? I would hope so. If you can't at least *try* and solve an issue with a bit of eighteenth-century bopping, accompanied by novelty-value, loud-patterned clothing these days, well, stop the world, I want to get off.

Ubud is busier than I've ever seen it. Walking the regular paths you're swept along in a constant flow of tourists, locals, expats and visiting literary types wearing glasses and crochet and floaty skirts. The buses have been squeezing themselves through streets so tight it's a wonder none of them have got stuck, or at least taken out a line of parked motorbikes yet.

Having River staying at the villa has meant that important media-type business aside, it's been an equally nice few days of getting to know him better, though I can't help but secretly curse the fact that I've gone and got myself a full-time job at the exact same time he's here. I'm also still writing a few things for BAWA, the Bali Animal Welfare Association, though they must be very busy as I can't always get hold of people over there. Hmm.

I'm not going to complain because that would be silly; being part of the festival is amazing! But you know what it's like when you meet someone you want to be around all the time. I had all sorts of things in mind to do with River: romantic strolls, escapes on scooters, gazing at the moon, blessing our new connection with a frangipani-scented ceremony of our own, another Yog-Off, one that I'd join in, somewhere sexy ... but no. It's not to be. There's work to be done and blogs to write and Tweets to Tweet and intoxicated old writers to scoop up off the floor.

Drunk people are 'a given' at writers' and readers' festivals, right? I mean, it's no great secret that writers are drunks. If we're not high on caffeine, convinced that three cups of coffee before 8 a.m. is the only way to get a thousand words down by 10 a.m., we're propping up bars, swigging gin and tonic, moaning to all who'll listen that the coffee kept us up till 2 a.m. and we've been way too sleep-deprived to write anything decent for weeks.

There's an old writer here (I'm not mentioning any names) who has been seen staggering 'round town on several occasions since the festival began, completely off his trolley. Yesterday he practically fell into our minibus as he accompanied my new friend Claire (who lives in Java and is here to blog) and me into town from the headquarters at Indus Restaurant. He reeked of booze and started slurring something about a session that morning, at which point Claire whispered, 'I was there. He was drunk.'

So he was drunk in public at 9 a.m. and he was even more drunk in our minibus at 5 p.m. This was impressive work by any writers' standards. When we deposited him at his request on a street corner, somewhere on Monkey Forest Road, he stood there on the broken paving slabs looking puzzled, in broad daylight, with no shoes on. Somehow he'd managed to leave them back at the headquarters. His shirt was unbuttoned, too, like he'd undressed and redressed himself in the dark. Bless him. People were looking at him like he was mad.

Drunken mad men in high heels were part of the scenery where I used to do all my work, in Sydney's Kings Cross — so much so that I'd barely register the men with no shoes on at all. Here in Ubud, Bali, however, well, you just don't see people like that. Especially not westerners, and especially not westerners over the age of sixty, muttering jumbled nonsense in a foreign language with their shirts undone.

Anyway, so far, I think the Ubud Writers' and Readers' Festival has been a fascinating study of humans in general, and there really has been some great stuff to attend and blog about. Being British, I'd never heard of the Australian singer Paul Kelly before, but he reduced a room to tears when he played a song called *How to Make Gravy*. Look it up, you won't be disappointed.

I might not have met many super-famous people or got to swan around all la-di-da-ishly with a glass of champers but suffice to say I'm surprisingly fine with that these days. I am, however, invited to the Closing Party tomorrow at Blanco Museum, and the after-party at the nearby Bridges Wine Bar.

Bridges is renowned for being one of the classiest, most expensive joints in town, but it's also one of the only places you can buy decent wine by the glass in Ubud, so naturally all the drunks will be congregating in that one spot. River might come too, as the offer of free, drinkable wine in Bali is one that few people can refuse … even healthy-living, busy web developers with damaged feet.

I'll be strapping my shoes on tightly, of course, and buttoning up my clothes with extra precaution, just in case he can't make it and the drunk tries to lead me astray.

Araknophobia ...

Holy crap, there's been an arak attack! A nurse from Australia has been poisoned by drinking *arak* laced with methanol in the exact same bar that Russ and I were drinking in just weeks ago, the Happy Cafe in Senggigi, Lombok! She ordered a jug of Happy Juice while on holiday with her mum and now ... well, here's what the *Sydney Morning Herald* says:

> Jamie Johnston, twenty-five, a nurse at the John Hunter Hospital, suffered brain damage and kidney failure when she drank a rice wine known as *arak*. She has been receiving treatment at Darwin Hospital for the past three weeks.

Yikes. That poor girl. How awful. And to think, Russ and I sat in that *same* place with the staff for ages and drank whatever they gave us as they taught us all those swear words in Indonesian. This could have been us. I mean, obviously after what happened to me as a result of my last — and I mean *last* — experiment with *arak* I would never have downed any when we were there anyway, but still, that's scary. What if Russ had decided to drink some? What if it was him now lying in hospital, his insides full of the same nasty toxic chemical compound that's usually used to make anti-freeze?

Russ definitely expressed interest in trying *arak*, until I told him how it made me hug my hotel toilet for roughly four hours as I vomited up my stomach lining (I didn't tell him about the muddy knees, or the rice paddy snog, ssshhh). Even when it's not maiming your insides and eroding your brain, it's still likely to make you beg barmen to ride you to nightclubs on their motorbikes ...

Back in 2009, there was a similar case of bad news involving the drink, when at least twenty-five people were killed. Four foreign tourists were among those who died after drinking *arak* cut with methanol and apparently dozens more locals spent a long time recovering in hospital.

Even though it's rare, things like this do look set to happen again, especially if growing tourism keeps Indonesians on the lookout for ways to cut costs and boost profits. *Arak* is popular here because it's cheap and an Indonesian government crackdown on imported alcohol means a ludicrous liquor excise puts the normal batch of wines and spirits out of many restaurants and bar-owner's budgets.

In fact, the whole alcohol business, especially in Lombok, is allegedly operated by the 'mafia' and there's only one supplier, so they can pretty much charge what they like to bring booze to the table. I've done some sniffing about, but finding any official rules, facts or figures about the alcohol industry is hard because of this corrupt monopoly.

Anyway, if you're wondering what *arak* is like in its pure form, it's a strong and slightly bitter spirit made primarily from fermented rice and palm sap ... a kind of rice wine. It's also not to be confused with the aniseed-flavoured drink from the Middle East, which is also called *arak* and is *much* nicer.

Sometimes in Bali, *arak* is poured on the ground as part of an offering to the spirits, in particular our good friend Dewi Sri, the goddess of rice. It's not just used for drinking purposes, which is another reason why careless manufacturing processes can sometimes slip through the cracks.

In a 'sick' way I'm glad to know how ill that drink made me feel, because if I hadn't had such a terrible time with it before I could have been tempted to try it with Russ in Lombok and … ugh. We can only hope that this latest tragedy is a lesson to the manufacturers to take extra care, and to tourists looking for a cheap drink to be more wary, too.

10/10

How do you doodle-do?

I've made friends with a group of guys who spend their days like many Balinese, sitting down outside the local temple.

Putu, Made and Wayan are always very busy doing nothing. Sometimes they're drinking rice wine out of a plastic bottle. Sometimes they're smoking cloves. Sometimes they're asking people if they'd like any transport. Sometimes they're stroking their cocks.

I always admire these birds as I walk past. Nine times out of ten they've got them sitting on their laps and today, as I flashed them all a grin, Putu, Made and Wayan beckoned me over for a chat. They let me take their photo and when we'd established that I didn't need a taxi, I sat down with them and learned a bit about their pride and joy.

Putu's cock is the smallest: white with speckled feathers towards the back end and an impressive chocolate-brown tail plume. Made's is very handsome indeed: blue–black on the underbelly and chestnut red on the top. Wayan's cock is the

The Cock Posse – it pays to have friends in high places

biggest and boasts so many colours it looks like it's wearing a chicken-sized patchwork onesie. You should've seen the love shining in the trio's eyes as they ran their fingers through those feathers. They've raised them from little chicks.

I was quite surprised to see that each bird seemed to be taking all this stroking and fondling quite nonchalantly, like contented little puppy dogs used to the attention. They seemed to encourage it by putting their heads back and inviting their owners to ruffle the feathers on their necks. I didn't think chickens made good pets, did you? But then I guess I wouldn't know; I've never had one. I wasn't allowed any more pets after my rabbit froze solid in its hutch and my hamster escaped and nibbled a perfect square patch in the bottom of Mum's sofa (true story — it was weird).

As soon as the three cocks were deposited back in their wicker baskets, however, all hell broke loose. I actually jumped up as what looked like a feather bomb started exploding in Wayan's basket. It looked a lot like they were vocally rebelling against the fact that they had to live behind bars: *'We thought you loved us, you bastards, release us at once!'*

I've noticed these birds flaring up in the past when I've been walking past their patch. They make more noise than the dogs and *cock-a-doodle-doo* at all hours like malfunctioning alarm clocks. The sudden joint hissy fit was quite disturbing. Cocks can *turn*, don't you know?

The guys didn't bat an eyelid at the flapping frenzy. Wayan motioned for me to sit down again, and Putu, who's the best at speaking English, told me that the cocks are left on the sidewalks like this to get them used to the sounds of the streets. They can squawk and kick up as much stink as they like, but they need to grow unafraid of commotion and loud noises, so that when the time comes for them to take their place in the cock ring, they won't be distracted.

The cock ring?

Yes, the … oh, grow up.

The cock ring is very special. As much as Putu, Made and Wayan love their cocks, they will eventually bind metal spurs to their legs and place them in a circle of doom where feathers will fly and blood will spurt and one bird will die in the ultimate sacrifice to appease the evil spirits. I shuddered in the sunshine.

These poor cocks, thinking they're so loved, so respected, being talked about with pride and all the while they're on death row. I know their irritating friends wake me up way too early every morning, but they're only doing their job. It's very rare that I actually wish death upon my alarm cocks.

I found myself looking at them sadly and plotting their release in the middle of the night. I could save them! But then, they can't fly very far … it would be pointless, really. Plus I'd have to set my alarm even earlier than they'd usually wake me.

'Do you give them names?' I asked.

The Cock Posse laughed, and so did I. Of course I was silly to suggest such a thing. It would be a little much to give them names and then watch them die and then eat them, wouldn't it?

'My cock is called Bayu,' Wayan piped up.

Guess not then.

The western equivalent of all this would be akin to raising a cat from a kitten, plumping it up with Whiskas, cuddling it, telling all your friends about its cute little habit of playing with the bottom of your curtains and then driving to the zoo and feeding it to a lion. But even death is not the end of the story for the cocks in Bali. Waste not want not and all that; once they've been sliced alive by blades, they'll be speared and sizzled on sticks, covered in peanut sauce and devoured by the very same mouths that kissed their pecky little heads on a daily basis.

Cockfighting (despite its religious overtones) is an exciting gambling sport in Bali and according to my new friends, the majority of men own at least one cock each. When they reach the age of three, the clock is ticking. Apparently it won't be long before Putu, Made and Wayan's birds are old enough to enter the battlefield.

'You want to come to cockfight?' Wayan asked me, puffing on a clove cigarette and flicking the ash onto the street.

Hmm. I wasn't sure how to answer that. Did I want to watch a bloody bird murder in a sweaty sea of shouting men and risk getting stringy chicken entrails tangled round my thongs?

Depends how much those cock-a-doodle-dos piss me off at 4.30 a.m., I suppose.

The burp that was more than a burp ...

This morning, River went off on his motorbike in search of some art. He has a new place to fill back in Montana and intends to cover every wall with paintings of Buddha, koi and rolling green landscapes featuring people in pointy straw hats. He plans to put it all in a box and ship it home before he leaves (very soon, sob) for the final leg of his Bali trip in Seminyak.

I waved him off and warned him not to injure his other foot, and as I watched him turn the corner and speed off into the green, I felt a pang of something weird. What the hell was I going to do with my day? I never normally have a problem finding things to do and the thought was only fleeting, but with River suddenly gone I felt a gap and it sort of bothered me. And then I felt bothered that I was bothered by such a thing because he's leaving me for good pretty soon and I have to get used to it. Hmm ... I could be in dangerous waters.

Anyway, as Bali would have it, I wasn't alone for long to over-analyse things because up popped a message from my friend Laura (another girl I met through writers' group) inviting me to come and 'share.'

In my usual friendship circle, the concept of 'sharing' means buying a bottle of wine, heading to someone's house and bitching about our jobs and boyfriends. We all 'share' *loads*. We might even cry unashamedly as we tremble under the weight of our sorrows and inflict everyone we know with Merlot-fuelled melancholy, a contagious disease that spreads and builds and burns through vulnerable women under the guise of help or comfort.

Until today, actually, I don't think I'd ever sat down with the sole intention of 'sharing', especially not with strangers. I was intrigued.

I caught a motorbike taxi up the street to her villa (still haven't found the guts to get a motorbike myself) where I found five other ladies already sipping herbal tea sitting on comfy sofas on her wooden deck. As we looked appreciatively over the rice paddies and talked about everything under the sun, I found myself thinking I could have done with this sort of intra-personal sharing a long time ago … and by that I mean with cammomile tea instead of wine.

Everything came out on that deck as people found the confidence to discuss things that had been bothering them for weeks, even years, in some cases. This is all highly confidential stuff and I'm not about to go into specific details, but it seemed like just offering or receiving a supportive smile was enough to feel good. Sharing is a different kind of 'giving back', I think. An invisible charity.

One lady expressed concern over heading back to her old job in the entertainment industry having spent so long out of the loop during her round-the-world-travels. I think we could all relate to that, in some way. I know it's sometimes hard to remember the tiny details of the lives we've left behind once we've been gone for a while, but the fact that we have to face them all again when we might not feel ready, well … it's a common topic of discussion here in Bali, especially among women. Many people who stay here never dreamed they'd be here for so long. Such is the magic of Bali!

We discussed how leaving Bali for her old life isn't something to fear. It's just another challenge and perhaps if she's so worried about going back to her old industry, maybe it's a sign that she should head in another career direction when she gets home.

Another girl shared her feelings on being bullied as a kid and how it's affecting her still. Together we decided that branching out on her own to explore new places and experience different people might never have crossed her mind if she hadn't had to learn how to be strong. Talking made us all feel more confident about our powers to adapt and change as women.

I shared my thoughts about travelling around so much, not having any real roots. We discussed how perhaps I've grown attached to River so fast because everything else in my life seems so up in the air and unstable.

'It doesn't sound like it's him you'll miss specifically, rather that you'll miss having someone there when it feels like there's nothing else,' one lady said, wisely.

I thought about this. I'll definitely miss River specifically, because he's awesome. But yes, I'll miss having *someone like him*, and something …

'Think of him as a friend who was sent to you for fun,' another lady continued. 'If you keep him as a friend, you won't cling to the romance, or lack thereof, and you won't be let down when he goes. You'll just be grateful to have had so much fun together while you could and you'll carry on being friends.'

The words of the poem sprang back into my head: *kisses aren't contracts, kisses aren't contracts.* Why does it take some women so long to realise this? And why, when we do realise what an idiot we're being over a bloke, do most of us keep on doing it anyway? I can take this advice and work with it but for some reason thinking of anyone as a 'plaything' or someone 'sent to me for fun' is quite hard. I voiced my concern, only to be offered an angel card.

Angel cards are a bit like tarot cards, only they have nicer pictures on them and don't seem to do anything except offer individual messages of hope and encouragement. They're a bit like glorified fortune cookie messages, I suppose, only they cost a lot more and you wouldn't want to eat the packaging. My message was from an angel called Adriana: 'I am leading you toward the answer to your prayers. Please listen to and follow the steps I am communicating through your intuition, thoughts and dreams.'

As it was read aloud, everyone nodded in silent understanding with small knowing smiles on their faces. I found myself doing the same thing. Shit ... was I about to say *namasté* too?

I noticed throughout our 'sharing' that one of the girls was burping quite profusely. As do we all, I burp a lot when I've eaten something huge but in the presence of others I usually try to contain them. These particular burps, however, were performed loudly and proudly. They were dignified and distinguished. Each one permeated the silence between confessions as a sound to be acknowledged, not hidden away and ignored. They were multi-dimensional and had meaning.

Eventually, the burper saw me smiling and as she exhaled in pleasure, she sighed, 'It's such a release, a beautiful release.'

I had burp envy on the spot. As suspected, these weren't just burps, they were another means of evicting all her worries. By sharing her thoughts and concerns, she was physically getting lighter. It was like watching the metamorphosis of a grounded caterpillar who once wiggled and squirmed but was now soaring as a butterfly on the wind. There are so many ways of sharing, if you really choose to do it. It just depends on how much confidence you've got to express yourself and take the advice that people give you.

I thought of my message from Adriana. Apparently she's leading me towards the answer to my prayers, but I haven't really been praying. I admit I have rather selfishly been wishing River would stay a bit longer but he has a plane to catch to Thailand and I doubt a printed angel on a piece of card is going to make him re-think a plan to explore another country he's never seen before, no matter how close we've become.

As I headed back the way I'd come, refusing the offer of a ride in favour of walking through the fields, I thanked Dewi Sri for sending River into my life in the first place. Without really knowing what he's done, he *has* become a friend. He's helped me to feel like what I'm doing right here and right now is OK, and that it's fine to feel unstable and insecure in a new place ... even OK to feel a little bit needy sometimes. And in turn, I've helped him out when he's needed it on the course of his own journey. We yoga'd together at a crossroads, had some fun, and now we're both just heading out into the world a little bit less lonely than we were before we met. I'll always be grateful for that.

When it comes down to it, I might not be able to physically burp my worries away, but along with the importance of sharing, I have definitely learned the importance of letting go.

13/10

EARTHQUAKE!!!

The same fault line that generated the 2004 tsunami runs just south of Bali, a fact that became glaringly obvious a few hours ago. I was, you see, just involved in a terrifying natural disaster of the earthquake kind. Seriously. I was sitting in a cafe, sending an email

to a very nice photographer called Sidd that I met at the Writers'
Festival closing party at Bridges (ssshhh, River didn't end up coming
and we got chatting, and that was it, I swear), when the earth literally
moved beneath my feet. I'm all shook up like Elvis right now.

The earthquake, which I now hear was a massive 6.8 on the
Richter scale, began on the cushion under my bum. It grew
stronger as it wobbled the table, making me realise that no, it was
not a result of last night's *nasi goreng*. Neither was it a very large
truck full of coconuts rumbling past.

Previous to the shakes I'd been trying to ignore a Dutch family
who were smoking and chatting noisily at the next table. Their kid
was running round the cafe shrieking and I was contemplating
moving seats so he wouldn't spill my coffee … normal, everyday
thoughts and things and movements. That was when the universe
chimed in.

I looked up to see the plants swinging and the trees swaying
in the rice field out the back and all of a sudden the annoying
family were grabbing their rambunctious rug rat and high-tailing
it out to the street. For a split second I thought, 'Should I take my
laptop?' And then I thought, 'Should I be Tweeting about this?'
And then I ran for my life.

The quake lasted almost thirty seconds. As I stood on the road
watching the signs shaking in invisible hands outside the nearby
stores, I felt my knees quivering. At one point they practically
buckled. My mind and my body were both out of whack,
trembling with the world. Holy shit! Would I die in Bali? Would
I become a statistic? Would the last thing I ever thought in the
public stratosphere be, 'This Dutch family is really interrupting
my procrastination, right now. I'm trying not to work!'

The Balinese staff were grinning and laughing, finding the
humour in it all far faster than the westerners were. They're used

to it, I suppose. Even though I was scared, I grinned and laughed, too, mostly because the situation was so ridiculous and I had no other way of relating to it in a logical manner.

For a moment I was terrified that the entire earth would split apart like a scene from a disaster movie and suck me deep down into its bubbling core. I pictured Bruce Willis arriving with harnesses. I pictured beautiful houses tumbling down hillsides, their bamboo pieces floating away on widened rivers like cocktail sticks in an ocean. I saw myself holding onto a rock with one hand, the rest of me dangling into the abyss, my thongs falling one by one into the flames and melting like candle-wax.

'Save yourselves!' I would shout to the dogs and the people and the geckos who'd have crowded round the edges of the even-more-broken pavements, wide-eyed in horror. 'Run while you can!!!'

When it was over of course, I hated myself for getting so scared. 'Don't be so silly, of course you weren't going to DIE! Pah? *Bali kopi*, please Wayan, *terima kasih!*'

But I felt I had to blog about it straight away, because the horrifying thought did cross my mind that it might well be the last piece of communication I ever have with the world, and it's in these moments that you feel the most alive, isn't it? It's in these moments, perhaps, that you *should* open your heart and show a tiny piece of the vulnerability you feel every single day but never share. What if it's your last chance?

Twitter went crazy with thoughts along the same lines. My friend Pip, who's supposed to be coming to visit me in the very near future, isn't really sure if she should still come but sends her love. I texted River who felt it too in Seminyak where he's now staying. Messages from friends to say they're thinking of me, messages from others to say how glad they were that it wasn't too serious, all plopped into the inbox and a seed was planted. This could happen again.

Upon further investigation, I discovered that we are *very* much at risk here on our little Island of the Gods. It seems that Bali and its visiting holidaymakers have been lulled into a false sense of security as far as things like this are concerned. Back in 2004, when the December tsunami claimed the lives of 230,000 people in fourteen countries and devastated coastal communities, Bali was untouched, shielded as it was by the protecting embrace of Java and Sumatra. However, should another earthquake occur, Bali and its bustling tourist attractions sits just twenty minutes (by the speed of a tidal wave) away from the fault line.

One website is telling me that some 'experts' in Europe have indicated such a quake may be long overdue. After the quake in 2004, all the aftershocks occurred to the north of its epicenter. It's quite possible, then, that extra tension has built up along the fault line to the south, where we are.

My friend Pip and I were going to have some fun by the beach, but now I'm just a teeny bit worried that we'll be swallowed whole by the raging ocean. I'm worried for River. I've just Googled, 'how to prevent a tsunami' and apparently, you can't. You can, however, be prepared. One website says: 'To lessen your chances of being affected by a tsunami, stay at a hotel at least fifty metres(160 feet) above sea level or 3.2 kilometres (two miles) inland from the beach.' They're really very specific about it.

You're also supposed to stay high (not like *that*). The largest wave that hit Aceh Province — nearest to the quake on that fatal December day — was thirty metres (a hundred feet) high.

'Well, that's OK', you might be thinking, 'If I go to Bali, I'll just book a room in the highest high-rise building!'

But wait. Due to Bali's building-height regulations, nothing here can be higher than a coconut tree, which are only about thirty metres tall. And in past tsunami events, waves as high as sixty metres have been known to strike the surroundings.

It takes just one second for the world to change. What if this happens again? What if something worse occurs and I don't get a warning, or a chance to say goodbye? Is this the price I'll eventually pay for not staying put in my own country, where leaves on a train track causing a ten-minute delay is about as close to a natural disaster that England ever comes? Who knows? But I can't live my life in a hard hat clutching doorways.

The truth is, if the Bali gods continue to decide we should tremble and suffer in their wake, well, I guess there's bugger all we can do about it.

15/10

Om not so sure ...

'What did you have for lunch?' I asked my Sound Healer as we found ourselves the only two people in the studio.

'I had some gluten-free bread with honey, some spirulina and two cacao beans.'

Oh.

'What did you have, Becky?'

'Um ... Chicken and mash. And a beer.'

It was with definite trepidation that I made my way to today's Sound Healing session with Diana. It was uncomfortable from the start, really, not least because I was secretly 'going commando' beneath my turquoise linen trousers. I ran out of underwear two days ago and as usual I have no idea when Ayu will return my laundry.

I digress. Diana seemed really excited about the session and we'd both been offered it half price, so in spite of minor doubts I thought it would be silly not to give it a shot.

Sound Healing, in case you haven't heard (tut), is basically the concept of sound harmonics working to free us from disharmonious energy patterns. It's using the voice and various instruments as conductors to express thoughts and emotions we might be storing inside. Kind of like a colonic, I suppose, except the shit comes out the other end.

While Diana, myself and another two ladies laid down flat on our backs on yoga mats, our guru explained how the healing tends to work. There was some mention of mantras and the power of *om*, which made me feel slightly nervous.

'Today we're going to concentrate on our soul sounds', she said, walking around us as I closed my eyes, feeling the vibrations of her footsteps shake the studio floor and ricochet right through me. Suddenly, my thoughts were spinning.

What if my soul doesn't have any sound?

'I like to follow my heart compass', our guru shared. 'Just take a deep breath and on the exhale, make a sound straight from your heart.'

OK, chill out, Becky. You can do this. Wait, though! Should I start with a high-pitched om *or a low one? What's the protocol? Am I even qualified to say* om?

The chanting began without me.

Diana was emitting a mid-range frequency that sounded like a panpipe on a loop. The other two ladies were humming in harmony; whether that was intentional or not, who knows? There were no limits, no volume restrictions. Any noise was OK, right there in that room. The only things listening were the cockerels and the dragonflies. Nothing and no-one was judging us.

What the hell.

I took a deep breath and then took the plunge. The sound *om* came out, long and loud and free. It felt good. It felt bloody awesome actually. I did it again. There weren't any angels appearing in bursts of white light but did I feel an incy-bit different for the release?

Our guru proceeded to tap on an instrument, which I visualised might have been a blow-up cushion packed with frozen peas. She '*om*med' a very professional-sounding *om* at various octaves that put the rest of us to shame. It rang out around the room — a Tibetan bowl to my cheap china plate — but I couldn't quite get comfy.

Due to having no clean clothes, I'd been stupid enough to put a bikini top on with a huge tie-up bow at the back and the knot was digging into my spine beneath my T-shirt, causing me to lie at a crooked angle. That, and the fact that I had no knickers on, were suddenly totally interrupting my healing. I tried to focus on my heart compass.

Concentrate. Concentrate.

The sound-making and frozen-pea bag-banging went on for quite a while, to the point where I thought I couldn't take it any longer. Just before we were allowed to take a break, however, we were encouraged to partner up, sit opposite one another and vocalise our trapped emotions in a stream of unbroken sound. This sound, we were informed, didn't have to include words, but it did have to last for five whole minutes.

Five whole minutes of making continuous random noises in someone's face? Even singing drunken *karaoke* takes more preparation than she was offering us time for. The thought was immediately debilitating. What would I do? *Om* might have cut it with my eyes shut, flat on the floor in my own little world of no underwear, but looking into another human's eyes? I couldn't do it, to me or to them. I'd have to come up with something different.

Back in 1999, when I'd stand in Ritzy's, teetering on four-inch heels, shouting flirtatious comebacks at the boy I fancied in an effort to be heard over *NSYNC, continuous talk was a Friday night certainty. I'd have a Bacardi Breezer in one hand, my glittery Union Jack flag handbag in the other and a repertoire of random wit and charm at my disposal. Talking random talk was never a challenge back then; twelve years on and it's crippling. There was even a stopwatch timing me.

Our guru looked on as we buzzed and whirred and ommed a bit more on our way to mending one another's broken soul energy fields. I tried not to laugh. I squirmed like a worm with its head chopped off. I tried to look like I was healing. I failed. As I ommed pathetically with my eyes dancing nervously round the room, I found I was looking everywhere but my partner's face.

When it was her turn, however, she sang for the entire five minutes. She smiled as she did it, at the start. It was beautiful — a melodious monologue straight from her heart. It actually blew me away, not just the sound she was making but the emotion she was showing, too. It was building with every note, bubbling up inside her like a fountain and spilling over down her cheeks. She closed her eyes. She was letting go, breathing out pain and inhaling freedom literally inches from my face. It threw me off guard. I looked away.

I felt awkward and a little bit envious. There she was, fantastically falling apart, reaping the rewards for putting her soul on the line, giving and receiving at the same time. She was obviously cleaning out some seriously dusty emotional cupboards in front of me, whereas all I'd been thinking for the last twenty minutes was *I'm still hungry, that chicken didn't fill me up,* and *I wonder if anyone knows I've got no knickers on?*

I felt so small I could have followed a lizard through a crack in the floor.

I'm still not entirely convinced I'll ever be able to immerse myself fully in anything like this. I stand on the brink of it occasionally, but I never jump off the edge. There's always that invisible wall that shoots up between me and anyone who goes the slightest bit mystical on me. It's almost as though I descend from mild understanding, to humouring, to actually fearing anyone who threatens to bring me out of myself, all in the space of five seconds.

Even after two months in Bali, I panic at the thought of this soul extraction. I can practically feel the cloak of self-preservation wrapping around me every time, tighter and tighter till it becomes a gag. Something inside me still screams: *Don't touch me, don't touch me!* at the hideous monster, a shadow of myself, creeping up on me slowly, threatening to open me up against my will and spill my innards all over a studio floor.

Don't touch me, don't touch me! I yell internally. *Don't you get it? I don't want to be like you.*

But they can't hear me. They're too busy singing in my face.

I'm still screaming as the monsters close in. They can sense that I'm weakening, with every yoga pose, every Sacred Spice, every *om* I emit in a silent room. They can sense that there are probably only so many more times I can put up this fight against myself, and win.

The only white Mangku in the village ...

The other night I was invited to a full moon ceremony by Sidd, the photographer I met at the closing party of the Writers' Festival, and it was really rather good. It was the first proper ceremony I've attended in Bali. It was held in the little village of Bona, about three kilometres outside of Ubud.

There are ceremonies every time there's a full moon here. The moon affects everything — the tides, how the crops grow, how the animals act and how humans behave. The moon's influence on our lives is at its strongest when it's full, so the Balinese see this phase, known as *Purnama*, as the best time for planting, healing and completing any projects they may have been waiting to close. Some people even believe that bathing in frangipani-scented water by the light of the full moon will help wash away your sins and keep you looking young and sexy (one to note for further experimentation, perhaps).

This full moon, according to Sidd, was extra special because it was also the annual cleansing of the village temple; a laundry day if you will, to rid it of badness, recharge the goodness and generally start the cycle of protection anew.

The village of Bona is known for holding particularly extravagant ceremonies and has one of the most beautiful temples I've ever seen. It also has the reputation of being home to one of the most powerful healing temples, which could be why I feel like the energy shifted somehow; like the old moon died and a new one burst through the sky to shine enlightenment on my clouded brain. Hello, Bali! There you are, Bali!

Anyway, Sidd currently lives at a place called the Svarna Dvipa Bali Cultural and Healing Centre in Bona; a visionary place constructed for the villagers and whoever else might like to drop in. It's managed by an Australian man called Budhi. Budhi has been here in Bali for eighteen years and was so well respected in the local community that he was asked to become a *Jero Mangku*, a huge honour.

Jero Mangku are highly regarded in Bali, as these are the people who, quietly and without fanfare, devote their lives to taking care of the spiritual health of their fellow villagers. They don't live in any kind of defined zones, rather they are active within their community and unless they choose to wear their 'uniforms', consisting of casual clothing, usually white, there's nothing to differentiate them from everyone else in their village. A *Jero Mangku* is like a friendly uncle to all. They are also responsible for the happenings in the temples where the Balinese worship Brahma the creator, Vishnu the preserver and Shiva the destroyer.

The Balinese *desa* (village) is typically host to a set of three temples, each representing an aspect of the village's life. The *Pura Desa* is in the middle and is where meetings and official celebrations are held. This is home to the spirits who protect and bless the villagers as they go about their daily lives. The *Pura Pusch*, or temple of origin, is where founders of villages are worshipped and where we were headed for our full moon ceremony. And the *Pura Dalem*, the temple of the dead, is where tribute is paid to the netherworld and the hidden forces of darkness.

Outside the village in the rice fields is a fourth temple, called the *Pura Subak*. This one's maintained by the irrigation organisation and farmers and is of course where our good friend Dewi Sri, the rice goddess, is worshipped.

Budhi sees to it that daily offerings are made to the gods and spirits who inhabit these sacred places and if asked he will also conduct any ceremonies that take place. He's a very busy man.

It hasn't all been plain sailing, however. Budhi says he fought the initial request to become a *Mangku* because he was scared he couldn't do it. His Bahasa Indonesia wasn't all that great and he really wasn't sure he was up to the job in general. That was when he got sick.

'When something's your destiny you simply can't ignore it,' he told me as he, Sidd and I tucked into plates of rice, spicy chicken and *tempeh* around the common room table at the retreat. According to the Balinese way of life, if you choose to ignore your destiny, there will be consequences.

As soon as Budhi accepted his fate as a permanent part of the Bona community, he got better, his life got back on track and he's now enjoying every new challenge that comes with having such an important (unpaid) job.

Talking to Budhi before the ceremony, it felt like things were really sinking in. Is it possible to know people for just an hour, yet feel like you've known them for ages? Budhi and Sidd and the others who sat with us around the table all have such a sense of calm about them, like life just washes over them and nothing ever ruffles any feathers. Maybe they weren't always like this, but it's definitely the impression they gave me as we chatted.

It wasn't all hippy talk and spiritual analyses either, not like I've encountered with some, or maybe most, of the people I'd met in Ubud so far. It was matter-of-fact and humorous. It was lessons in Hindu culture mixed with un-appreciation of Apple products. We discussed netherworldly forces sprinkled with talk of advertising, travelling with musicians (which Budhi used to do) and writing books. These are people who have lived, eaten, prayed and loved and know who they are. I felt like myself with them … like I could express anything I wanted and ask any question, and actually get some answers. Budhi also generously extended an invitation for me to stay there at the retreat whenever I felt like it. Such a nice *Mangku*!

When it was time to head to the full moon ceremony, Sidd dressed me up in the traditional Balinese dress. For women, there are a few main items that are usually worn for such occasions. The first is a *kamben*, which is a patterned sarong tied at the waist and reaching the ankles. The *kebaya* (blouse) is traditionally made from lace, featuring long sleeves and buttons all the way up the front. The *selendang*, a long and decorative sash that's tied around the waist on top of the *kebaya*, completes the ensemble. The outfit was all white and cinnamon–red and according to Sidd it was fine that my bra was showing through the lace of my blouse as it wasn't so long ago that Balinese women used to walk around with their top halves naked anyway. The Dutch put a stop to that. What were they *thinking?*

I'm not going to lie, I felt pretty sexy as a Balinese lady, even though I was roasting. In the heat of the night my body was pretty much suffocating with my arms and legs in sleeves and a long sarong, but *if that's how the Balinese must dress, that's how I must dress*, I thought, as we stepped out into the light of the lovely new moon.

In the centre of the village, the action had started around the *Pura Pusch*. A huge procession was in place with beautifully dressed women carrying giant offerings, or *banten*, on their heads as they walked, one after the other, through the main village street.

These *banten* are giant offerings made for important ceremonies and are stacked to the max in a Christmas-tree shape. Typically, they feature fruits like mangosteen, mangoes and bananas at the bottom and are topped with cupcakes, huge slabs of sponge cake and sweet treats that look a bit like blocks of pink Rice Krispies.

These yummy things are topped once again with smaller offerings, usually flowers in pandan leaf trays just like the offerings you see all over pavements and in doorways in Bali being showered regularly with holy water. I've since learned that sprinkling holy water over an offering is intended to bring the life back to the plants that were killed in order to be part of the offering in the first place. The Balinese really are a *very* thoughtful people, aren't they?

We stood on the sidelines and watched the parade until it was time to go into the temple. Here I was told to follow Budhi's lead, so I knelt barefoot next to Sidd and went through the ritual of holding various flowers in my fingers and up to my third eye, thanking the gods of the temple for blessing us. Each flower, once used, was to be placed in my hair, I was told, as a gateway to the gods. We were sprinkled several times with holy water and handed a bowl of rice so we could press several grains to our foreheads and temples. This action is to signify a request to the gods to bless your mind. If you stick it on your throat, it's a sign to bless your heart. I stuck it on both for good measure. We also had to eat three grains to embody the blessing of Brahma, Vishnu and Shiva.

Afterwards, I got to practise my Indonesian on a lot of new people as we all gathered to chat and watch the young girls of Bona perform their traditional *Legong* dancing. This is dancing of the most spectacular and kaleidoscopic kind. If you haven't seen it, hop on YouTube and prepare for some serious costume envy.

Girls learn to dance the *Legong* at an early age and it involves a series of intricate moves, especially with the hands and fingers, mostly while holding a fan, plus a lot of skittish eye movement.

Gossiping Legong dancers discuss the word on the street

In a whirl of gold, pink and turquoise they moved for at least an hour and if my thighs were sweating beneath my tight sarong, I can only imagine how hot they must have been in all that make-up and heavy headwear.

Aside from the dancing, people were talking all around the temple — mobile phones rang, children skidded about and motorbikes still struggled to make their way through the throng. It was a bit of a carnival atmosphere with *gamelan* (a clanging musical ensemble), masks instead of clowns and women carrying leftover offerings of chickens and papayas instead of toffee apples and fairy floss.

When it was over, Budhi had to leave and witness a friend of his go through the ritual of dying and being reborn as a higher level of priest (as you do), so Sidd and I walked by the light of the full moon through the rice fields back to the retreat, where I'd left my regular clothes. As I traipsed through the grass behind him I realised that there really is something incredibly sexy about a young western man in Balinese clothing. When the young Balinese dress up they look ridiculously handsome to me, too, all foreign and dark and mysterious, with those beautiful smiles radiating almost as much light as the moon. But I'm sure there are only a few white men who can pull off a patterned *kamben*. Sidd is one of them. He also wore a *udeng* — a traditional white headdress. He was to me in that moment a young, handsome emperor showing a wide-eyed poor girl his magical kingdom (I think I've watched way too many Disney movies in my time).

On the way back to Ubud, dressed in our regular clothes, we sped along the narrow ledges of the rice fields on Sidd's bike, throwing up mud and stones and watching cats and rats scatter in the headlights the whole way back to the street. There was no-one around. As quickly as the crowds had appeared carrying the *saban* and colourful *banten* on their heads like lemmings brandishing fruit and biscuits, they'd dispersed into the night, leaving only coconut husks in piles, snuffling dogs barking after our wheels and the fading smell of incense.

'Did you have fun?' Monet croaked, popping out from behind his painting as I climbed into bed back at the villa.

'I did actually, thanks,' I said, looking once more at the light in the indigo sky through the gap in my curtains. I don't know what it was exactly … perhaps the start of a new cycle born with a brand new Bali moon? It might have even been the insight of a *Jero Mangku* and a wise young man in a well-fitting *udeng*. But something was definitely different.

K9 terrorism ...

I've decided to move out of my villa. It was a tough decision but seriously, the only time I've seen the pool being used was when Russ and River stayed. I've never even been in it myself. Stupid, right? I think I like knowing I have a pool more than actually being in it, if that makes sense. I suppose it doesn't really.

I don't really need such a big room, either and I really can't justify the 5,500,000 Rp it's costing me each month to live in this place. I'm also not particularly keen on living in the rice fields now that I know a little bit more about what's often sacrificed in the name of building all these villas. And that's not all. I'm sick of being chased by those stupid dogs every night when I walk or cycle up my pitch-black street.

'I've been trying to help you, idiots!' I screamed at them last night as they made a dash for my pedals. But I don't think news of my marketing work for BAWA has reached them.

On that note, I haven't been given as much to do for BAWA as I hoped. It started well but I think the people in charge are too busy to delegate. Poor things, they're all just so frazzled. My emails go unanswered, even the ones with work attached. I also found out that one of the girls I made friends with when we went on all our field trips to the clinic, and to a local school to witness the educational talks they give on animal welfare, has actually given up her volunteer position and moved to Sanur with her boyfriend. I'm not sure why, but things have gone a bit off-track. Maybe it's for the best. I'd feel a bit weird working for the good of Bali's dogs when every single night I want to murder some of them before they can do the same to me.

In other places in the world, I'd be fearful of the human monsters lurking in the shadows. Here in Bali, though, I trust the humans. The village people on my street are lovely; their dogs, however, are pure evil.

Last night one of them snarled from a temple entrance as I peddled past, before bounding down right in front of my tyre, causing me to swerve. In a carefully planned terrorism attack I was suddenly surrounded. The original snarler plus four of his mates were hot on my heels, barking and making threatening snaps at my legs as I pedalled twenty times harder than my shaking calves wanted to allow. It was frickin' terrifying! When I finally made it home I was shaking and went as far as locking my door. I even took the key out, should this vicious street-savvy breed of beasts have learned how to bypass basic human security systems. It wouldn't surprise me. They're smart. And they have no respect *whatsoever*.

This morning, having hurtled down the street again only to find them all sleeping in doorways (don't be fooled), I parked my bike at Bali Buddha to have a nice, calming, healthy cup of ginger tea and read the 'good news' paper. Big mistake.

The *Bali Advertiser* tells me an Indonesian man who left his nine dogs to starve while he was away on holiday was recently decapitated and eaten by the pack of hungry hounds when he returned home. Oh yes.

'Police found Andre Lumboga's body ripped to shreds on Monday Sept 5th after a neighbour reported a horrid smell coming from his house in the Batam Centre district of the Riau Islands, a province of Indonesia, northeast of Singapore in the South China Sea.'

OK, so not my specific neighborhood, but still …

'We suspect the dogs were hungry, so they attacked Andre because they had not been fed for fourteen days,' says the article (it's not the greatest journalism ever, really).

'Police chief Eriyana said the man's skull was found in a different room to his body.'

I couldn't seem to locate the paper's usual positive spin on this piece of news, although it's kind of apparent that justice has been served in this case, albeit in a tragic way. Seriously, no wonder these dogs are so angry, if this is the way they're being treated.

So yes, it's onwards and probably downwards I must go. I'm pretty sure I'll be able to land a month in a homestay for less than three million rupiah, and hopefully I'll be able to walk home at night without feeling the need to yell British and Indonesian profanities at animals … (we can thank the guys at Lombok's Happy Cafe for something, after all).

I really do love my beautiful, clean room and the marble floors; Diana, Ayu and her sweeping; the rice paddies all around us; and the farmers who have taken to clanging their aluminum cans on strings day and night behind the pool to stop the birds pecking away at the harvest. And of course I'll really miss Monet and our nightly one-sided conversations.

But unless I move, I'm pretty sure it's only a matter of time before the 'K9 al-Qaeda' decapitate me on the street and eat my liver.

20/10

SeminYUK and the last goodbye...

'Let's get our tits out, maybe he'll give us a discount! I've been here nine fucking times, mate, trust me, I know what things cost.'

It was after this comment from the drunk Aussie blonde at the next table that my visiting friend Pip and I made our swift exit from Ku De Ta yesterday afternoon. There were two girls and two guys, fresh from a tough morning frying themselves like eggs on the beach. The guys were bare-chested and covered in tattoos (of the horrid kind, you know, like anchors), and the girls removed their tank tops as soon as they sat down, revealing bikinis that were so small, their boobs were pretty much on display when you looked at them sideways. Once they were settled with four more large beers, they went about ordering vast amounts of sashimi:

'Aaah yeah, let's get shit-loads of this raw fish stuff, it's so fucking cheap compared to at home, ain't it!'

I'm aware stuff like this makes me sound old, but there were *children* present (tut) and also, this is not Bondi Beach, it's Bali. We tutted profusely as we made our exit and made sure they heard.

I think there's a lot of 'this sort of thing' going on around Kuta, and I've largely avoided it so far by opting to base myself in Ubud. That's pretty touristy too, of course, and I wouldn't count it as the *real* Bali … at least not the kind I got to glimpse with Budhi and Sidd the other night, but it's a long-shot from having to hear semi-naked, foul-mouthed twenty-somethings vocally demonstrating their disrespect for everything they lay their eyes on.

Pip wanted to see the Aussie holiday haven that is Kuta and Seminyak, so we made our way down for the weekend. I tried to do some work in a Kuta coffee shop at one point as Pip went shopping, and it was like setting up a desk in a rave, with five competing DJs blasting tunes through the door at once. I saw more Bintang items than I could count. There were even girls in Bintang dresses carrying Bintangs, shouting at boys in Bintang shirts, also carrying Bintangs in Bintang stubbie holders. It made me wonder if the Balinese working in Kuta view all westerners as hideous drunks.

We asked the taxi driver on the way back to our rented villa (which I made sure was more than two miles away from the beach, in case of a tsunami during our visit), 'So, Kadek, how do you feel about all the drunk tourists in this area?'

'The Australians?'

'Um ... OK.'

'It is just their culture, you know? They like to drink, it's not up to us to judge them.'

'Do you like beer then?'

'Yes, I like a beer ... but I don't need twenty.'

I overheard someone say the other day that they thought Bali was basically Australia on a budget. Whether that's a fair assessment or not, the Bali Central Bureau of Statistics (as quoted in the *Bali Advertiser*) tells us the number of Australian tourists in Bali reached 432,480 during the January to July 2011 period, putting Australia at number one in the top ten sources of Bali's foreign tourists. In fact, Australians contributed to 27 per cent of the total number of foreign tourists (1.58 million) coming to Bali during the same period. Kadek must have ferried a lot of drunks about in his taxi cab.

Anyway, there's no nice way to describe Kuta. It was probably stunning, once. In 1970 it was just a small Balinese village, home to no more than 9000 people. There were just two hotels and no restaurants there at all. By 1975 there were more than a hundred hotels and twenty-seven restaurants in Kuta. It's gone downhill ever since. It's the place where Bali's spirit comes to die. The beach is the most disgusting beach I've ever seen, and I'm from England.

The pollution isn't all the beachgoer's fault — the monsoons also bring rubbish in from other islands, trash which officials are supposed to remove up to five times a week. In April (2011) a scathing article in *Time* magazine, with the headline 'Holidays in Hell: Bali's Ongoing Woes' brought added attention to the fact that Bali's infrastructure is by no means keeping up with its development. It also pointed out that in early March, the Bali authorities warned tourists that swimming in the sea in Kuta for over thirty minutes could cause skin infections.

Perhaps as a result, also in April, 100 cubic metres of unwanted trash was taken off the beach in a mass clean-up and in late August, vendors selling food were banned on the sand to stop littering. Also, in 2010, a surf school partnered up with Oakley and Hard Rock Cafe to provide a hundred recycling bins to keep Kuta Beach clean. As far as I can see though, nothing seems to have helped. It still looks like a giant in the sky tipped his dustbin over it.

Why people would want to sit on it all day, I have no idea. Perhaps they don't notice how grim it is through that Bintang haze. I guess the surf is good. I don't know much (make that anything) about surfing but it must be something special if you can endure wading through all that crap, and possibly contracting something nasty, just to get to a wave. It makes me so sad that such an incredible, spiritual island is being destroyed right before our eyes.

Thankfully Seminyak (roughly ten minutes in a cab from Kuta, depending on traffic) wasn't all yuk. Call me a snob but after seeing Kuta, Pip and I hightailed it back to our villa-with-a-pool and hid with the two exceptional bottles of wine she had to pay a man 100,000 Rp to let her bring through customs. She watched him put it in his pocket and decided not to tell him how many packs of tampons she was smuggling in for me, too.

Pip and I have known each other since 2003, and some of the craziest nights of my life have been with her. It wasn't too many years ago that the concept of taking a holiday in Kuta alone might have sounded quite appealing. I recall one Christmas Eve in New York, Pip and I met a group of handsome young fisherman (and a dog) trying to sell a bag of fresh oysters to Lower East Side bars and restaurants. Somehow we all ended up back at my place in Brooklyn, where we strummed the guitar out on the stairwell till the early hours, drinking tequila and experimenting with the effects of catnip on humans.

As I crawled around on all-fours pretending to be a playful kitten, the fishermen, Pip and I agreed that yes, this was indeed the *greatest* Christmas ever … just as the dog decided to jump at my apartment door from the inside, locking us all out with the key inside.

Luckily … well, not for her, a poor lady was suffering an asthma attack in her bathroom downstairs and the fire brigade were already on site, trying to get her out. We yelled down at them to help us and before long, two strapping hunks (at least, I remember them that way) were beside us in the stairwell, getting ready to bash the door down among a heap of bottles, a bag of oysters, two drunken girls, an abandoned guitar, some catnip and some fishermen.

'Wait!' Pip yelled. 'Do you have to break the door down? Can't you just go in through the fire escape?'

They looked disappointed. Clearly the lady with asthma hadn't given them enough drama for the night and they were dying to batter something in the line of duty. Eventually, though, they retreated, climbed in through the open fire escape on the outside of the building and rescued us, just as the trapped dog and my severely territorial apartment cat were about to embark in a fuzzy brawl on the kitchen floor.

Ah. Those were the days … but yes, the point *is* (and I do have a point!) that even with nights like that behind us, Pip and I would never ever have sat in a Bali restaurant and got our tits out. Ever.

It was Seminyak again that bore witness to another girl-and-boy goodbye. Just metres from the spot where CK and I bid each other farewell back in September, just after I first arrived in Bali, I hugged River for what may have been the last time.

I know, I know, I already said goodbye to River in Ubud, but seeing as we were both in Seminyak and he hadn't caught his plane to Thailand yet, we decided to meet up again and all have dinner.

It was nice to be able to have a second goodbye with him as I guess life has been a little less exciting since he stopped living in my bedroom. And plus, I know at least that by keeping River as 'a friend who was sent to me for fun', he can no longer turn into an object of obsession and can therefore do nothing to get under my skin. Damn, I think that 'sharing' session really did help, you know!

As he sped off on his motorbike with his foot almost completely healed, I didn't feel so alone. I felt full of him, and happy that the universe had first put his bendy body in my path with that sexy Parsva Bakasana move at Boom Boom. Thailand would look after him now.

Pip and I headed back to Ubud together with a new sense of appreciation for the lives we've led and, in a funny way, how far we've come since our crazy days. Singing in hallways with random fishermen was fun, but these days a weekend in a private villa where we can sip from nice wine glasses, escape tsunamis and still hear each other talk is way more appealing these days. Guess that's growing up for you.

I didn't really realise how much I'd adapted to the quiet life since I moved to Bali. But seeing what seems to be polluting the island that I'm really growing to love, I sincerely hope Ubud, or anywhere else for that matter, doesn't turn into the new Kuta, or SeminYUK.

Facing the fear...

It's time. I need to get behind the wheels. I say 'wheels' because a motorbike has two and while my bike is very handy, I need to go faster. I need to go further. I need to bulk up like a biker chick and face my crippling fears before the terror overwhelms me completely and I go my whole time in Indonesia without ever doing it.

Ugh. I feel sick.

My friend Nyoman (of *arak*-night, rice-paddy-snog fame) offered to take me out on a motorbike for a few hours and teach me the basics. He said he'd even show me what to do if I hit a dog, which seemed very kind of him. Hate to miss out on that part. Back home, bumping off a dog would land me in jail, no matter how I did it, probably. No-one ever works the concept of not killing one into a step-by-step guide on how to drive a vehicle. It would make it much more exciting if they did. Imagine swerving around stuffed puppies and stiff dobermans in the supermarket car park with your dad in the passenger seat doling out handy tips. What fun!

So many people keep telling me I'm going to have to face my fear of riding if I'm going to see the *real* Bali. The *real* Bali is a place I'm hearing more and more about these days. I'd like to go there. I'm not sure where it is exactly, or if the *real* Bali is somewhere tourists *should* be going, seeing as we've already stomped all over some very nice areas of the island as it is. But after the other night in Bona I can sense it just beyond my reach.

The *real* Bali is croaking coded secrets with the froggy chorus in the darkness, creeping through the mosquito mesh with the *bang, bang, bang* of the metallophones and the xylophones in the distant *gamelan*, getting even more intriguing every day. I want it to whisk me away like it did when Sidd sped me off into the sunset and dressed me up like a local in a *kamben* and *kabaya*; when I knelt beside him in the Bona Pura Pusch and felt those first three splashes of holy water run over my head and totally ruin my hair. Take me with you, *real* Bali. Show me who you are! But please don't kill me on a motorbike as you do it (gulp).

You probably don't need me to tell you that the way people ride motorbikes here is terrifying.

The *Bali Advertiser* tells me today that the World Health Organisation has released figures that show motor vehicle accidents are one of the world's biggest killers. Motorbikes claim the most lives and it will come as no surprise to most that Southeast Asia is the region that tops this list.

The Balinese, of course, have absolute faith in healers and mystics and psychics, which also contributes to the problems on the roads. Why? Well, if you've been told you're going to die by drowning when you're forty-five, what harm can come from speeding down the street at full throttle on your motorbike with no helmet on when you're eighteen?

Anyway ... I'm supposed to be convincing myself to get a motorbike, not to forget about it. OK. Some positive things: not only will a motorbike get me out of Ubud, it will cause me less pain than cycling. There are so many bloody hills around these parts! As I've said before, all those scenes in *Eat, Pray, Love*, where Julia Roberts cycles around incessantly, waving at everyone with not a sweat patch in sight, are LIES. That infamous grin would have had to be edited in from scenes in *Pretty Woman* had she really pedalled her way round Bali. It's not easy. She would've looked like shit.

But every single day at least three people die in motorcycle crashes in Bali. On a daily average, 150 accident victims turn up limping, seriously injured or already dead at the main hospital, Sanglah. I meet someone every week who's been in an accident. Look at River, for example. His wheels skidded on some gravel, his thonged foot got caught and it took him a month before he could even walk without bandages.

On some days, doctors here tend to 300 people. There are countless youngsters on the island currently being fed slush through drinking straws by their parents, existing like cabbages, not really living, because they didn't wear a helmet.

Riding drunk is a problem here, too. I often get motorbike taxis home, usually a result of answering the call 'Transport?' from a group of guys standing round on a street corner. Wayan Number 9 helps me out when I need a car, but there aren't any official motorbike taxi drivers in Bali. Most are just friendly local guys looking for some easy cash. After a few rum and Cokes, I'm less cautious and don't give a crap how I get home, as long as I don't have to walk and risk being eaten by dogs.

I never really know who my drivers are, or if they're safe. I'm a trusting kinda girl. It's just what everyone does. Yet every time I make it home safely and stare at my face in the bathroom mirror, I thank my lucky stars because what if that smiley guy who'd left his mates on the street corner in order to take my life in his hands for two dollars was drunk?

According to the same article in the *Bali Advertiser*, which has taken a positive spin on things (naturally), the World Health Organization has considered making some changes to the rules in the hope that the trouble on the roads will go away. I can imagine the conversation at headquarters went something like this:

'Why don't we lower blood alcohol limits?'

'That's a great idea! But, wait. Do we have equipment to test those limits here?'

'Er … no. But we could offer instant assessments for all kinds of narcotics?'

'Excellent solution. But, wait. Do we have *those* here?'

'Hmm. No, I don't think we do.'

Silence.

'We could lower the speed limits?'

'OK. This could work, yeah. But we'd need speed limits in the first place, wouldn't we, in order to lower them?'

'Ah, yes. You're right.'

Silence.

'We could enforce the rules on seatbelt restraints and helmets?'

'Great idea. But we already do this. It's a nice way for police officers to score a bit of extra cash before waving them on their way again, unprotected, remember?'

'Hmm.'

Long silence.

'Shall we go back to the drawing board?'

'OK. We'll get some *nasi campur* on the way.'

It's really not looking like things on the roads will be changing any time soon. Still, I suppose if jumping on my own motorbike is the key to seeing the *real* Bali, I've just got to pad myself up and get on with it.

23/10

Shakes on a plane ...

On the plane to Bali in September I met a lovely lady from Perth called Jane who sat next to me. We started chatting and it turned out that she'd just sold her house and given up everything she owned in favour of living on an ashram in the foothills of Mount Agung. I shut my book instantly and gave her all my attention.

This ashram is run by a guru called Ratu Bagus, a self-realised master who receives his teachings from the 'light' and passes them on through a form of meditation involving shaking. It's an art. You stand on the spot, shake your body and you heal.

Ratu's power as a Brahmin, teacher, healer and community leader has been praised internationally and Jane was very excited to be flying back there to shake three times a day in a room full of people. In fact, Plane Jane was positively powering the aircraft herself with her soaring spirit.

'Ratu Bagus means good king,' she told me, beaming, before spending the best part of an hour describing her healing process and the various things that go on around the ashram. Apparently, it's about to become one of the most sought-after healing spots to visit in the world. I was hooked.

The ashram has been around since 1987 and is situated in the east of Bali, about ninety minutes north of Denpasar. Ratu lives there with his 'spiritual' family, which I think probably means they're not related but spend a lot of time sitting in silence together and not wearing deodorant. Since 1993, when a group of Italians discovered the amazing work Ratu Bagus was doing and took him to Rome with them, western students have been drawn there, too, to experience his highly transformational inner work. They stay for weeks or months at a time in order to heal themselves of all sorts of illnesses ... or just to be close to his greatness.

A group of Balinese who live there are expert shakers with years under their belts. Ratu's mum, who's in her nineties, also shakes and everyone staying there helps with running the ashram.

Ratu is apparently quite creative in his approach.

Let the shaking commence!

'He has a wicked sense of humour, even though he's incredibly powerful,' Jane said, as visions of Dumbledore in a flowery sarong whizzed through my head. 'He shows us how to truly heal ourselves by fully opening our hearts and helping us to connect to Divine love.'

Plane Jane doesn't know how long she'll end up living on the ashram. All she knows is that it's where she belongs. It occurred to me there and then that maybe this lady had chosen to sit in that particular empty seat, on that relatively empty plane for a reason.

Perhaps this is how it happens, I remember thinking at the time, getting romanced by the notion of being spiritually selected by destiny as we soared through the sky on the way to Bali. Is this how the start of *me* starts?

After some further research, I've now booked my place at the ashram in December. Apparently by then, Ratu Bagus himself will be back from his teachings abroad and ready to get back to work in Bali. I shot Plane Jane an email. She's still there and doesn't anticipate leaving before I get there (not surprising, seeing as she's sold her house), so I'll know someone there, which makes me feel a bit better about connecting to the Divine without any of my usual friends around to pull me back again.

I never thought I'd go and stay at an ashram, but I'm really quite excited about shaking things up a bit!

25/10

Bali: why bother?

Ooh, there's been some drama today. A journalist from Australia's *Sydney Morning Herald* has written a pretty scathing report of her time in Ubud during the writer's festival and it hasn't gone down well at all.

Pip sent me the article from her desk back in Sydney with a note that said, 'Well *I* liked it,' so it was the first thing I read when I woke up. The Twitterati were already fuming.

This journalist didn't have a very nice time here because of the 'touts'. Apparently these people, constantly chasing her down the street offering their services and flogging their 'wooden penises' and 'plastic skeletons having sex' shouldn't be out in public at all. Her actual words were: 'I developed a resentment of locals, which I'm sure is undeserved. I just wish they could see how bad their touts are and lock them away in a dark room.'

Oh dear.

Another snippet causing concern is: 'This tout smiled and asked if I wanted "transport". I smiled and explained very politely that, in Australia, if a woman gets on a motorbike with a stranger, that is called prostitution.'

People aren't liking that one at all! As many people have pointed out in various forums, getting on a motorbike does not in any way link the rider, nor the passenger, to prostitution in Australia, does it? I mean, I don't know for sure because I've never dabbled in the bikie circuit over there, or the selling-my-body-for-cash circuit for that matter (honest), so I can't say with absolute certainty that the journalist in question didn't research this paragraph completely before committing it to a computer. I just don't know.

She might in fact be the greatest journalist on Earth, poring for hours over this theory in secret and finally concluding this shocking fact to be true. But when it came to writing it down, she screwed it up. She didn't *tell* us how long she spent interviewing prostitutes on the streets of Melbourne, or Koolyanobbing, or Tittybong, or Pimpinbudgie, or Burrumbuttock (I admit, I Googled 'small towns in Australia' for this and would you believe these places really exist? Australia is amazing!)

She didn't tell us how many bikie boys she followed down darkened alleyways in search of red lights and the cracking of whips and the squeaking of cheap plastic passing as leather, hugging gyrating bodies in floor-to-ceiling windows. If she'd only added a little validation to the sentence, we may have read it differently.

Another cracking sentence: 'Then I started pretending to use my mobile phone as I walked, which oddly enough actually worked, save the odd, determined "Miiiisss ..."'

I don't know why I didn't think of this!

Seriously, I know you can't expect every visitor to learn another language just in case they need to say 'no thank you' to a taxi driver, or refuse a wooden penis (which are officially carved as symbols of fertility). It can be annoying having to tell twenty-five men in the space of ten minutes you don't need a ride ... hell, the other day I was asked if I needed a motorbike taxi while I was actually *on* a motorbike taxi! But one of these days you're going to want a ride, maybe two in quick succession, and these guys don't want to miss their chance.

Wayan Number 9 told me once that Ubud taxi companies or drivers can't have contracts with hotels the way they can in some places like Nusa Dua because the hotels here have all agreed to use drivers and staff from the properties' surrounding villages. Even then, hotel employees will often get to the customers first with their own, slightly cheaper offers of transport. In order to be a taxi driver you're supposed to have a government licence, but lots of people don't bother paying for one. It's expensive to do things legitimately.

If the police catch someone without a licence, Wayan Number 9 says they'll just accept a bribe and send them on their way, like they will if they catch a westerner without a helmet or an international driving licence. It's a dog-eat-eat world, the world of Bali taxi driving. The journalist continues: 'Then I thought, is it just me? Do other Australian tourists find the whole tout behaviour thing charming or amusing? I mean, do they see it as part of a carnival atmosphere that you just laugh off? I thought it was vile. It didn't reflect well either on the Balinese or on the tourists; it was a lowest common denominator tourist hell.'

As we know, Australians currently account for 27 percent of international visitors to Bali and tourism itself generates almost US$3.5 billion a year. Bali needs Australians: drunk, obnoxious or otherwise. And most of the drunk ones love Bali. It has good surf, cheap booze, wooden penises and men who love to ferry women around in exciting motorbike thrill-rides, whether they think they're prostitutes or not. What's not to love?

The idea of trying to correct opinionated foreigners would probably not occur to many Balinese, at least not those living peaceful lives selling their produce and services in tourist towns. My lovely friend Ibu-T (who also helps me with my visa stuff) came into Clear Cafe the other day, practically in tears.

'Becky,' she said, 'I am so upset … my customer … I just had to tell him I can't help him anymore.' She flung herself down in the chair opposite me miserably.

It emerged that this customer, a middle-aged man from Australia, had propositioned her. He told Ibu-T that she was beautiful and that he liked her, and that he found her attractive. He told her that if she felt like spending a night with him, he would be fine with it and it didn't matter to him that she had a husband and a child, as long as it didn't matter to her.

Ibu-T was distraught. 'Becky, I love my husband,' she said. 'I'm in love with him, and I love my son and I would never cheat. Why would he think that I'd cheat? Why would he think that I didn't love my family?'

I told her that the man was clearly a horrible, slimy sleaze-bag and not to worry about it. But whereas most of us would be tempted to give the bloke in a question a good hard slap about the face before storming off into the blue, to a gentle Balinese lady like Ibu-T it would be the height of rudeness. Instead, she took his proposition straight to her heart, where it festered and burned like an offensive cigarette in an ashtray. And even though it smouldered and hurt, she still felt she shouldn't do anything about it. She told him instead that she didn't have the time to work with him anymore, and left it at that.

'I often wondered what these touts would think if their sister or mother got on a motorbike with a strange man,' the journalist continues. Well, to be honest, probably nothing. Everyone rides a motorbike in Bali. If she'd spent longer than five minutes observing the traffic instead of talking to imaginary people on the phone, she'd have noticed.

If a husband who'd been waiting ages for his wife to come home were to ask 'What took you so long, Ibu?' and she replied, 'Well, I was going to hitch a ride with that man we've seen around but I didn't know him and I wasn't sure it would be wise,' he'd probably be quite shocked. If a bike's going up the street and there's space on it after the rider's loaded up five chickens, three children, nine brooms and a wardrobe, why the hell wouldn't he carry a woman too?

I guess I can understand that it's hard not to be ignorant here at times. There's so much to learn and take in and you're obviously going to get some things wrong (and yes, I suppose this is a bit of a personal disclaimer!). I feel like an idiot most of the time myself. But still, for this journalist to put her opinions on the page of a national newspaper without really even *trying* to understand anything at all about the culture is a bit of a shame.

It's also a bit of a shame that the Balinese, who had the misfortune to encounter her here in Ubud, are going to think Australia is a country full of pillion-passenger prostitutes.

28/10

Water, water, everywhere!

I had a choice of visiting one of two places when it came to extending my visa at an Indonesian Embassy. Neither of them was in Indonesia. One was Bangkok and the other was Singapore. At the time of decision-making and flight-booking, Bangkok was suffering at the mercy of the worst flooding in more than half a century.

'A high tide beginning very soon may exacerbate flooding, which has already killed 373 people and swamped factories north of the capital,' screamed the news.

Naturally I chose Bangkok.

So here I am, sitting in a cafe just off Khao San Road, waiting for … well, I don't really know. Gaby (who still lives here) and I are both tapping away at our computers, same as usual, keeping a close eye on news feeds for word of impending disaster, but so far I haven't seen so much as a puddle. The sun is shining, a guitar is strumming, the husky tones of a male singer accompany our coffee and we're contemplating Thai for dinner. Maybe we'll catch a movie. It's all quite strange. And in spite of the weirdness here, it's also weird *being* here.

The further away from Bali I get, the more 'back to normal' I feel and I'm not sure this isn't a bit unsettling. I'm starting to like the way life in Bali is so different, and how it's really starting to bring out a different, almost calmer side of me. Gaby, however, sees these changes from another perspective and has said she's one step closer to disowning me. When I met her off the plane and we hugged in a shopping-mall Starbucks, I was sporting my turquoise trousers, thongs, no make-up and a Bali patchwork hold-all I bought from the Ubud market. She was

119

not impressed. I might not smell of hemp yet, but I'm starting to consider the word *namasté* and of course I'm spending December in an ashram. I can see how she might think I'm going off the rails.

Anyway, it's hard to believe that dikes just north of the city are currently struggling to hold back a three-meter-deep wall of water that has already bogged roughly 10,000 factories, buggering up the supply chains of gigantic, seemingly indestructible companies like Toyota and Apple. Crocodiles have been spotted on doorsteps. Residents in northern Bangkok are catching fish in their kitchens and slurping noodles with their feet hanging off chairs piled up over waist-deep floodwaters.

'For people who choose to stay in Bangkok, we have a plan for a food-storage centre,' a man of importance has just announced on the telly. 'Electricity and water should not be a problem, for now.'

It's like the end of the world has dawned. Mum even posted three kisses to us both on Gaby's wall. 'Stay safe xxx'.

As arranged, I stopped by the embassy this morning, visa documents in hand, only to find the gates shut, bolted and blocked by stacks of sandbags. Every door is blocked by sandbags in Bangkok right now.

'Open in three days', a bored-looking security guard said, pointing to a sign in Thai.

I stood there in front of him, clutching my envelope and passport, looking at the gates as though they might suddenly apologise and open.

If I can't get my visa extension here in Bangkok, I'll have to leave the country AGAIN in thirty days, on a plane ...'

I looked at him, hoping perhaps my inner monologue of concern would transcend the language barrier. He grinned.

... OK. If it's open in three days I might be able to get the visa in time to make the flight back to Bali, but it'll be cutting it fine and I can't really take that risk. What if I missed my flight? AirAsia will never let me change my flight at such short notice. Hmm. What to do, what to do...

He grinned some more. Obviously my thinking-face was amusing.

I suppose I can't be too annoyed here, can I? At least my house isn't underwater and I don't have crocodiles sleeping on my porch. I can't complain at all about my stupid little visa problem because in the grand scheme of things, it's not even a problem. It's just going to be expensive, flying somewhere else in another thirty days just to visit another embassy.

Thousands of people have reportedly left Bangkok, but thousands more are still here and the city is marching on, like always. Except ... we've just heard that the Twilight-themed Halloween party has been cancelled. Not good.

There are other parties, of course. You can't stop a city like Bangkok from throwing a bash if there's a good enough excuse. I have a feeling people would party in this city even if they had to swim there and float around the event on inflatable chairs. But Gaby says she wakes up every morning never knowing if today's the day she'll find her belongings floating around her room and have to evacuate. It's a big, scary world away from what I've been used to in Bali. I feel very fortunate and blessed. I've told her she should come back with me.

When I get back to Ubud, I'm moving into my new homestay in the centre of town, on a street with considerably fewer stray dogs on terror patrol. Putu, the lovely lady who runs the place, has offered me a very nice room for the monthly sum of 3,000,000 Rp, for which I'll get a basic bedroom and bathroom and her home-cooked breakfast every morning. There's no swimming pool, but it's just down the street from Bar Luna, which I happen to think is an excellent trade-off.

When I first walked in to check out the place, Putu was bathing her two-year-old son, also called Putu, who was giggling and splashing about in a plastic bathtub. Her husband Wayan was looking on, smiling in the sunshine. It was like a scene from the start of a movie or something. You could almost see bluebirds landing on their shoulders. As she wiped the soapy suds off her hands to grab a room key and show me round, she chattered cheerfully about all the people who've stayed there so far and how they always come back because they love her banana pancakes.

Mai Malu, which means 'come now' (in a very innocent way) only opened in December, so the rooms are really nice. I looked at a good few guesthouses before I found this one, and I can safely say that it's a far cry from some of the others in town. Some were disgusting and dark and damp, and looked like they hadn't been touched-up or even cleaned in years.

If you're looking for a homestay in Ubud, my best advice would be to do what I did and spend a morning walking around the area you want to stay in, and look at all your options. A little research will definitely pay off. It seems to me as though most landlords have raised their prices drastically in the last few years without doing anything much in return. There are some good ones around if you're willing to put in the legwork, as most won't have websites. If you want one with a swimming pool expect to pay roughly 150,000 to 300,000 Rp a night or slightly less if you're staying long-term.

So … back to Bangkok. Like I said, I've told Gaby she is more than welcome to fly back with me to Bali and stay with me and Putu and Little Putu and Wayan until things get a bit better here, but she's grown an attachment to the city and wants to stick it out with her friends. Well … she *says* that, but I think we both know she's afraid of making a new attachment to a fashion-free lifestyle and the ever-growing possibility of smelling like hemp. So I'm returning to Bali alone.

05/11

Trouble in paradise …

Going through the airport in Denpasar always freaks me out. I see those signs reading 'WELCOME TO INDONESIA! DEATH PENALTY FOR DRUG TRAFFIKERS' and rather than be appalled by the terrible spelling, as I am most days in Southeast Asia, I automatically think the worst — that someone's snuck half a kilo of cocaine into my Winnie-the-Pooh suitcase.

The visa stuff doesn't bother me, really. I may have failed to get my six-month visa, for which you have to leave the country to get, but another thirty-day tourist one has covered me for now and my good friend Ibu-T can take care of an extension on my behalf for what seems to be a set fee. Drugs are a different matter. I don't think you can buy your way out of that little issue in Bali, no matter how much cash you try and flash.

I've been reading Schapelle Corby's book, *No More Tomorrows*, which didn't help my state of mind as I wheeled Pooh through customs the other day. The more I read, the more horrified I am by the whole thing. Did she do it? Did Schapelle, who's now going out of her mind in a Kerobokan Prison cell, really attempt to smuggle 4.2 kilograms of marijuana into Denpasar in her boogie-board bag back in 2004?

The media have been pointing fingers all over the place since it happened, but having seen a bit of what goes on around here, I would be willing to bet she didn't actually do anything wrong. According to the book (which of course, might not be 100 per cent accurate) the bag of cannabis found in Schapelle's bag was never fingerprinted to check where it came from — not by the Indonesian custom officials nor by the police. Requests to watch airport CCTV footage were denied and Schapelle's case was barely covered at all in the Indonesian press. It seems to have been swept under the carpet (probably with a really big broom).

I could go on, because I really do feel bad for Schapelle, imprisoned on an island most people are running around calling paradise. But I won't.

At the end of the day, Bali's a nice place. But it would be a bit silly to think — and indeed report — that everything's peachy here in our little esoteric wonderland.

When I looked around for more information on visitor's hours, I found a tour company set up specifically for visiting Schapelle Corby. Don't worry. It takes about three seconds to recognise it's a hoax:

> Actually get inside Schapelle's cage and spend up to thirty minutes just metres away from her. This tour is recommended if you want to take up-close photos of Schapelle, or if you want to try and talk to her on a personal level. For safety reasons Schapelle must be chained up during all cage visits, and should not be approached under any circumstances.

I'm not so sure Schapelle would find that funny.

Apparently, CK's friend was allowed into Kerobokan for a visit a while ago and all he had to do was take some food. I think he went to see some of the Bali Nine.

For those unfamiliar with the story, these nine Australians were arrested in 2005 in a plan to smuggle 8.3 kilograms of heroin from Indonesia to Australia. The stash was valued at approximately A$4 million, though they're now paying for it with their lives. Two of them, Andrew Chan and Myuran Sukumaran, are on death row, while the rest are serving life imprisonment in Kerobokan.

As a result of reading Schapelle's book, I've been wondering more and more about the prison. It's kind of weird, I know, but you know when you get an image of something in your head and it's all you can see? She paints a pretty gruesome picture. I've only ever seen it from the outside, driving past in a taxi. It's kind of eerie.

My friend Sarah, who took me to the Green School that time, knows a lady called Joanna Witt who works in the prison on a project to teach the inmates silversmith skills. I'm not sure if she works directly with Schapelle, but she does work with Si Yi Chen, another member of the Bali Nine. I'm shooting her an email to find out more. It's quite nice to hear that there are some good things going on in there, especially as all the media reports seem to be so negative.

Over a hundred tourists are suffering in Kerobokan Prison now for drug crimes. Some are there because they bought drugs, sometimes sold to them by corrupt, undercover police, and freed only after lining someone's pocket with an extortionate bribe. Examples are made of a few petty criminals here and there to maintain the appearances that Indonesia simply won't tolerate such behaviour. More recently there was the case of an anonymous fourteen-year-old Australian boy sentenced to two months in prison after he was convicted for buying 3.6 grams of marijuana from a Kuta street dealer. Luckily, he escaped a life of confinement in Bali and after a harrowing ordeal that will no doubt haunt him for life, he was released and is now back home wearing a balaclava (seriously, he wore a balaclava in public the whole time!). But in a third-world country where money talks and corruption is rife, the drug problem continues.

Travel forums are full of tips on where to buy magic mushrooms in Bali, as well as horror stories from people who've experienced the competition between cafe owners to sell the biggest trip. A loophole means that mushrooms, while not entirely legal, are tolerated. The problem is they are often mixed in drinks with other substances so you never really know exactly what you're taking. The Gili islands, in particular, while not a part of Bali, are supposed to be a 'shroom-fan's paradise and there are no police on the islands yet, either.

These mushrooms grow on cow and buffalo shit and I'm not entirely sure if they're washed or not before they're blended into your trippy banana and Redbull smoothie. Can't see why they'd bother; you wouldn't want to go washing any of that yummy psychoactive psilocybin off too, now would you? I guess I'll find out soon enough. My friend Dacey and I are all booked to go to the Gilis for my birthday.

When you consider what Indonesians have been through during the Dutch occupation and then that terrible General Suharto dictatorship (who's like Voldemort here by the way; you just don't speak his name because people get very upset), it's easier to understand why there are so many contradictory views on narcotics in this country. Despite a strengthened anti-narcotics law, which passed in 2009, the head of Indonesia's National Narcotics Agency (BNN) estimated that five million people were still dependent on or using drugs in 2011, which accounts for three per cent of Indonesians between the ages of ten and fifty-nine. Scary. It's a country of contradictions, but if there's any doubt in your mind about what's allowed and what's not allowed, do yourself a favour and assume that nothing is.

I read that the sales of plastic wrapping and padlocks for luggage have gone up since Schapelle was convicted. Luckily, no-one has tried to deposit heroin in any of Winnie the Pooh's cracks yet but needless to say I watch my baggage like a hawk the whole time I'm anywhere with strangers these days. The last thing I want, aside from subsisting on a diet of white rice and rat droppings in a prison cell, is to be heading back to the UK in a balaclava.

08/11

People don't choose Bali ...

'Man, since that full moon I've just been all over the place.'
'You're a Cancer, aren't you?'
'Yeah ... oh right! That'll be why, of course!'
— Overheard in Clear Cafe, Jl Hanoman, Ubud

Ubud itself gets its name from the word *Ubad*, or medicine, referring to the healing herbs growing wild around its jungle and rivers. Some might say it's this healing reputation that has drawn people to Ubud; those who feel the need to touch base with their innerselves, or change their lives.

The energy here is so strong that sometimes the forces collide and make you go a bit stir-crazy. They can also crisscross and block until none can move at all ... kind of like a cosmic traffic jam. This is when people might experience delays in their everyday lives.

In a big city, if this happened you'd probably never notice, right? If something doesn't happen as it should you tut in minor irritation and do something else instead. After all, you don't feel normal unless you're being pulled in a zillion directions anyway, right? *Hair appointment, lunch date, meeting with boss, dinner party, obligatory shag with equally knackered other half* ...

But sometimes in Bali you can be sitting quite peacefully, alone, with no agenda whatsoever and you'll still get this overwhelming feeling of restlessness. It's enough to make a sane woman think *is it me?* Or is it *really* this island that's twitchy?

Ibu Kat told me back in June when I first met her, that lots of people believe Bali itself to be the womb of the universe; the beating heart of all things feminine. And if Bali's the centre of womanly power and Ubud is pretty much the centre of Bali, we're living slap-bang in the girliest energy vortex on Earth.

'Just look around you,' Ibu Kat said as we sat sipping our yummy *arak* in Bar Luna. 'See how many strong, powerful women there are here? Every one of them came here for a reason, even if they don't know what it is yet.'

And then, looking at me over the rim of her glass, she said the most intriguing thing of all: 'People don't choose Bali. Bali chooses people.'

Yesterday in writers' group I met a girl called Zara from Alabama and straight away I felt like I'd met her before. After sharing our thoughts and scribbles out loud, we arranged to meet later at a pre-arranged raw dinner party, full of even more people neither of us had ever met.

At a table full of strangers, it emerged that Zara has been going through some emotional difficulties and as part of a long, self-healing, round-the-world trip she's stumbled upon Ubud and is finding it almost impossible to leave. She says she feels a magnetic pull … like she has to be here, although she's been feeling quite drained because something with equal strength seems to be pushing her out.

'Like what?' I asked over a heaped plate of lettuce.

'I feel like something's watching me at night in my hotel room,' she said.

It was then that Bob piped up. Bob's also a member of the writers' group and he works with energies.

'Is your hotel near the river?' he asked mysteriously, popping a forkful of grated zucchini into his mouth.

The Balinese are afraid of living close to the river because of the River People — restless souls who, we've learned, travel up and down the waterways and cause trouble. Ibu Kat had a dog taken from her by these spirits once; an event she describes in her book, *Bali Daze*. One day, the dog felt the urge to sniff out the steep riverbank, though he'd never gone there before. He got stuck on the slopes and had to be rescued, but several days later he did it again and never came back. He was eventually found with a broken neck.

As Ibu Kat's *pembantu* Wayan Manis wiped her eyes at the sight she said sadly, resolutely, 'The River People wanted him'.

The Balinese are so cautious when it comes to these spirits that they let all the ignorant westerners live in their wonderful waterside properties, while getting *themselves* inland, where it's safe. They bathe in the rivers, of course. You can't go five kilometres without seeing a gaggle of bare-butted men chatting happily as they sud themselves clean by the side of the road, but they rarely occupy waterfront homes. These spirits are inclined to take over houses, you see. It takes a lot more effort and a lot more offerings to keep them out. Bob described what they look like, too: 'They're practically human'.

Bob has a friend who identifies the energy of certain plots in Bali, using two metal rods. It's a bit like divination, I suppose, but he searches instead for bad vibes so people know whether or not it's safe to build their houses. He once identified a really bad energy which he said could be a warning from the River People in the corner of a plot of land that was soon to host a new home, but the building was erected anyway. A few years later, a western lady who'd found herself bedridden in that *exact* spot died of cancer.

I noticed Zara was getting paler and paler as the conversation continued. I think we were all wondering which rampant spirit might be holed up in her hotel room.

Bali's society, I'm learning, consists of two inherently ambivalent spheres, which they control with ritual behaviour. To the Balinese, absolutely everything has its allotted place, which is why both good and bad forces are acknowledged with offerings. The highest and most holy spot in the heavenly sphere, or 'upper world', is reserved for the gods and their revered ancestors. The lowest spot in the sphere of the underworld is home to evil spirits and demons.

There's a middle world, too, where we humans live. A *real* Middle-earth. In Bali, humans are considered to be a sort of microcosm, a miniature version of the greater world, if you will, and as such we're participants in all three worlds. The supernatural is very real and is not something to be taken lightly. Humans can be affected by the darkness at any point, if we fail to appease the evil forces.

Talking on this topic for long at a party would usually see the weirdo initiator ostracised in a corner, but here in Bali, ghosts, energies and spirits (not the boozy kind) are obviously subjects of merit that can make for hours of mesmerising conversation. Zara, Bob and I were just getting into the haunted rice fields around the ARMA Resort on the outskirts of Ubud (according to legend, there are fourteen-foot beings who float above the ground there) when one bearded man, having overheard our chit-chat, took the liberty of sidling up beside me at the table and telling me I wasn't even there.

'This is all just an illusion,' he said, gesturing across the colourful bowls of veggies and grains with a giant sweep of his arm. 'You're a fool if you honestly think any of this is *real*.'

I frowned in Zara's direction. There's always someone who has to take things too far.

Still, I can't concentrate a lot of the time here. Everything's out of whack. I feel compelled to do certain things and go certain places for no explicable reason and when I give in to these urges, nine times out of ten I soon find out why. I'll meet someone nice, or helpful, or someone I can help somehow, or someone I'd been thinking about contacting anyway. Perhaps this is just a coincidence; just what happens in a small town. Or maybe it isn't.

As Bob pointed out last night, if Zara hadn't been so miserable in her hotel, she wouldn't have come into town for the writers' group, and she wouldn't have met me. And if she hadn't met me she wouldn't have come to the dinner party and discovered the *real* reason she'd been feeling so miserable ... those pesky River People! And if it wasn't for the River People we definitely wouldn't have had a 'girl power' sleepover at my homestay, discussing other weird energies and everything in between less than twenty-four hours after we'd met. Well, I couldn't let her go back to her haunted hotel!

Bali seems to bring people together at the strangest times for the weirdest reasons, but I'm learning to trust it. It's just the way it is around here. Even so, what Ibu Kat said is still getting to me. Did Bali really choose *me* to come here? I felt the pull back in June, but I didn't know why. Did it choose her and Zara and my friend Susan who survived the boating tragedy that took her family? I meet strong, inspirational women here all the time and they're definitely not all here to *Eat, Pray* and *Love* hot Brazilians.

I wonder, are these energies around us working some kind of invisible magic, or are they only there because we're choosing to *think* they are? We haven't appeased or indeed intentionally ignored any good or bad forces since the day *we* were born, so why shouldn't all of this elude us? Are the things we see and feel here all an illusion, like beardy said? Am I real, or did I *used* to be real but now I'm just losing myself to this fairytale world of good and evil, stuck in the Middle-earth with my linen trousers on, sitting at raw food parties, a fake who still has no idea about *Saccharomyces boulardii.*

Sometimes I get so confused looking for answers in this place that I can't even remember what the question was.

10/11

Villa Kitty...

We all love cats. Even the people who say they don't like cats are lying, I'm sure of it. I had a terrible experience with cat ownership in Dubai — mine was a right little diva and I had to give her away to an Arab after she crapped on my bed one too many times. But I got over it. What's not to love about those little wet noses, those twitchy whiskers, those tiny little kitten paws obsessed with the hem of your skirt or frayed jeans? Cats and kittens make the world go round, not money. If all the money ran out there would still be kittens and that would make everything OK.

And I'm not just saying this because I'm thirty-one and single. I'm NOT.

Well, maybe my current love of cats *has* got something to do with being thirty-one and single. I never thought about it this way. Maybe this is how it starts. I don't have a boyfriend, I don't even have a web-developer from Montana living in my bedroom anymore, but here in Bali there are just so many kittens offering cuddles, who needs a man? I can hug and squeeze and play with and feed and sleep next to and ...

Yeah, this is definitely how it starts.

I don't care, though, because whereas dogs and I seem to disgust each other, cats and kittens in Bali deserve a lot of love and attention and yesterday I spent the whole afternoon at a place called Villa Kitty, full of people who think the same. Villa Kitty. What an awesome name. When I first heard it, my imagination built a stupendous pink castle in the shape of a cat's head. Massive it was. The doorway was a grinning mouth and the ears were windows, out of which poked the little button noses of a million lovely cats, all waiting to play with me.

When Wayan Number 9 dropped me off in the car and it was just a little villa, I had to hide my disappointment. Dubai would have built the cat's head.

Villa Kitty is an operation set up by a fantastic lady called Elizabeth Henzell and was started in 2009 as the 'Cats and Kittens' section at BAWA. After landing some funding of her own in early 2011, Elizabeth was able to take her growing brood of rescued cats to a purpose-built shelter, and it's from this tranquil spot that she and her twelve staff work tirelessly to provide veterinary care and sterilisation programs for the kitty-cats of Bali.

I was invited to brunch, something Villa Kitty does once a week for friends and supporters. We sat outside the cat compound, watching the resident dog Kanga, who has three legs, hop about like a comedy cartoon character. Elizabeth told me how she's still having trouble getting the proper help she needs to turn Villa Kitty into a *yayasan* (a foundation registered and approved by the government). Apparently, as a non-registered company they're not allowed to take volunteers, even though BAWA has legions of them begging to help. To get the *yayasan* status, Elizabeth must go through officials in Jakarta, a place that doesn't seem to think a foundation for cats is particularly necessary. They hate cats in Jakarta. I'm not sure why ... what on Earth did cats ever do to Jakarta? Google tells me nothing. Until a way around it all is uncovered, Elizabeth and her co-founder must spend $3,000 of their own money per month, plus whatever donations they receive, on buying everything the cats need to survive in their care. And more support is desperately needed.

Villa Kitty also plays host to children from such places as the Jodie O'Shea Orphanage. The orphanage, which was founded in 2005 in memory of a lady who died in the Bali Bombings is home to over fifty children aged from two to eighteen. Elizabeth has seen miraculous results in the kids who've been brought from Denpasar to Ubud to play with her cats. We're talking kids from broken homes, kids who've suffered terribly from abuse, kids who haven't smiled or shown emotion in months, and their faces lighting up when handed a kitten! The power of cats should not be scoffed at!

But there's so many of them here at Villa Kitty needing homes. *Where will they go if no-one adopts them?*, I mused as we sat there eating lunch. Sometimes, Elizabeth says, it seems the twenty-four hour care and devotion of twelve people just isn't enough.

I offered to help writing copy for the official Villa Kitty website, like I did for BAWA. If they can get word out, maybe more help will come with donations and people looking to adopt.

There's a problem here, though. Foreign breeds of cat can *still* be bought from the Denpasar market — a market that's teeming with every creature you could possibly want to purchase. Elizabeth told me that one of her staff brought back a monkey once, thinking he'd rescued it from a life of misery. He may have saved one, but he paved the way for another to be ordered in and sold to someone else. It's all about supply and demand.

Expats like 'nice' cats and dogs. They like cutesy breeds like Chihuahuas and Pekingese, which don't cope well in this environment. The animals get sick and who do their owners come to for help? Elizabeth's vets; the vets who are already flat-out working to help Bali's own animals.

Treatment of a foreign cat is probably what started the current outbreak of feline panleukopenia at Villa Kitty, a contagious disease which must be curbed before it claims any more kitty lives. But it's not just diseases that are killing kittens in Bali. The story of Yola and Splasher almost had my thirty-one year old single self sobbing on the floor.

Splasher was a big, strong, 'street-fighter' tom, and Yola was a timid ginger kitten. To everyone's surprise, the two were so inseparable that Villa Kitty had to look hard for an adoptive family that would take them both together. Eventually, the right couple came along (or so they thought) and the two went off to start their new lives, being spoilt and adored. Unfortunately, the adoptive family had no idea that cats are supposed to be fed, and can't actually find their own food and water. Villa Kitty's policy to check up on their animals two to three weeks after adoption saved their lives, but only just.

Yola came back to Villa Kitty so thin that they had to put her on a drip immediately. For her sake, they brought Splasher back too, only to find he was not the same cat. He'd lost one and a half kilograms and was covered in wounds. He was so traumatised from fighting with other cats for food that he now wouldn't even trust the humans who used to take care of him.

Yola was put in Villa Kitty's sick bay and pined for Splasher, but Splasher couldn't even look at Yola. It was almost as if the pain of seeing her so sick was too much for him. Eventually, her little *meows* won him over and he lay beside her. Since then, he's only left her side to stretch his legs and to visit the toilet.

When I saw them they were both stick-thin and fragile. I was shown photos of how they looked before and the difference was staggering.

'How people can treat animals like this is beyond me,' said Elizabeth, practically in tears herself as we looked at them lying miserably on the floor in their own little enclosure.

The most shocking thing in the whole story, though, is that it was an employee of another animal welfare association who abused them. Someone who's been trained in animal welfare and who should have known better is responsible for their starvation and consequential organ failure.

Yola and Splasher are getting plenty of love and care back at Villa Kitty but the future doesn't look bright. It's quite possible, says Elizabeth, that their friendship is the only thing really keeping them alive.

There are so many animals in Bali that need help even though so many of them have already been treated for disease, and hundreds more are tucked away, being looked after by people like Elizabeth and her team. I'd take some in myself if only I could (and not just because I'm thirty-one and single!).

The Balinese are being educated in animal care and slowly but surely there's a noticeable improvement in the general welfare of domestic and stray animals in Bali. But to the regular westerner used to seeing cats and dogs bouncing with health and vitality, it does seem like there's a frighteningly long way to go.

Underwater balloons and the broken boat …

I popped my head above the water to see Papaya was still swimming furiously ahead of me, the orange tip of his snorkel a beacon against the vivid blue of the sky. I'd lost the coral reef ages ago and had been staring at sand on the bottom of the ocean for the past five or ten minutes through my cheap, leaky mask.

'I see turtles!' Papaya cried, waving frantically from his position in the deep. His excitement rippled across to me on the waves but I was starting to freak out. How much did I want to see a giant green turtle, and how much did I not want to drown?

'Come here, Becky, I promise I show you turtles, they're just over here!' He was pleading from afar but I was treading water, aware that the beach on Gili Trawangan was miles away in the other direction. Reluctantly I shook my head. 'That's OK, thanks anyway,' I called, before turning around and flippering it back to safety. While turtles are very cool (and I was even more enamoured with them at this point, for reasons I will soon explain), I'm not about to die and get eaten by them.

I saw Papaya the next night. He danced up next to me in Tîr na Nôg (the grimy beachfront establishment that proves there really *is* an Irish pub wherever you land on Earth) and announced, 'I saw turtles!' A grin stretched across his face. 'Lots of them. Huge big ones.'

Dammit.

When one of my best friends, Dacey, decided to come to Bali for my birthday we also booked a little side trip. It takes just three hours, door-to-sizzling-sand, from Ubud to Gili Trawangan and as we stepped off the speedboat in luminous sunshine along with hordes of shirtless men, I could tell it was going to be a happy birthday.

There are three islands making up the Gilis, just off the coast of mainland Lombok. I hadn't heard much about any of them before I arrived in Bali. Gili Trawangan, at three kilometres long and two kilometres wide, is the biggest and most action-packed, but you can travel between the three quite easily on a small boat for about three dollars.

Some people are calling Gili Trawangan (Gili T for short) the new Ibiza, as you really can party around the clock. If you want to lose your mind on those 'not legal but tolerated' magic mushrooms, you've got it. If you want to indulge in a bit of skinny-dipping at 7 a.m. with a backpacker you've only just met, you've got it ... though the Gilis, like Lombok itself, is Muslim territory, so it's best to be discreet with that one. You can also opt to do nothing. You can hire a bike and find a quiet spot and just lie there finding faces in the clouds.

The middle of the island is a maze of streets they call The Village. It's still muddy and undeveloped, so chickens scratch in the dirt and local kids zoom around on bikes in the dust, and you can still find a *warung* with a *nasi goreng* for a dollar. There's also a giant hill to climb in the centre, which Dacey and I discovered provides a perfect sunset view over the majestic Mount Rinjani (and a very good opportunity for a million mosquitoes to make a delicious all-you-can-eat buffet out of your body).

It's a hard life for me and Dacey at the Pesona Resort,
Gili Trawangan

Backpackers sweat it out in the cheap homestays along these back streets so they can blow the money they save on booze. Dacey and I chose to stay on the seafront (I wasn't staying in a hovel on my birthday!). The more salubrious establishments offer nicer rooms with air-conditioning, which is well worth paying for — Gili Trawangan is hotter than hell.

Dacey, Winnie the Pooh and I headed straight to the Pesona Resort. It has a *shisha* lounge right on the beach in front of it so it's pretty easy to spot, thanks to all its *hookahs* and cushions. We were instantly welcomed with a couple of beers by the British owners, Sumeena and Sandesh, who answered all our questions and informed us of all the parties within a two-minute radius that were set to occur during our stay ... very helpful information indeed, although even as we arrived in broad daylight, it did seem a bit like every single place was already having a party.

The Gili Islands (the smaller Gili Air and Gili Meno included) have been luring more and more people over from the mainland since the 1980s, especially during monsoon season when other parts of Indonesia are getting drenched. Cheaper places on Gili T start at around $7 or $8 a night (ours was roughly $45) but at them you won't get a pool, or free Wi-Fi, or an Indian menu featuring a truly sensational butter chicken curry, or a lovely couple who know exactly what you want on an island birthday holiday.

Taking their advice on my birthday itself, Dacey and I accepted an invitation onto a 'party boat'. As we handed over our money to a smiley man at one of the dive shops, we had extremely high hopes of spending the afternoon sipping champagne on a pristine catamaran. We couldn't wait to get on board, lie back in our new bikinis near the DJ (who'd love us and want to play *all* our favourite songs) and claim our rightful places on the trampoline, where we'd stretch our arms through the netting and waggle our fingers at the ocean life below us.

As we queued on the pier and the rickety wooden boat approached us at the speed of a handicapped snail, we looked at each other in concern. An Indonesian party boat, it seems, is actually a random bloke's fishing vessel, which he happens to live on … with his two dogs. An Indonesian party boat has no DJ. It does have netting to sit on but it's so sea-savaged it feels like it might snap, so you don't really want to risk it for too long. To make you feel better, an Indonesian party boat does still have booze.

We sailed away with twenty five others into the turquoise ether, plastic cups of vodka and Coke in hand, ready for the sunset. And the sunset was sensational. The more I drank the more I thought it was all pretty great ... and then the engine died.

It was dark. We could see the hazy lights of Gili Meno in the distance so we knew we weren't far from land, but the power of our captain's additional motorised dingy wasn't great enough to tow us back to Trawangan in anything less than seven hours. Suddenly I was sober. And annoyed. A stranded captive being slobbered on by dogs, on my *birthday*. 'Noooooooooooo!' I wailed at Dacey, who was by then too busy drinking on the roof with a fit man from Sweden to care.

It was 8 p.m. Sumeena and Sandesh had organised birthday drinks back at Pesona and I still needed to shower and wash the sea out of my ears and ... apart from all that, I had a man to get back to; a man who'd been playing on my brain since he'd taken me eighteen metres under the water that same afternoon and blown me up a balloon on the bottom of the sea.

***

I learned to dive a few years ago in Jamaica with a big, grinning Rasta man. I did several more dives in Nicaragua after that, but by the time I got to Gili T I hadn't done any diving in ages. I needed a refresher course. Dacey had never done any diving before but she was keen to try. There are fifteen diving operations on Gili T. On our first day there, we walked into the first one that grabbed our attention, and I met The Diver.

After a brush-up on skills in a swimming pool, our first foray into the sea was a twelve-metre dive to a site called Shark Point. We saw no sharks, unfortunately, but I was too caught up in the moment to care, as The Diver pointed out snapper and pufferfish and triggerfish and eels, one after the other. As Dacey and I flapped and flailed our arms (even though we had fins strapped to our feet), The Diver slid gracefully through the deep, a slick fish, perfectly at home in his personal aquarium.

At one point The Diver grabbed my hand and pulled me to the floor to show me several 'Nemos' (common clownfish) hiding in the swaying stems of the anemones. We swam with parrotfish, sweetlips and groupers, watched mantis shrimp scuttle over coral and under rocks, admired crusty hawksbill turtles take flight and glide to the surface like flattened angels above us. And then, out of nowhere, I found myself swimming over a giant green turtle.

The sight of this *huge* thing, the size of a satellite dish, was amazing; so peaceful and still, chomping on something green, as his little fishy friends performed a spa treatment on his long scaly neck and fins.

A local initiative called the Gili Eco Trust works to preserve the turtle population around Gili Trawangan (among other things). Their ingenious strategy was to involve the people who were once poachers and pay them instead to find turtle nests, so they can be kept under surveillance and protected until the eggs hatch. The babies are then kept in giant tanks until they're about six months old, when they're big enough to fend for themselves and be released into the sea.

We swam together for a while, side by side. He was almost as big as me. At one point, he looked straight at me as if to say 'what?' and when his thoughtful eyes met mine I was hooked. When we finally got to the surface and I pulled off my mask, I kicked myself for staying away so long. How could I have ignored this big, wet paradise that's been stretching all around me, jagged and wavy and oh-so-mysterious and full of wondrous beings? Bloody hell. I had to go back down.

The Diver invited Dacey and me to have some drinks that first night, and on a nitrogen high we accepted. Drinks turned into dinner, which turned into more drinks and some crazy dance moves in the Irish bar. By the time Dacey left I was a giggling cliché, oblivious to anything else in the room except him. And so it was that I found myself swept away to his ramshackle house, as swiftly as he'd swept me through the ocean that morning.

On my birthday, we took a camera down on our second dive. As we swam with our flippers in sync, just the two of us this time, my imagination of course provided even more props. He was a merman and I was a mermaid! With our fingers entwined we were twisting and twirling like only those with tails can move, on our way to an underwater ball. We were the envy of everyone in the sea. The sensational crustacean band was playing a special song to accompany our kisses. Sebastian the crab may have even been there. We were dancing in the deep, frolicking with the fishes, splashing our fins and breathing in bubbles. We belonged in that kingdom.

And then … back in the real world … when he actually did take out his regulator to blow me up a purple balloon, I knew no birthday would ever compare.

I am *such* a girl.

***

'You have to tow us back,' I told the captain, who was starting to look embarrassed that people were beginning to realise the engine had died on his crappy vessel. I could feel my merman fading and I was damned if I was going to miss another dance with him, on land …

The captain looked perplexed but when I shamefully threatened to cry he agreed to abandon ship and take a boatload of us back to Gili T.

Within an hour I was washed, dressed and pressed against The Diver for a night that ended the way all the best nights end, you know ... when you refuse to sleep without just one last kiss, without at least one part of you touching the other's body, whether it's a finger entwined with another, or a leg wrapped around another, or your hands in the other's hair. Salty from the sea air, dirty from the dusty tracks, sweaty from dancing with our feet in the sand, we didn't care. I didn't care.

As the boat sped away, taking me and Dacey back to Bali and its storm clouds, I watched the Gilis turn from giant landmasses to three small dots in the distance. I didn't feel sad at all. The Diver was a dot too. Another island in an infinite sea. A speck of hope. Everything glimmered and shone and I could still feel his light, still see him blowing up that balloon with his brown eyes laughing behind his mask. As the dots got smaller and eventually disappeared, The Diver remained; a grain of sand caught on the breeze, reflecting in the sun.

There were no promises or commitments made, no contracts in his kisses. But for once, surprisingly, that felt OK.

21/11

Mule jewels ...

The guards were peeling a bunch of mangosteens when I entered Kerobokan Prison but as I went to walk past they stopped what they were doing, wiped the juice from their fingers and the smiles from their faces and tried to look official. Joanna Witt walked straight past and I was told to sit in front of the guards and wait for permission to enter.

Joanna, I think I mentioned, is coordinating a project beyond the scary gates aimed at teaching the prisoners silversmith skills. I went along for the day to meet Si Yi Chen, who is one of the Bali Nine currently serving a life sentence for being a drug mule. The silversmith program itself is now his day job, and along with eight others he spends every day in a special room inside the prison from 9 a.m. to 3 p.m. making jewellery for a line he calls Mule Jewels.

I smiled at the guards from my hard wooden seat, noticing they were all wearing huge, spotless black and white boots like something from an army clothing commercial. One of them offered me a mangosteen so I peeled it and ate it as they all eyed me suspiciously. I decided I had better flirt to ensure I got in, so I spoke in Indonesian and batted my naked eyelashes.

Prior to my visit I was told to make myself look as unattractive as possible. This isn't really something I have to be told lately, but respectful clothing is encouraged in Kerobokan because of the large component of Muslim prisoners and staff ... and also because some of these men have not had sex in *years*.

Wearing the wrong clothing and receiving a few cat-calls is not, however, the biggest concern when it comes to heading into a building full of criminals. As we chatted in the car on the way to the prison, Joanna reminisced about a time she used to enjoy the odd conversation with a tailor who'd work sewing the guard's uniforms in the silversmith's room. One day, he climbed onto the roof with the hope of escaping and after he was caught and relocated to another prison, Joanna found out that this chatty guy (who she'd assumed was a drug trafficker, like 90 per cent of the prisoners in Kerobokan) was actually doing time for murdering his friend. The unlucky victim's head was found on a beach in Gianyar, while the rest of him was found in Kuta.

In a prison you never know who you're talking to or sharing a cell with. Some people in Kerobokan, if they're extremely poor and can't buy their way into anything better, are forced to share cells with up to thirty other people.

The heavy metal doors swung open and a little man in a bad *batik* shirt ushered me through. Handing my mangosteen peel to the guards I waved them goodbye and followed him through a series of walkways, taking it all in. Kerobokan Prison is a scary place. If your soul's not crushed automatically by the dark foreboding walls and crumbling paint, you're trying not to shiver at the deceivingly cheerful outdoor grounds with their tennis court and temple, and tower block reading SUPER MAXIMUM SECURITY, surrounded by open drains. It doesn't smell nice. Men stare when you walk past. I was glad to reach the silversmith room.

Joanna used to buy jewellery in Bali and sell it in Japan, mostly in the Tokyo subways. For the last eighteen years, however, she's been an active member of the Ubud community and the work at Kerobokan started in February of 2010, basically as a way to help rehabilitate the prisoners and to keep them out of trouble. The effort is funded by the parents of the prisoners involved and partially by Joanna herself.

It looked like any other workshop. Shabby pink paint clung to the walls, a painting of distant palm trees displayed a Bali the inmates never get to see, and a kettle was boiling away in the corner. The prisoners were all chain smoking. One young girl was welding with a blowtorch.

Si Yi smiled and stood up with his hand out for me to shake, and as I shook it he offered me some green tea; proper green tea from a bag his parents brought him over from China. It was probably the best tea I've had in Bali.

Born in 1985, Si Yi looks older and appears wiser than his years, hardly surprising considering his lifestyle. In 2005 he was arrested at the Melasti Hotel in Kuta with three others and his share of a total of 8.3 kilograms of heroin in a suitcase. Whereas his life was changed forever, it hasn't necessarily *all* been a negative experience. He's since discovered a talent and a passion he never knew was in him — Si Yi's line of Mule Jewels is gorgeous. He practises Taoism and as such, every piece he makes has a specific meaning.

'When I make them, I send them out into the world with positive messages,' he told me as we went through some of the silver charms they've made, which he keeps in a little drawer at his work desk until they can be sent to the shops. Joanna's Yin stores, which are scattered throughout Ubud, and the Ocean shop on Gili Trawangan sell these Mule Jewels, so keep that in mind when your magpie eyes go scouting for precious pieces in Bali. You could be helping these guys.

Everyone on the program works on commission. All proceeds go right back to the program and to the prisoners themselves who use the money to help make life a bit more bearable behind bars.

When she's not at the prison itself, Joanna is helping out with marketing. I decided to get a little gecko bracelet made to remind me of Monet and I sat with one of the guys as he sketched it from scratch. Apparently, it will be ready in under a week — a personalised piece made by the prisoners, which will not only be a beautiful piece of jewellery but will also, in some small way, contribute to the life of these prisoners. Without the funds to buy their own food from a snack shop, they are supposed to live on five pieces of sugary bread, a quarter of a papaya and one unripe

My beautiful Mule Jewels gecko bracelet

banana per day. And that's just for the foreigners. The Indonesians get rice three times a day with a finger-full of vegetables and the occasional egg.

The biggest problem with the silversmith program, Joanna says, is motivating the prisoners. When she first started working with Si Yi, she'd arrive at Kerobokan to find him still asleep. When he'd finally get around to joining her, he'd be quite depressed and commented a lot on the guilt he was feeling about putting his long-suffering parents through such a bad time.

After several months Joanna had had just about enough of this. She told him outright, 'Hey, I'm here to help!' She told him yeah, sure, other things in his life were shit and monotonous and boring, but she was there to change things for the better and if he wanted her to keep on coming, he'd better pull his act together.

The next time she arrived for a session, Si Yi was up, ready and waiting, and from that point onwards he set about putting 100 per cent of his energy into learning the craft.

'When I get out, I want to work with silver,' he told me as he carefully put the jewels back into their little bags. And he definitely will. You can tell by talking to him that Si Yi is immensely proud of what he's achieved so far in this little pink room with a view of barbed-wire fences and broken glass. Before the Bali Nine drama saw him being sentenced to life in what's dubbed Hotel Kerobokan (because you can check out anytime but you can never leave), Si Yi used to work in a mobile phone shop.

I also met Myuran Sukumaran, another member of the Bali Nine, who is doing a lot of good things inside the prison while he serves his time on death row. He showed me the room where they create and print designs on T-shirts, which they sell. He also showed me the art room, in which at least five prisoners were kneeling on the floor, covered in paint and lost in their creations. Most of them were painting surreal images of twisted bodies and Dali-esque melting items, men and women with long eerie limbs. The many ghosts and spirits were perhaps manifestations of their troubled minds (it's no secret that drugs are a big issue inside Kerobokan), although Si Yi told me about a ghostly figure who stands on top of the Super Maximum Security tower at night, eternally searching for a way out.

So what does Joanna think of Schapelle Corby's book, and others that have been written about life inside the prison? Well, actually, she doesn't think very highly of those who've penned 'largely fabricated' memoirs about what it's like to live there. Often, she says, they're written to satiate the desires of a hungry media and the prisoners don't benefit at all while they're still inside. She said to Si Yi one day: 'If you want to be famous, don't be famous for being an imprisoned drug trafficker. Be famous for being an amazing jewellery designer.' Her advice seems to have stuck.

'I'm so proud of Si Yi and the group, and what they've accomplished,' she told me on the way back to Ubud, with the rolling Bali plains looking even more beautiful in the context of the freedom they represent. 'It's pretty hard to avoid the negative things that are happening in the jail, but this group is producing some amazing designs and pieces on a daily basis. I take my hat off to them. They are some of the most changed and successful people I have ever met.'

I know none of us can truly imagine what it must be like to live behind bars anywhere, especially in Bali. But the next time we read something terrible about life inside the Kerobokan Prison, perhaps we'll also think about the good stuff that's happening in the same building, thanks to people like Joanna.

23/11

I'll have a big Maca please...

'Is this vodka raw?' my friend Jen from San Francisco asked, pointing to the spirit listed on the menu in Bar Luna. Obviously she was joking, but something inside me groaned and it wasn't just my stomach. Unprocessed. Uncooked. Mostly organic. That's raw food. And it's all I've been consuming for the past few days. I'm bored as hell.

It's not a hard regime to follow here in Ubud, obviously. Raw is the new black, the new *filet mignon*, the new pie and chips. It's everywhere. You can't take five steps in Ubud without hearing the word uttered from a lycra-clad yogi's lips, or see it springing healthily in abundance from a restaurant menu. Everyone's going raw and while I've shunned the idea until now; something about my somewhat debauched trip to Gili T made me think again.

For the benefit of others like me who have almost no idea about this stuff, raw food is very good for you and consists of unheated food, or produce cooked at a temperature less than 46 degrees Celsius (115 degrees Fahrenheit). This retains all the goodness and nutrients that blitzing it at high temperatures would usually eradicate.

The side effects I've noticed so far are vastly improved digestion (essential in the run-up to my very first colonic, apparently) and a slight weight loss. The weight has shifted most noticeably from the little fold in my tummy, which caused a spate of frantic, vain Gili photo deleting, (oh come on, we all do it).

Anyway, yes, the tummy's a teeny bit trimmer now, which could also of course be attributed to yoga and dancing in an increasingly more ecstatic fashion, but aside from these wonderful side effects, I'm not experiencing the higher energy levels everyone raves about. Not so far, anyway. The other day at Ecstatic Dancing I practically passed out. There I was, about to do the infamous fairy flutter from one side of the room to the other when I felt a wave of ickiness swamp my being. I had to stop mid-flight and re-assess. The carrot juice I'd had for breakfast was not sufficient for an ecstatic fairy and did nothing to top up the egg, lettuce and raw milk cheese salad I'd had for dinner the night before.

I made plans to attack Clear Cafe's raw chocolate cake as soon as possible. Surprisingly, raw chocolate is encouraged and is absolutely, one hundred per cent NOT bad for you.

Things I can eat this week are seeds, fish, eggs, meat (as long as it's *carpaccio*), raw fruits and vegetables and non-pasteurised, non-homogenised dairy products. So yes, cheese is in, but it's not very tasty cheese. Some would argue that it's better, of course, but to me it's the dairy equivalent of switching your boyfriend for his less attractive twin brother; it's a pleasant enough experience but you're still missing that intimate, comforting connection you could only ever have with the original. I think I'll ignore this imitation raw-invader and savour the prospect of a sweet reunion with a slab of creamy blue. (Am I missing the point of all this?)

'You're missing the point of all this,' my friend Jen said, scanning the menu once we were back in Bali Buddha where I've been eating most of my meals since I started the diet. The point of all of this is to purify my body by consuming fewer toxins and calories. You are what you eat. But that's exactly my point; I'm eating miserable, boring food and I'm getting progressively more miserable and bored as a result. Perhaps raw food only works on a physical level if you're psychologically ready for it? A nice raw vodka might clarify things ...

The waitress approaches.

Some of the stuff on the menu sounds vaguely edible. It will also be washed in an eco-friendly produce wash, thank goodness.

I could have a *Live Food Platter*, featuring *jicama* (a sweet, root vegetable that looks like a turnip), dried tomatoes, cucumber and raw flax crackers with raw food spreads. I could also have a *Raw Food Energising Spirulina Ball*, or a *Pineapple Goji Ball*.

A *Maca Superfood Alternative* sounds interesting. I read the description aloud: 'Maca is an adaptogenic plant, which means that it works on the body according to the needs, age and gender of the person taking it'.

152

Sounds pretty incredible to me. Too incredible to be true, actually. Sounds like swallowing a robot, doesn't it? Jen continues the description: 'It encourages the glands within the body to produce the needed hormones by balancing the pituitary hypothalamus'.

Oh, does it? (Do I dare admit that I've got no bloody clue what that means? I've got no idea at all and quite frankly I'm getting a headache. Did I come out for lunch or a lesson in agricultural techniques from the future?)

'Maca affects the entire endocrine system including the sex glands, adrenal, thyroid and pancreas ...'

The waitress is tapping her notepad. I must choose. Will it be a *Maca Jahva*, a *Mocha Jahva* or a *Maca Jahva Gelato* milkshake? I panic. I don't have Wikipedia at hand. All I know is that reading the word Maca over and over like this is making me want a Big Mac. It's all I can do not to shove her aside, hop on a bike and hightail it to Kuta where the drunken bogans, oblivious to the crazy raw world up the road, are ordering Triple Pounders in ignorant bliss.

Just as I'm trying to figure out what the hell all these items are without sounding stupid, I'm asked: 'Would you like some nut milk?' This upsets me further. I've been through this before. I refuse to accept that there's anything healthy or indeed *right* about accepting milk from a nut. This is quite possibly the most perplexing menu I've ever read.

I look around. Everyone looks quite content, crunching away. I'm not sure if they understand what they're ordering and eating, or whether everyone's playing this silent game of lucky dip for fear of admitting that they too are stumbling blindly, yet faithfully, through a raw food movement that actually mystifies them. Either way, I feel the strange need to show the world the wonders of my newly balanced pituitary hypothalamus … so fuck it, I'll try it. What harm can come of it?

'I'll have a *Maca Jahva* and an *Energising Spirulina Ball* please.' And then I will go to Pizza Bagus and hope no-one there knows me, or sees me walk out with a box full of stuff I understand, like cheese and king prawns and hot anchovies … Oh shit, I can't, that's not raw. Dammit.

OK, just bring me some nut milk, then. Whatever.

This is hard.

Black magic and the Village Voldemort …

If anyone ever mentioned black magic to me before, I'd picture witches and warlocks, clandestine and cloaked, reciting curses around cauldrons. It would also remind me of a brief phase I went through at college when a bunch of friends and I got our hands on a Ouija board and spent every night in a garden shed summoning up the dead. We spiralled into a pretty dark place that summer. I don't think I even realised how dark it was at the time, but when a psychic I was interviewing for a college radio project took me aside and told me (without knowing anything about me) that I really shouldn't be messing with things I didn't understand because I was 'inviting evil spirits into my life', I chucked that thing away faster than Harry Potter could say 'Wingardium Leviosa'.

It did, however, leave me with a major fascination of all things freaky — magic spells, voodoo, ghosts, all that stuff. Psychics too, apparently.

When I first met Sunni it was his sad eyes I noticed first. Sunni has found himself the victim of black magic here in Bali, courtesy of a horrible woman in his village. She lives alone in a small house, the proverbial cat woman I suppose, surrounded by trees and hopefully cobwebs and some pointy hats, but I can't prove this bit. Sunni's been telling me stories about her powers lately as we've been sitting around the homestay compound. I got my phone out to record some of them but weirdly, nothing recorded. Hmm.

This woman's husband had graduated to the very highest level of black magic that a human can reach. He was the Village Voldemort, if you will, and before he died she learned everything she could possibly learn from him.

Sunni says her interest in her husband's 'hobby' wasn't suspicious to anyone for a long time. Lots of women in Bali learn a little black magic in order to protect their newborn children from evil spirits, who sometimes like to snatch them when they're babies. They also learn it to control their naughty, straying husbands because accusing them publicly of doing 'the dirty' is not encouraged in what's still a very male-dominated society.

The men rarely notice when they're being controlled … apparently they just tend to feel a bit lazy, like they can't be bothered to leave the house anymore … but according to Sunni, not even the women know the evils they unleash by indulging in a little bit of magic.

'What they do is invoke *karma*,' Sunni told me, stirring palm sugar into his coffee cup as we sat on the steps. 'They do something they think is small and they get their husband back. He stays at home and things seem better, but the magic they've done opens the door for more spirits who want to take control.'

Sunni says black magic is more common in Java where they actually summon spirits to stay in their shops and hypnotise people into buying their stuff. He says it's happening here in Bali too. Even in Ubud.

'No way. Which shops?' I asked. My eyes were popping out of my head. I told him how just the other day I felt totally compelled to buy this crappy bracelet with an Indonesian coin bound in the middle by stringy plastic and I would love to think it wasn't a terrible purchase decision on my *own* account. What if all the stuff I've been buying since I got here has actually been programmed into my skull by a greater power? That would explain the turquoise trousers. Only the darkest, most evil force could have got me to fall in love with *them*.

But I digress … Sunni, this wonderful, super-smart man with sadness in his eyes, doesn't even know why this woman chose to attack him. Lots of people around him started getting sick first. 'They'd go crazy, start talking to animals. Their minds weren't there,' he said.

He was concerned, like everyone else. He prayed a lot, but then it started happening to him, too. For roughly one month, Sunni went crazy. Putu at my homestay can vouch for it; he was a shadow of his former self.

'I would talk to the chickens,' he told me. 'I would call people up and they'd say that what was coming out of my mouth was Sanskrit. It wasn't Sanskrit, it was another language, one of the spirits, but no-one knew what it was so they called it Sanskrit. In my heart I knew what it was I was saying, but no-one else could understand me.'

Sunni found himself taking showers four times a day, always at the same times. And after each shower he'd feel a different spirit take over his body, like a ghostly tag-team was at work in his bathroom. He didn't sleep more than a few hours a night for more than ten days straight.

Eventually, in the brief moments of sanity he could grasp between the madness, Sunni knew he had to get help. A friend of his father's knew a powerful healer and medicine man, so one night, almost driven to complete despair by the voices in his head, Sunni hopped on his motorbike and made his way over there. It took him a long time to make it. He had to stop four times due to the spirits, who he says were screaming and trying to force him off the road. At one point, he thought he was truly going to die.

'I saw a truck ahead of me but I was going really fast. I tried to brake but my hands wouldn't move from the accelerator!'

Sunni sped along towards what seemed like inevitable death from a head-on collision, hearing the conflicting voices of the spirits and a male ancestor, whom he believes was trying to help him.

Just metres away from the oncoming truck, Sunni says his hands were miraculously released and he was able to swerve. At this point, he saw spirits everywhere in shadowy form on the roadside, up in the sky and in the trees. They were surrounding him, he says, because the head of all evil spirits had chosen to jump inside him. He was essentially, at that moment, the king of evil, hurtling along on a motorbike. Sunni believes it was the overpowering good of his great ancestor that helped him reach the healer.

It took numerous sessions to get the evil out of him.

'I went to different people,' he said. 'One medicine man took me back to the woman's house, the woman who worked the magic on me, because he wanted to show me what had been causing me so many problems.'

I followed Sunni's eyes to a nearby tree.

'We stood on her land and when I looked up I saw a huge, black spirit, high in the banyan trees. It had lots of smaller spirits floating around it. The woman is using magic to send them all out and hurt people, because the more people she can affect, the higher up she will go in the ranks of black magic.'

'So she's *still* doing it?' I implored as he turned back to me and I met his eyes. I was there with Sunni by that point, in the witch's garden, looking up at the cold, dark mass in the treetops, holding a magic wand. I was Hermione next to Harry and Ron. We had to stop her. We had to *do* something!

'Yes, she's still doing it. No-one can stop her,' he said.

What? 'Are you sure? What about your ancestor? Can't he do something?'

Sunni shook his head gravely. 'We can stop the spirits with magic of our own. We can even kill her, but we will only experience bad *karma* ourselves if we do anything. She will keep doing it until she dies.'

He said it so matter-of-factly: 'She will keep doing it until she dies,' like he's resigned to the fact that this spell-casting queen of mental destruction is destined to wreak havoc like her late husband did, while everyone else just sits back and tries not to be killed. The Balinese don't mess with *karma*. *Karma* is a bitch.

'We did some healing work so they don't come into my house anymore,' he said, before explaining the general Balinese practice of sharing with the supernatural, bits of which I'd heard before.

'The spirits are the lowest in the power ranks. Then above them are humans, and above humans are the gods. The spirits were here first, so if we build a house on their land, of course they're not going to want to move out!' Sunni told me. 'That's why we make offerings. We tell them thank you for letting us be here, too. We give them gifts so they know we respect them and in return they stay out of our homes, most of the time. They can only go as far as the front doors. They live outside.'

I didn't say it out loud, of course, but a lot of things started to make sense as Sunni explained all this.

'We never pray to the spirits, only the gods. And we only pray to the gods in the temples. If we pray to the spirits they will think they're powerful, and that we believe they have equal power to the gods, when they don't. You see? Black magic goes against these rules, but it is still just as powerful as white magic.'

I remembered something Bob had said at the raw dinner party when we sat around discussing Bali's energy and the appearance of River Spirits, and I wondered if it was true. He said the main way of telling what's human and what's a spirit is the upper lip. A spirit trying to take human form will always have a flat, taut piece of skin above the upper lip, whereas most humans have a mild indent from the nose down. Sunni nodded.

'I've seen them,' he said. I shivered.

I'll be looking at everyone's upper lips from now on. I bet you will, too. Admit it. You're trying to think of who you know with a weird mouth. I'm going to go all Dana Scully on people with funny mouths from now on. It could get awkward.

I admit, I had to fight a mild urge to beg Sunni to take me back to his village. Part of me, the part that messed with that Ouija board when I was seventeen, wants to stand in the witch's garden and see if I can see anything other than mangoes and butterflies in the trees.

There are aspects of Bali that are evil incarnate. Offerings keep the demons at bay and a show of smiles and flowers and trickling water features hides what's really happening behind the scenes. But it's also the fairytale world I've always imagined exists, where good conquers evil and *karma* kicks arse. It would be stupid for us all to be cynical or frightened as we walk about looking for witches and flat upper lips. But in spite of Bali's colourful and sunny disposition, when it comes to magic it's clearly still a very complex world of black and white. And you don't want to mess with that.

Naked jungle yoga and The Carpenters ...

Jen was all excited when I met her for breakfast this morning, as she's about to head into the hills up north for a five-week yoga retreat in a place called Bali Eco Village.

'Does it have Wi-Fi?' I asked. It's always my first question. I hear the word 'retreat' and I picture longhaired-hippy cult members who've lost all touch with reality traipsing around dew-soaked gardens holding their arms up to fluttering birds and butterflies. I imagine them singing songs by The Carpenters while these pretty, winged creatures perch happily on their outstretched fingers, all bathed in a lovely ethereal glow. I'm not sure why I imagine stuff like this. I just think that, much like The Carpenters, a retreat seems like something that can be equally joyous and miserable at the same time. I also suspect that people 'retreating' probably never know which emotions they're really feeling because everyone else is messing with their minds.

Anyway, obviously I'm just hypothesising because there are lots of different retreats out there and I've never actually 'retreated' anywhere myself. Of course, I still have the Ratu Bagus shaking thing to look forward to. I can't believe I'm really taking myself up there ... *on my own* ... especially after hearing so many stories about what goes on. Hmm. But I'm intrigued and my phone has unlimited Internet access, so if I do start wearing tie-dye combos and singing songs about rainy days and Mondays, my multimedia accounts of it on Twitter will make sure someone comes to rescue me.

'They do have Wi-Fi', Jen confirmed after double-checking the website, and we both breathed a sigh of relief as we ignored each other again to check our email.

Jen's particularly excited, not only because being on the retreat will help her not to eat and drink the usual amounts over the upcoming Christmas period (she's not allowed out till January 1), but because she's been handpicked to learn a special kind of yoga from the one and only Arshia.

'Who the heck is Arshia?' I had to ask. And when I was told the whole story, I practically had to scrape my jaw off the floor. Arshia is the most *awesome* woman to have ever walked the face of the Earth.

'Now ... go and make yourself a cup of tea.'

'Are you back?'

'Did you remember the cookies?'

'Are they raw?'

'OK.'

Arshia was a competitive athlete who in her youth ran around the savannahs with the Masai in Kenya. At a young age, she decided to ditch the African wilds and study metalworking in Bali, a trip that made her question everything she'd ever known about the universe. It propelled her into moving here permanently on a personal, spiritual quest.

At just twenty, already an expert in yoga thanks to her grandfather (a strict Indian yogi and explorer), Arshia packed her bags for the Balinese jungle, where she set up home with her yoga and meditation guru, Vireshvar.

On a search for the extraordinary, they lived among the vines and critters for no less than seven years, practising yoga by the river, in the nude. Sometimes they'd hold their poses for up to three hours at a time. *Three hours!* Imagine that. Three hours in the nude, in the jungle. Imagine the mosquitoes zooming into open cracks with gay abandon. Imagine the snakes and the spiders all manoeuvering around and over these weird and intriguing fleshy statues ... eek. Brave. I wouldn't do it.

Arshia and Vireshvar lived in a little bamboo house, buried their supplies underground to keep them nice and cool, ate raw garlic to keep them strong and free from illnesses and drank the blood of scorpions. Apparently, the scorpion blood worked as many wonders as the garlic, though Jen says Arshia would probably admit she prefers garlic.

For the entire seven years they had no electricity; no creature comforts in the jungle, just creatures. In fact, Arshia and Vireshvar lived in what was considered an extremely spiritual area that scared the bejesus out of most Balinese. As a result, they barely had any contact with the outside world while they were there — a modern day Adam and Eve, frolicking alone in their garden.

Suspiciously, however, their little bamboo home was burned to the ground just ten days after a corporate hotel chain decided to steamroll the valley. The hotel's still there and what has become the 'Beverley Hills' area of Bali is going strong. But what was once their their outdoor yogic wonderland of great power and spirituality is mostly appreciated for its property value these days.

After the fire, Arshia and Vireshvar realised the time was right to leave the jungle (or what was left of it), but their quest for the extraordinary wasn't about to end. At first, Arshia was surprised to learn that other people were practising yoga. It hadn't been anything major in the western world at all when she'd first left for Bali. The concept of a yoga mat was shocking and so was the idea that the practice had erupted into an expensive, consumerist pastime, but that was something she had to get over.

Arshia has since worked hard to encourage people from all over the world to practice the kind of yoga they feel is right for them (predominantly Ayurvedic), while helping those who want to learn it her way (and no, that doesn't mean naked, sorry).

And so it is that after more than twenty years of teaching and talking on intangible subjects like the spirit world, tantric philosophy and meditation, Arshia is orchestrating the retreat that's promising Jen a whole lot of much-needed Ayurvedic rejuvenation. Vireshvar, in a separate venture, offers vedic astrology readings in Ubud.

The beauty of Ayurvedic yoga when compared with other styles, I learned, is that it's all about enjoying life as a human being. It's centred on emotion, feelings and getting back to nature. But Jen herself doesn't have to hold a nude pose in a jungle for three hours to get a taste of what it's like to be alive. Oh no. With Arshia she can learn how to feel connected *all* the time.

As well as holding regular retreats and sessions in Ubud, Arshia practises the traditional Indian Odissi dance and takes care of her son. What a woman. I'm dying to meet her, ask her what it's like to drink scorpion blood (I'm a Scorpio, would it give me magical powers?) and maybe even take a few classes with her when they're back from the retreat next year. I almost wish I could join them, if only for a bit, to spend some time in the light of this incredible woman whom Jen says always brings a very powerful and humbling presence to a room. But alas, I can only 'retreat' once this side of Christmas and I still choose the super-shaking and fully clothed Good King Ratu Bagus.

Jen's going to tell me *everything* as soon as she gets back, which will bring me one small step closer to extraordinary myself, I suppose. And I've made her promise that if she so much as hums a Carpenters' song while she's out there, she has to let me know so I can save her.

27/11

Singa-poor...

There's nothing quite like arriving in another country knowing you've got no money, especially when it's Christmas time in Singapore. My new Aussie bank card was delivered to my old address in Sydney last week, where my old flatmate no longer lives. We had to cancel both my current and new cards 'for security purposes', rendering me unable to withdraw cash in a foreign country. Excellent.

Anyway, no-one wants to hear about boring banking issues but suffice to say it was too late to cancel my visa trip to Singapore, so I left the staff at Bar Luna to sign for my *new* new card (as you do when all else fails), packed what pennies I could scrape together and headed off to one of the most expensive cities in the world.

Maybe I've been in Bali too long but Singapore looks like Santa threw up all over it. I've never seen so much twinkling, so much glitter or throbbing neon in such a small proximity. And, of course, it's scorching outside, which doesn't quite match the festive cheer; not to my British eyes at least. You can't do Christmas shopping without a woolly scarf on, surely?

Maybe I'm just PMS-ing but some things got to me as I wandered around, penniless like a hobo with my Bali patchwork hold-all. For starters, I felt really unfashionable … and no, not just because of my Bali patchwork hold-all (it's practical, OK?). I realised today how behind the times I am. There's no fashion in Bali. None at all. It's all very nice and twirly and floral and summery, but as Gaby pointed out when my turquoise trousers made her cringe on my last visa trip to Bangkok, it's not fashion.

After a while you start comparing *batik* items and appreciating one over the other, because it's all you see. The inner voice tries to warn you that no *batik* items are ever, *ever* good. It tries to tell you that even by being in the shop *with* the *batik* items you're letting yourself go, but you shush it because it's all there is and if you don't appreciate at least something made of fabric every now and then, you'll go mental.

ZARA's mirror repulsed me. I really have let myself go. A stretched and sun-faded black tank top, a frilly knee-length skirt, thongs and no make-up was what my reflection displayed, right there in the middle of a public place. I avoided my own eyes with shame.

The things I heard upset me, too. I know it's nearly Christmas, but is it really necessary to blast Cliff Richard at full volume through Carrefour? A few years back, such festive, musical treats would have filled me with happiness but for some reason it all just seems fake and annoying to me now. Bali's constant twanging can take its toll but I'll take the *gamelan* over Cliff any day.

Anyway, I'm sitting here in an Irish pub called Dubliners (of course), waiting for my friends Saxon and Kate to finish work so I can cab it to their house. They're making me a lovely roast dinner so we can sit around a table and reminisce about the Sydney days. They've promised wine. As I may not have mentioned yet, good wine is a mythical substance in Bali. They make their own, called Hatten, but Bali being a sub-tropical climate, this wine is not good. In fact, it would be better for sprinkling over your chips with a dash of salt than it would for drinking with a nice meal. I always give Hatten 'just one more chance' even though it's disgusting. I'd rather pay for and then moan about a shit-wine experience than not have one at all. It's just who I am.

The common visa run is an expensive, somewhat corrupt inconvenience for most expats in Bali. In every coffee shop you visit you'll overhear someone harping on about their terrible, time-consuming trip to Bangkok or Singapore and the vast amounts of cash they have to hand over for 'the paperwork'. It's really quite boring to listen to after a while, because when you think about it, the bonus of being able to live just a little bit longer in one of the greatest places on Earth should more than make up for it. We all like a good moan, though, right? And it *is* a pain in the arse, heading off to another country just to hand your papers over to some gum-chewing woman who doesn't even look up as she examines your passport.

In Singapore you have to hand your stuff in by 11 a.m. and pick it up by 4 p.m., so naturally I envisioned a day of sweeping my way round clothes shops, stocking up on essentials like dental floss (which you can't seem to get in Bali), hair-removing cream (which you can't seem to get in Bali), and visiting the cinema to see Twilight's *Breaking Dawn* (which you can't seem to do in Bali).

In the end, it was a very productive day and I managed all these things, except the sweeping through clothes shops part. In hindsight, having no bank card was probably a blessing. It's been a very long day though, so far. It started at 3 a.m. when Wayan Number 9 picked me up from the homestay and drove me to the airport. Then I got on the wrong plane. Yes. I got on the wrong plane. Don't ask me how. I was just settling down in my seat, untangling my iPod headphones when the bloke in front of me exclaimed: 'This plane's going to Kuala Lumpur?' before standing up and pushing his way off the aircraft with the urgency of someone who'd just discovered a bomb under his seat.

Er... what?

I scrambled for my stuff and stood up. Somehow, we'd both been allowed on the wrong shuttle bus and taken to the wrong plane. I'm not sure if it was the airline's staff or some gross inefficiency in the shuttle-bus team that was to blame but in all my time travelling this planet, this has never happened before. I found myself elbowing bemused passengers out of the way and following him down the steps onto the runway, where we were immediately surrounded from all directions by men in orange jackets with walkie-talkies.

Eventually we boarded the right plane. After failing to get my visa in Bangkok due to the floods, I really didn't need to wind up in Kuala Lumpur with no hope of getting anything again. Mind you, had that plane been heading to New York, or Jamaica, or the Maldives, or Hawaii ... well, that would have been a different story. Buckle me up, sister — I'm going on holiday! *Your fault, not mine.*

Back to being annoyed about Christmas cheer. This worries me. Am I turning into a Scrooge already, at thirty-two? Perhaps it's because I'm rootless and Christmas is about family, so on a deep, semi-conscious level I feel uncomfortable because I don't feel included. Hmm. Nah, fuck it, I *love* Christmas. I just don't like Cliff Richard singing at me as I buy hair remover. It makes me picture him watching me in the bathroom, looking all sinister, covering his privates with mistletoe and wine (ugh, sorry).

It's nearly time for Saxon and Kate to finish work. A home-cooked dinner and their comfy couch await, and in spite of a horrible day in twinkly, Christmassy Singa-poor, I'm feeling lucky to have such lovely friends here looking after me. With the help of one glass of Chardonnay in this Irish pub (I can always budget for wine) I'm adopting my new, Ubud, spiritually-sound attitude from this point forward. Who cares if I have no money right now? Hopefully the staff at Bar Luna will have signed for my new bank card today, I've saved a heap of money on all the crap I would have bought that I just don't need, *and* I finally have my long-term Indonesian visa. Hurrah!

Such is my reputation that I know my friends will choose to assume I really flew all the way here just to see the Twilight movie. I'd like to make it clear right now that this is not the case, although I'm not too proud to admit that if I'd had more time and money, I would have watched it twice. I'm a teen-vampire-loving *adult*. I can do what I want.

29/11

Death of the alarm-cock ...

When Putu from the Cock Posse sent me an SMS to say, 'I got tiket for cockafaithing you want visit?' it took a while to put two and two together. English as a second language, plus the iPhone's autocorrect function, does not make for easy understanding. But a cockfight is what Putu was suggesting and being intrigued, if somewhat disturbed by the concept of watching his beloved bird battle to the death with blades strapped to his skinny feet, I took him up on the offer.

I just got back. I feel like I need about three showers.

The event took place under a circus-style big top, constructed with metal rods and plastic sheeting. I've never been anywhere so hot and sweaty in my life and I don't think that's an exaggeration.

My ears are still ringing, too. A cockfight is a cacophony of human, mechanical and animal sounds unlike anything you've ever experienced. First you have to weave your way through a million motorbikes outside, some still revving under the feet of their enthusiastic riders, others parked so close together it's a wonder they don't get tangled up like a giant metal puzzle.

Then you have to pass the clothing stalls (any excuse for a quick sale), the ancient medicine men plugging potions made from ground-up animal skulls, the fruit sellers with durian and mango in fly-swarmed piles, the sticks of greasy *satay* browning slowly over hot coals…

'Hurry!' Putu shouted, three steps ahead of me, as I battled through the *satay* smoke. 'We don't want to miss start!'

In the main stadium, we pushed our way through the rowdy human jungle with the skill of a pair of Amazon warriors. It turned out that it was Putu's friend's cock fighting, not his. It was nice of them to include me in the witness stand for the spectacle, although I'll admit I felt a bit sick when I got my first whiff of the arena. It wasn't exactly an attractive scene either.

Roosters squawked and doodle-doo'd, men bellowed, clove cigarettes sparked alight and emitted evil plumes above the madness. Aside from the girls carrying woven pandan leaf trays of drinks and snacks on their heads, I was the only woman there. Generally women don't watch these fights, so me in my bright-pink *sarong* and T-shirt, clutching a digital SLR stood out like a sore thumb. I've never had so much male attention in my life … or so many men asking me if I like their cocks (sigh).

Cockfights, which are commonly known as *tajen* (the *taji* being the blades bound to the birds' feet) are held for one of two reasons in Bali these days; either as a ritual at a temple or purification ceremony, or as a sporting event, just for gamblers.

The ritual itself is known as the *Tabah Rah*, which translates quite literally as 'pouring blood'. Oh yes, this is not stuff for the faint-hearted.

I found it hard to know what to wear, actually. What does a western woman wear to a Balinese bird murdering? I opted for the *sarong* because it's easily washable and I didn't want to get anything too nice all blood-splattered, and I really didn't want men ogling any more than I'd been told they would. But I should have just gone for shorts. Many of the sweating men were shirtless and resembling drowned chickens anyway.

'This is a *real* cockfight!' Putu had enthused on our way to the village of Sukavati, about three kilometres out of Ubud. Two more grinning friends I hadn't met before were in the back. He was banging his hands on the steering wheel with glee and I realised the car was filling up with testosterone as quickly as the air-conditioning could fight it.

Today's 'real' fight was held in honour of the dark moon, which started yesterday. Just to clarify, when there's no visible moon in the sky the Balinese offer a sacrifice to keep the evil spirits from descending, which they tend to do in darkness. The blood of a battle-weary cock seems to work.

No-one knows for sure when cockfighting started in Bali. There are ancient texts which suggest it has been happening for centuries, with one inscription citing a fight in the year 933 CE. In 1971, President Suharto declared gambling illegal, which of course is in line with Islamic teaching, but a loophole based on the religious significance saw to it that the ritual continued. It seems impossible now that the Balinese would stop their gambling, even if a serious crackdown were enforced. I've never seen so much cash being flashed in my life. Small bets are usually made, but according to Putu, people make loads of them. Entire family fortunes are lost all the time in Bali because of cockfighting.

Sure enough, in the stadium, shirtless men were waving millions of rupiah about in their hands, making bright-pink fans from the banknotes to fight the heat. It was like being in a P. Diddy music video. And aside from the bets being made on the birds, there were other games happening on the sidelines. Cards, dice, old coins, chips, anything you can imagine were being used as a means to gamble. There was one game that looked a lot like Twister, but with different depictions of gods and demons instead of coloured dots. The guys weren't twisted all over it, they were simply sitting around it in a giant circle, smoking and throwing cash onto the various characters, like Pictionary mixed with Poker. They wanted me to bet. I gave them 20,000 Rp. I lost it within two milliseconds.

The cockfight was one huge, unsexy scene of roughly two thousand loud, perspiring men, but with no alcohol. I guess the equivalent in British terms would be a footy game at Wembley Stadium with no beer.

I fought my way to the front to get a better look, using my telephoto lens as a weapon.

The expert spur affixers were hard at work in one corner, tying the blades around the cocks' legs with red string. Putu told me that these spurs are only sharpened during eclipses, or when there's no moon, like last night, and these blades should never be seen by women. I did avert my eyes after he said that … but it's too late now. Whatever befalls women who look at blades on chicken's feet is about to befall me.

The circle of men around the birds were hushed as the feathery fighters were placed in the middle of the ring. Then a bell sounded and they were off, squaring up on one another like Tyson and

Holyfield, ready to fight. The stadium erupted once more and in a whirl of feathers, sweat, bellowing and squawking, the first injury became visible as the white bird turned red and fell over.

Another bell sounded. I looked at Putu who was in a trance. I knew he'd placed a bet on the wounded bird, but he never told me how much. Putu's pal, the cock's owner, a big, burly man with tattoos, looked pretty pissed off, too, scowling on the sidelines, a boxer's coach witnessing the decline of a prize-winning prodigy.

A bird's owner identifies with his cock to the extent that the bets made on it are seen as an extension of his place in society. According to my research in the local library in Bali, in a book whose name I have now forgotten, letting your cock fight is putting your own masculinity on the line. Whereas bets are *supposed* to be small, the real gamble is risking one's own pride, even when it is part of a temple ceremony. I have to say, on reflection, for an 'offering in light of the dark moon' it didn't seem very holy to me. I wonder if it really was a 'real' cockfight, associated with religion, or whether we'd all been duped into parting with cash for the hell of it.

Anyway, the interval took roughly two minutes, during which time the poor, injured cock was tended to (meaning his spurs were tightened), allowing him to fight another round. Unfortunately for him, after the bell rang for the start of round two, the bigger, stronger cock he was fighting finished him off within seconds, much to Putu's annoyance. At least there's a bit more fresh *satay* on the menu in town, I suppose. And he still has his own cock to stroke when he gets home.

There are usually nine or ten matches in a cockfight session, with the winner of each fight going on to tackle another bird. It can carry on for up to four hours, so I'm told, but I'd had enough after one. The whole scene was a bit too much for me. Like most women who are sheltered from the bloodshed, I'm definitely not man enough for this sport.

Putu and I exited the stadium and the gory pit of feathers, entrails, blood and shit, leaving his pals to carry on gambling. It was enough to put me off chicken for life. Probably. Unless it's in a warm caesar salad with crispy bacon bits and a boiled egg, covered with dressing. Mmm.

Whether I witnessed a 'real, religious' cockfight or not today, I can tell you one thing; the sound of those infuriating *cock-a-doodle-dos* in the mornings now will be tolerated with a tiny bit more compassion.

29/11

The final kirtan ...

I've just had to cancel my colonic, which I have to admit I'm a bit relieved about. My new bank card has still not arrived (at least the gang at Bar Luna haven't seen it) and I can't very well show up for a draining and not pay afterwards. What if they decided to pump it all back in again? Anyway, I'll reschedule ... I'm told it's an Ubud experience I don't want to miss (even if I secretly do) and plus I don't want to have been torturing myself with all this raw food without completing the cleansing process.

Having no money has been a sort of initiation into a different lifestyle. While trying not to spend any more than is absolutely necessary, I've been partaking in a lot more indoor activities this past week ... and no, not of the naked kind. There've been none of those since Gili T, unfortunately (although The Diver and I are still having very nice textual relations, thanks for asking). No, I've actually been sitting in my room, playing guitar.

Even though I'm a bit crap, it's always been a sort of hobby, a therapeutic practice, I suppose. Back in August, when I found myself being digitally stalked by a bloke I met in Thailand, I found remarkable release in penning a song about it. The first bit goes like this:

> He messaged me on Facebook, said he'd fallen in love
> And I said what did I do to deserve this?
> So he emailed me again and said, no, really I love you
> And I started to get a little bit nervous
> Then he emailed me again and sent a DM on Twitter
> Said I love you, I love you, I love you
> And he comments on my status update, every single day, it's
>   insane
> I just don't know what to do
> It's not like he's physically there
> But seriously, now I'm scared
> 'Cause he's poking and Tweeting, requesting Skype meetings
> And Facebook's not safe now, I swear.

I couldn't show anyone this song because a) it's shit; and b) my stalker would have seen it, but my borrowed guitar and I had hours of fun together, bellowing it out at high volume in various terrible arrangements. With no guitar once more, however (I had to give it back), I was as blocked as my stalker is now from my social networks. I couldn't even finish my song.

Perhaps because I'd been putting it out to the Baliverse how much I'd been missing my musical buddy, my friend Dave from writer's group spontaneously offered me the use of his before he left for California. I get to look after it until he comes back here next year. Hurrah!

The thing is, though, this new borrowed instrument is a cheap, ancient imitation of the one I had before and it falls out of tune the second you so much as *look* at it. For a week it's been leaning up against Winnie the Pooh like an elderly senile person who used to be fun and intelligent but now mutters nothing but nonsense. I do like my guitars to be in tune, even if I'm not. I play a little every now and then in the hope that it will sort itself out, but I always wind up angrily shoving it back in the corner when it twangs apologetically under my fingers.

And then, out of the blue this morning, came Alissa. She sat on my porch step and held out a guitar tuner. 'Thought you might need this, if it was you I heard singing last night?' she said.

Oh dear God.

Alissa is in Ubud to record an Ecstatic Soul kirtan CD. She played me some of it and its jazzy elegance filled the grounds of our homestay with a million times more soul than my Facebook song ... not a difficult accomplishment really, but it was quite lovely. According to a sign I see often at the Yoga Barn, *kirtan* is a method of singing meditation that uses ancient Sanskrit mantras to call upon sacred energies, repel any obstacles blocking us and brings us back to the centre of our being. I keep meaning to go check it out, but, you know ...

Alissa has also experienced Bali's mysterious and magical generosity since she arrived last week. She came over from Australia looking for the best musicians she could find in Bali to help complete her sound. In typical Balinese fashion, they found her, and it didn't take very long. She acquired an incredible flautist yesterday, who's been trained by one of the best flautists in the world and today she's found *me*, a backing singer.

'Do you want to record with me?' she asked, before quickly adding, 'I can't pay you.'

I fought an internal battle. I've harboured hopes of becoming a famous singer since I was five, of course, but I'm not sure thirty-two is the age to start pursuing such dreams, whether I'm being paid or not. Plus I can't *really* sing that well and I'm not sure they have the budget for AutoTune. I'd look terrible in hot pants now, too. Where was she fifteen years ago? I guess I could go with something longer, or looser, maybe something with glitter. But wait, do *kirtan* stars even *wear* glittery clothing or wigs? I'd need a wig too. Something long and black and enchanting, to bring out my eyes. Not that I've thought much about this (ahem).

After a few seconds I decided that a *kirtan*-chanting backing singer didn't quite have the same ring to it as 'member of a girl band' even considering my current age and physique (and lack of vocal skill outside of a *karaoke* booth). Besides, I'm quite busy at the moment, being poor in my room. I thanked Alissa for the opportunity and said I'd think about it some more as she hurried off to look for a back-up backing singer.

I had a look at her website when she'd gone:

Ecstatic Soul is music that opens the heart and unravels the mind. Dipping into the nectar of the heart, ecstatic energy liberates the mind, allowing the river of life to flow unencumbered. Surrender to the soulful tones and be transported into the arms of the divine.

Sounds wonderful. And her music is soft, sensual and evocative — all very good things. But I suspect singing about unencumbered rivers would probably involve donning long-sleeved floaty tops and gargantuan waist-swallowing fisherman pants, and maybe not shaving my legs, and the attention of bearded hippies with questionable career paths. And B.O.

It's nice of her to deem me worthy of backing-singer status, but her final *kirtan* CD will have to be *sans* me (and undoubtedly far better for it).

I'm grateful that my guitar ... well, Dave's guitar, is now in tune, even though Bali's magic and I may have got our wires crossed somewhere in the spiritual divide. When I put it out there, that I'd quite like a guitar and a tuner so I could finish writing a rubbish song about stalkers on Facebook, it didn't mean I thought the time was right to become a volunteer *kirtan* recording artist in fisherman pants. Talk about throwing me in at the deep end, Bali.

I hope my bank card gets here soon.

30/11

Shake 'n' Pack ...

'Things are going well and very intense here. There's no way we can have visitors, it's really about bonding as a group,' said Jen this morning in an email.

She's still up in the hills with the naked yoga lady, Arshia, and this is the first I've heard from her since she left. So what I actually read in those two sentences was: 'No outsiders! Outsiders are unwelcome because they disturb the changing process and might oppose the part where we hand out the purple robes and special pills and attempt to cross over to a better world.'

Sounds a bit 'culty' to me, but I'm sure she knows what she's doing.

It's the time of year for 'taking yourself away' in Ubud, or so it seems. I'm heading off to the ashram and Ratu Bagus in two days' time and others have either gone home for Christmas or sought out a means of escape from it all by heading into the middle of nowhere and doing something weird till 'it all goes away'. I'm wondering if I'm not the only one who feels a bit out of place and hence slightly angry among festivities

If I'm honest, though, I'm a teeny bit nervous about the ashram. I saw Ibu Kat again in Bar Luna last night. She said, 'Oh, you're going at the weekend? OK, well, see you Monday', which clearly means she thinks I'll last two seconds. She's not the only one. I keep hearing mixed things. Originally I booked myself in for a week and then I met a lady in town who said she had a friend who went up there and absolutely loved it. Apparently she totally 'changed' and ended up staying two months. When I heard that, I promptly emailed Ratu's PA and asked if I could stay two weeks instead.

Then I met a guy at that raw dinner party a while back, who told me they make you smoke something weird before you start shaking, which appalled me so I promptly emailed again and said I wasn't sure two weeks would fit in with my schedule and could I please go back to one week.

Then I met a younger guy in Bali Buddha, a hottie no less, who said he'd spent three weeks there and got a lot out of it, and he'd never seen any weird smoking devices. So I thought, no horrible smoking *and* the potential of meeting a hottie ... well, shit, maybe I should just get the hell over it and stay a month, in December, and go cold turkey on everything Christmassy completely? I've got my bank card back now (finally!) so I have access to my money again, but staying on an ashram would mean I'll continue saving my pennies, too. What could there possibly be to buy in hippy-land? It's win-win. I emailed them back, and got this in reply:

'Christmas here is fun. There will be a tree and Ratu will play Father Christmas. We have lots of children and they will all get little gifts. It's always a very nice celebration.'

So there you go then. How good is that? Ratu himself is not just the Good King. He's frickin' Good King Wenceslas! Rather than ignore the festive season, Ratu Bagus himself is going to strap on a pot belly and an even bushier beard, and do good things for poor children. This sounds like the best Christmas ever. It'll be like living in a Little Orphan Annie adaptation. I wonder if they'll all shake while they're doing it? I wonder if they'll shake the whole time and spill whisky on each other and bake little Ratu Bagus mince pies with Ratu's face on them. I could play *Tomorrow* on Dave's guitar and everyone could clap along like only hippies can clap. That would definitely make me feel like less of a Scrooge.

I leave in two days time at 9 a.m., so I should arrive, according to his PA, 'in time for the afternoon session'. I'm still not entirely sure what a session of any kind entails … finding specific details on this is kind of hard, which is why I've been asking so many people. All I know is that it involves shaking on the spot for a length of time and that I should pack comfortable clothing. Plane Jane is still there, thank god. At least I'll have one person I sort of know.

As for coming back, well who knows? I've confused the ashram folk as much as myself with all my chopping and changing. I could be back on Monday like Ibu Kat predicts. Or I could decide to devote my entire life to the practice of shaking. I could never come back. It's not like I really have anything in particular to come back to, anyway. I'm the absolute target audience for an ashram, actually — a lost and wayward soul with no particular place to go; impressionable, single, slightly naive, in possession of an overactive imagination ideal for convincing myself and others that shaking on the spot several times a day is the one thing that will make a difference in this terrible, terrible world …

If they hand me a cloak and a pill, who will stop me? Who would even *want* to try and visit me out here, in Bali, in the hills, in the middle of nowhere, on an ashram, at Christmas?

Better get on with my packing … it could be the last trip I ever take.

01/12

The monkey and the mermaid …

I was contemplating a few last-minute happy-hour cocktails before my inevitably sobering ashram experience when I got a curious call from Budhi. Remember Budhi? He's the only white *Jero Mangku* in the village. He told me that Ibu Ayu Cantik had some trance healing to perform, and asked if I wanted to come.

There was only one thing to do; I donned my finest Balinese attire, called Wayan Number 9 and headed back to Bona. If you're wondering why I didn't ride myself there on a motorbike, don't worry, I'll come to that soon (ugh).

Sidd has gone back to Australia now, so it was just me and Budhi, and using our phones as flashlights we trekked through the rice paddies in the darkness towards the eerie chanting we could hear coming from the nearby Pura. Dressed in my *kamben* and *kabaya* once again, I knelt on the outskirts of the circular room next to a guy in his late teens, who introduced himself as Agus.

If I haven't mentioned this before, I always find it quite awkward wearing these clothes; not because I don't feel like a Balinese princess in them, all lacy and sparkly and pretty, but because the sarong is usually wrapped so tightly around my legs that it makes me walk like a penguin. It also forces me to sit with my thighs squeezed so closely together that it induces a kind of sweat that I can only describe as … actually, I can't describe it. It's just gross. Maybe I'm not dressing myself properly. But anyway, I tried not to focus on such a trivial matter. There was possession in the house! Possession by evil.

Ibu Ayu Cantik is a trance healer and medium. She's also the descendent of a priest, the highest caste in Bali, and is obviously paid huge amounts of respect in Bona. She's a petite lady, probably in her early forties, with dark flowing hair and bright red lipstick and she seems to float around the room, rather than walk. When she recognised Budhi she threw him the most gorgeous smile and I remember thinking, wow, she's probably one of the most enchanting and graceful ladies I've ever seen, which is fitting because *cantik*, pronounced *chan-teek*, means 'beautiful' in Indonesian.

Three people were already dancing when we got there, whizzing about on the terracotta-tiled floor with their eyes closed. The songs that filled the air along with the incense in the open Pura were mostly mantras set to whirly, twirly soundtracks. These, I noticed, were being played on an iPod Nano, controlled by a DJ playing to the forces that might choose to inhabit the people of Bona. (I wonder if Apple knows it's orchestrating the spirit world now, as well as this one?)

A huge altar at the front held hundreds of offerings of rice, jackfruit, mangoes, flowers and roasted chickens. Chilling paintings of demons hung on the walls behind giant stone gargoyles and Ganesh statues. I felt a bit nervous, but Budhi was smiling and chatting quietly to other people sitting around us. Every now and then another person would peel away from their place on the floor and start dancing.

The dancing looked normal, I guess, if a little bad. A little kid in a Spiderman costume was climbing on the railings around the Pura, his blue and red costume somewhat out of place but probably not as suffocating as my sarong. I was pondering the significance of wearing a superhero costume in a temple full of evil spirits, when something happened to Ibu Ayu Cantik.

She had started to vibrate. Two men grabbed her elbows as her eyes rolled back in her head and she flopped like a rag doll into their arms. Gently they helped her over to a chair near the altar and a semi-circle formed around her on the floor. Agus scooted up closer for a better look, so I did the same. It was like storytime with grandma. Ibu Ayu Cantik had even started speaking like an old lady. All dancing stopped, the Nano was paused and I found myself holding my breath.

During a trance, it's believed that a spirit or 'roh' enters the body of its chosen human, who then becomes a vehicle for that force, acting out its intentions. Budhi told me that during a trance, anything the medium says or does is considered to be said or done by the roh occupying their body and for people to ignore any messages would be most unwise.

By now, Ibu Ayu Cantik's features were contorting fiercely and through the crowd of people I saw her take some kind of clump from a pandan leaf, which she placed slowly in her mouth. She chewed noisily as she continued to speak.

'She's channelling an ancient ancestor from Mount Agung,' Budhi whispered. And she was. Everything had slowed: her speech, her hand-to-mouth coordination, her mannerisms. She looked physically older, even her skin looked darker against her white ceremonial clothing. Her juddering actions were so weird coming from a previously graceful lady in red lipstick … and then I realised, it wasn't red lipstick. Ibu Ayu Cantik's lips were stained from chewing betel nut, which grows in the tropical climates of Southeast Asia. It's known for suppressing hunger, as well as heightening awareness. Round and round in her mouth it went as she spoke — in Chinese!

Budhi says speaking in other languages is not uncommon when people go into a trance. Most of the time, they can't remember what they've said, or what they've done while under this spell. Some claim that when in trance, the *roh* inhabits a certain part of the spinal cord, which stops signals reaching the brain and causes amnesia.

'What's she telling them?' I whispered back.

Apparently, she had mentioned his presence in the room, although when she stopped with the Bahasa Indonesian and moved to Chinese, Budhi lost track.

She spoke as the old woman for about ten minutes, puffing on a cigarette, and then snapped out of it as abruptly as she'd started. The music came back on and all hell broke loose, as if Ibu Ayu Cantik had opened a door to the netherworld.

There were spirits flying in left, right and centre, slamming into the bodies of these seemingly normal people and making them jump, scream and writhe around on the floor with their eyeballs bulging. The dancing had turned into manic convulsions and almost every tile on the centre stage had a squirming man or woman on it. I shot back to the outskirts of the Pura next to Spiderman, but even he was looking concerned.

The young Agus, who'd told me previously that he started coming to the regular trance healing sessions a month ago because his hair was falling out and he didn't know why, was the next to be struck. He was sitting quite quietly on the floor, keeping himself to himself, when a huge force suddenly jolted through him, slamming him back against the wooden railings. He shuddered and shook on his bum as if a toaster had just been chucked into his bathtub. His feet were pointed straight out in front of him and he started shrieking in a tone that sounded nothing like the one in which he'd spoken to me before. Spiderman fled the Pura. Two little girls sitting next to him shot up and jumped on me, and if it wasn't for them I would have jumped on the woman next to *me*!

Ibu Ayu Cantik, now back to her normal self, hurried over and doused Agus several times with holy water, frangipanis flying everywhere. She helped him up and then shoved him into the crowd, where he stumbled, made sounds like an ape, pursed his lips and howled at the ceiling. Meanwhile, a girl of no more than twenty years was wailing at equal volume, with tears streaming down her cheeks. Budhi got up at the beckoning of Ibu Ayu Cantik and started dousing *her* with holy water, too. It didn't seem to work. She flung herself around the room, smacked hard onto the floor and with her arms to her sides and her legs stuck together with invisible glue she started flipping about, like a dolphin stuck in a boat.

For a couple of hours at least, the madness ensued. There was so much holy water on the floor we could practically swim in it. When peace finally returned, a small ceremony, which Budhi also directed, saw us thank the spirits and Ibu Ayu Cantik, and we all made more offerings, after which we got to nibble on eggs, rice and sweet palm sugar snacks wrapped in banana leaves. Cautiously, I sat next to Agus again, who had calmed down and resumed his usual temperament. He told me the spirit of a white monkey had entered his body.

'How did it feel?' I asked him.

'Like a monkey was in me,' he repeated.

'Yes, but how did it make you feel?'

'Like, a great white monkey entered me. I don't remember after that.'

'So where are these spirits when they're not inhabiting bodies?' I asked him, hoping they'd all been appeased and weren't still loitering with intent.

'*Neskala*,' he replied. 'It's the world we cannot see.'

I shuddered, in spite of my sweaty thighs. I never want to go to *Neskala*.

Budhi later told me that this world is very real. To the Balinese it is positively pulsating with forces unseen. It's full of *dewa* (deities), *leluhur* (all their beloved and perhaps not-so-beloved ancestors), *buta khala* (evil beasts and demons) and *panengen dan pangiwa* (knowledge that's translated as white and black magic, respectively). Most trance sessions usually entail the channelling of these four very strong forces.

Let's not forget that the Balinese, of course, are also closer to the natural world than us westerners who wander about switched off, or more often than not plugged into various gadgets. As such they're far more receptive to extreme experiences with possession and the supernatural realm.

It was most likely *buta khala* that possessed the open-minded Agus. With *buta khala*, the spirit of a beast will enter the human through the feet and can take the form of a host of animals, from a tiger to a horse to a snake. In Agus's case, of course, it was a monkey. A white monkey. I even saw his feet shake when it struck him!

I also saw a horse demonstrated by an elderly man in full neighing and galloping mode, and a fair few snakes slithering around people's ankles.

In the case of the girl in green, an ancestor or a *leluhur* had taken her over, most probably a baby, which was why she had no control over her arms and legs, although there's a legend of a mermaid spirit called *Putri Duyung*, who could also have been responsible for her fish-like mannerisms.

'It's hard to tell,' Budhi said, scratching his chin.

It's not uncommon for these people to ask for gifts in their trance state, to appease whatever's inside them. Unpeeled eggs are popular (hence our snacks), rice wine is often splashed about, even baby chicks are occasionally sought ... anything the force needs.

Anyway, being in a trance is good because out comes any sickness when it passes. Sometimes it happens straight away, but sometimes the healing is a slow process that can take months. The national health services in the west might turn us away and make us wait months for appointments, but I bet they'd hurry the hell up if we all started screeching like beasts and flapping around like fish in their car parks.

'So, do you have to be a special sort of person to go into a trance?' I asked Budhi as he drove me back to Ubud at midnight (the session lasted over three hours!).

'Not necessarily,' was his answer, though he explained that most *dewa* forces (the top, most important ones) prefer to enter the bodies of clean people ... not so much those who've lathered themselves beforehand in Imperial Leather, but those who've undergone the purification ceremony, like priests. Or priestesses, like Ibu Ayu Cantik.

I'm still finding it quite tough to digest what happened in that temple. To think my old life would have seen me heading to a bar for those cocktails at the end of a long day, but here I am in Bali getting home after midnight stone cold sober, sopping with sweat and holy water, having had a relatively normal conversation with a boy who was just possessed by a monkey.

It's hard to imagine that shaking meditation at an ashram can get any weirder than this …

Day 1 at the ashram: Finding Yourself – Advanced …

It is usually in the first couple of days that our blocks wake up, rather than our soul, and thus it can be highly challenging to stay the first full five days in the ashram. One sometimes wants to run away, sees things that seem wrong elsewhere, thinks 'this is not for me' or 'this might be good but I can't do it,' etc. This initial resistance often occurs during the first two to four days and is completely normal. Do your best to get through it with a positive mind and you will reap the rewards. You will get to see, feel and understand how powerful, positive and life-changing this shaking practice really is.'

— Ratu Bagus Instruction Manual

OK. I've been here one full day and yes, I want to run away. I really want to run away. I want to call Ibu Kat and say 'You were right, I can't take it, I'm coming back,' but out of pride, I won't. I won't leave, but I'm definitely thinking I can't do it, which makes me a textbook ashram virgin in Ratu's eyes. Great.

Currently the power's out around the ashram and all I can hear in the darkness is this terrifying wailing noise, like a pack of werewolves howling at the moon. I'm seconds away from the *Taman*, which is the octagonal-shaped structure where the 'shaking' takes place, and I just legged it from the session half an hour early because:

a) it's dark, so I knew no-one would see me; and
b) as I left, some of them were gurgling insidiously as they shook, like players in a Balinese version of *Thriller*. Not normal.

Maybe I'm even more freaked out than I'd usually be because the power's out. Yes. I'm sure that's what it is. Stupidly I thought we wouldn't have to shake in the silence. With no music to shake to surely the whole thing would be kind of pointless, right? Like staying at a rave when the DJ's gone home — who does that? My inner quitter rejoiced at the thought of *not* having to do what I came here to do, on the very first day I was supposed to be doing it.

But just now I watched roughly thirty silhouettes in the candlelight, trembling on the spot like zombies, all feeling 'Energy' I most definitely could not feel. These people can shake to the beat of their own drums, it seems. There's no escape from the shakes ever in this ashram, which is why I'm hiding in my dorm room under a sheet, shaking all by myself.

The first thing I thought when I entered the *Taman* at 1 p.m. for the 'afternoon session' was: *Shit, I don't know how to do this!* My first instinct was to try and dance to the music pumping out of some giant speakers on hinges around the walls, like we do when we dance at the Yoga Barn.

Oh, the lovely, easy, simple Yoga Barn. How far away you feel right now! Obviously, the Yoga Barn is baby stuff compared to what they practise here. I've only been here a day and already I can see that. The Yoga Barn is 'Finding Yourself, For Beginners'. I'm in an advanced class now.

Standing behind the lines of people all jiggling themselves into a frenzy on the spot, I started moving my own body, only to find my ego jumped straight into my brain and screamed at me:

'What the effing hell are you *doing*?!'

'Shut up ego, just shake will you!'

'No. I will not. You look like an idiot. You're embarrassing me.'

'Look, everyone else is doing it.'

'That's because they're weird. You don't want to be like them, do you?'

Peggy interrupted by jiggling up to my side. 'Don't try so hard. Just let the rhythm come from your heart,' she said. Peggy is a lovely woman in her fifties from Denmark, who's as towering and gangly as a giraffe, bone-thin and bushy-haired. She's been here since 2007.

'Try and feel the Energy. The Energy will tell you what to do.'

I took her in as she beamed at me, all happy and healthy, a fully fledged shaker in her tight purple top and leggings. By 'Energy' she was referring to the force field, the vortex, the invisible electrical grid that appears to be the means of all spiritual healing here at Ratu Bagus's ashram. Energy is a word that's whispered most excitedly among the residents here and always with a capital E. In its purest form it powers the place, and as I bopped up and down pathetically, I noticed it was starting to surge through other people with much the same magnitude as I witnessed that white monkey go ballistic inside Agus last night at the trance healing.

'Concentrate on a painting at the same time,' Peggy told me, probably noticing my inability to feel anything more than incompetent.

'Pick a painting of Ratu, any one you like, and feel the Energy. I like that one, over there.'

I followed her pointing finger to the front of the room, where a giant portrait of the man himself hung in the far left corner. He was pointing directly at us in return. Above him read the words *Om Swastiastu Ratu Bagus.*

Roughly twenty pictures of Ratu Bagus, the Good King, hang in the *Taman.* He's doing something different in each one; either grinning, or pointing, or looking very official in a white button-up coat. The idea is to channel the Energy that he sends out from the paintings, while shaking your body. If you lose focus, you're supposed to chant the mantra over and over, *Om Swastiastu Ratu Bagus. Om Swastiastu Ratu Bagus.*

'What it actually means', said Peggy, shaking furiously and thrusting her hands in the air towards the paintings as though experiencing some sort of seizure in an art gallery, 'is welcome into my life, light, love and hope. Welcome healing and connection, open-mindedness and positivity, welcome inner teacher, magic mirror, friend who's always been inside me. Welcome Sacred Fire!'

I'm still not entirely sure how all that can come from a bit of canvas, but I nodded anyway and tried to follow her lead.

Shaking isn't always entirely comfortable. I focused on clearing my mind, as instructed. I repeated the mantra several times but all I could think about — apart from the fact that I was talking to a painting — was that my boobs were jiggling up and down in my stretched and worn-out bra:

'Don't think about that, block it out, block it out …'

'But they're quite uncomfortable. Couldn't this cause stretch marks?'

'Don't think about it!'

'But you don't usually need a bra at all, this is quite exciting. Maybe you need a sports bra these days?'

'What do you mean these days? You're thirty-two. It's not like your boobs just grew … oh God, what if they're drooping already and that's why you need a bra?'

Don't think about it … *Om Swastiastu Ratu Bagus!*

Just as I'd finally fixed myself on one particular painting and started to get into the groove, Neil, a large-set man in his forties who's come to shake from the UK, transformed into a helicopter in front of me. With a shriek and a howl he started whirling around the *Taman* with his arms outstretched in a make-believe game of pilot-crashes-into-mountain. As he spun out of control the stench hit me smack in the face, as did a little shower; the stinky by-product of his exertions. As Peggy bobbed obliviously at my side, chanting the mantra under her breath, he was blessing me with his odorous ecstasy in tiny, wet, unholy droplets that landed on my arms and chest, making me gag.

Eventually Neil crashed to the floor and writhed like an octopus, delighted and triumphant. Any concentration I might have forged went out the window. And just as I thought his performance couldn't get any more unsanitary, he hurled in a bucket.

There are buckets placed conveniently throughout the *Taman* for people to do just this. I think it all has something to do with tobacco. It's not smoked, but it hasn't quite been explained to me yet.

The aim of a shake, so reads my instruction manual, is to tune into the Divine Energy, to shift the focus to *feeling* rather than thinking; to identify with your healthy and happy soul rather than with your mind and body. Once you're in touch, the Energy can work miracles.

Such a shame it smells worse than Ecstatic Dancing.

Ashram life with Ratu Bagus involves shaking three times a day, from 7 to 9 a.m., 1 to 3 p.m. and 7 to 9 p.m. There are roughly thirty people here right now, which seems like a lot, although Peggy tells me there are less visitors when Ratu Bagus himself isn't actually here. Apparently I'll get to meet him tomorrow. I'm already planning my outfit. It's not every day I get to meet a Good King … or any king at all, for that matter. I think I'll go for the navy blue OM top and leggings, perhaps a raincoat to protect myself from any future sweat showers, if I can source one in the middle of nowhere.

I *so* wasn't prepared for this.

03/12

Day 2 at the ashram: The King and I …

How to shake: Stand with your feet shoulder-width apart, with your hands parallel and stretched out forward, palms open to the front. The knees should be slightly bent so that the whole body can shake or vibrate easily. There are numerous other hand and leg positions or movements one can do. Ask a senior shaker to show you some. The position is not too important, it's more important to feel electric and hot inside.

— Ratu Bagus Instruction Manual

I've found solace on the roof of the *Taman*, which is a slightly nicer way of saying I've discovered a hideaway from the scary people in between shaking sessions. It happens to have a power point for my laptop. There aren't many power points around the ashram for some reason, but I think this one is up here for the cleaners, in case they need to vacuum the giant stuffed tiger I've just seen lurking in a cupboard.

Anyway, it's day two at the ashram and here I am in my octagonal rooftop haven, where no-one can see me. Some may call it anti-social or shunning the Energy. I call it self-preservation. It's nice up here in the sunshine, with Mount Agung keeping an eye on me.

The ashram grounds are stunning, all waterfalls and walks down grassy slopes with bamboo railings. There's even a swimming pool. They have monkeys in cages, fluffy white rabbits, two dogs and a captive (and critically endangered) Bali starling, but animal welfare issues aside, it's all very nice. It's so peaceful ... if you can ignore the agonised screams coming from downstairs.

In the west, our inner demons (i.e., fear, greed, jealousy etc.) are personally controlled or at worse, left to fester inside. Budhi — who's become a bit of a guru to me as far as things like this are concerned — told me that to the Balinese, these inner demons are as real as the demons and deities that overtake them during a trance. They're identified and dealt with promptly, rarely locked away and ignored, because no-one wants a real, live demon inside them, do they? My guess is that some of Ratu Bagus's Balinese students head back into the *Taman* after the shaking sessions to have another crack at getting rid of them when no-one's watching.

Ratu is one of many practised people in Bali who can exorcise these evils, as well as many serious, life-threatening diseases. He does it in an unconventional way by helping people fight their own demons, whatever they may be. To the community who live on this ashram, he really is a king who's worshipped and admired by his subjects. Some of his workers have been here more than twenty years.

When I expressed my concerns about talking to paintings this morning, I was told the images in the *Taman* are just there to help us focus on the Energy when Ratu Bagus is not physically present. 'The Energy comes from him and everything he blesses, like a battery,' Peggy explained. 'He's a transporter, but the Energy flows through all of us and it gets stronger the more we shake!'

'HAHAHAHAHAHA!!!!!' said my ego.

Jesus, you are so rude. Shut up.

Peggy gave me a little tour and I've got to say, all skepticism aside, the photos on the walls of Energy Orbs surrounding Ratu and his shakers are awe-inspiring (there are videos on YouTube, too). Apparently more have been captured around the ashram in recent years than anywhere else in Bali. And according to ashram chit-chat, more Orbs have been photographed in Bali than anywhere else in the world.

In one photo you can actually see the vague outline of Ganesh sitting on Ratu Bagus's head, outside a building in Rome. I did a double-take when I saw it, not least because Galactica Blanco told me she could see *me* in her crystal ball with Ganesh on my head. She also said she could see me meditating on a mountain. Maybe she just got her astral wires crossed and she was actually predicting my time with the Good King.

Anyway, ugh. Difficult. I want to believe so, so, so badly, especially when I see this stuff. But I also don't want to go insane and be shunned by all my friends. Hmm...

Chatting to the others in the dining room, I learned that Ratu Bagus has helped many western people heal themselves of some horrible things. Plane Jane found me sitting with my

Marmite on toast this morning. As we discussed serendipity versus coincidence she told me how her epilepsy has completely disappeared since she started shaking (no pun intended). She's been here over three months already but she swears she was actually healed after three weeks.

There's another lady here too, from the US, who was quite sick with migraines and is now much, much better. She's easy to spot around the place because she never stops shaking. I call her Permanent Mild Shake. The first time I saw PMS she was sitting in the kitchen on a stool, tapping her feet on the floor at the same time as talking and peeling garlic. The next time I saw her, she was shaking her whole body as she ate her lunch. It was like dining with a vibrator on the next chair — awkward. Plus, think of the indigestion.

Anyway, she seems happy enough as she vibes her way through the day; another Ratu Bagus' success story. According to Plane Jane, whomever here has had the courage and determination to go through Ratu's 'Energy Laundry' for any extended length of time will testify that their lives have indeed changed dramatically.

I met the Good King himself this morning. To my ego's disdain I was shaking like a pro, getting into *I'm a Barbie Girl* with a good bounce thanks to the handy tips in my instruction manual, when all of a sudden the room went crazy with even more wild animal noises. I opened my eyes and realised Ratu Bagus was standing there at the front, beaming like Buddha. It was like one of the paintings had come to life and spat him out into the room. For a moment I was quite stunned, and not just by his whiter-than-white outfit. There's no denying it, he really does have an incredible presence.

He walked around the *Taman*, touching people and standing on their feet, making a sort of tugging motion with his hands near people's chests as though pulling an invisible rope from their hearts. Big Al, a wiry man from England and his son, Little Al, went crazy when he did this to them, screeching and laughing like loony macaques and bouncing all over the place, right at the front of the *Taman*. Little Al in particular has a manic laugh that pierces the room in a pitch I'm pretty sure only dogs should be able to hear.

Big Al's wife, who arrived at the ashram from England late last night during the power cut, also gave a good performance. They're seasoned shakers, though. They shake every chance they get and this is a special extended family holiday for the three of them in Bali, during which they won't leave the ashram for three weeks. Highly commendable. God knows it was tough enough for my family to stay in Disney World without an argument.

One young Balinese boy was flung so far across the room in my direction by the Energy when Ratu walked past that he looked like he'd been struck by lightning. I had to jump out of his way! The whole show was quite spectacular and chaotically choreographed by the Energy. I'm surprised they didn't knock over the Christmas tree.

I'm still not sure if people can actually feel a different energy when Ratu Bagus is the house, or if they just *think* they can. I could definitely feel his presence in the room, which was a bit weird, but some people have told me they've actually had orgasms on the floor, such is the power of the Divine!

Ratu Bagus held my hand for maybe two minutes as I bobbed up and down in front of him in yet another badly fitting bra, but I'm sorry to say, I felt nothing different.

I've been thinking about this. Perhaps the power of suggestion is so strong here, what with the paintings and the instruction manuals and the blessed tobacco (I'll come to that, eventually), that people start to believe they're being transformed, when in actual fact they're just retreating further into their own impressionable minds and a world without friends. I don't know. I'm confused.

I can't imagine a point at which I'll feel the urge to scream in the face of a sixty-two year old, bearded man myself. Ratu Bagus is softly spoken, and short and plump like a pastry chef. Actually, you know the chef from South Park? Think of him, only Balinese. He really is lovely, and in spite of my cynicism regarding the actions of his 'subjects', I find him quite bewitching. In fact, as he turned his back on the shaking and went to sit in his little shrine behind the paintings, I watched the way his pert rear held its own against his crisp white trousers.

Jesus. OK, it's wrong of me to be admiring the bum of a sixty-two year old bearded wise man, I know. But you know what? There's something about him that's so intriguing and mysterious and I can't help it. I've always equated those qualities with sexiness in a man. Doesn't matter how old he is. Knowledge is power, as my dad used to say. And power is hot.

Anyway, I should get ready for the 'group sharing', which I think is happening on this very rooftop in about fifteen minutes. I'm feeling a teeny bit better about being here now, I suppose, but I don't think I'll share my new crush on the King.

04/12

Day 3 at the ashram: Bali's Most Haunted...

To feel and connect with the Energy in the shaking, we have to believe in it and in ourselves, even if we can't feel it yet. The moment we believe, we switch dimensions; we make a conscious choice to take that leap of faith and tune into the spiritual frequency — after all, what is there to lose? Suddenly we can feel it, like we're being shaken by the Energy; it is everywhere and something in us connects with it — wow!

— Ratu Bagus Instruction Manual

OK. Hmm. I don't really know how to say this without sounding like a weirdo, but today I caught what I'm pretty sure are Energy Orbs on video. ORBS. Quick, call Mulder and Scully!

It's day three and as we've established, I've been going through what's called the 'Beginner's Process', whereby everything seems stupid and pointless and I withdraw into myself and my ego, intent on gaining nothing from the whole experience and mocking it all to the very end. Everyone probably hates me.

BUT ... and I say this very loudly, that doesn't mean I entered this whole thing with my mind and heart bolted shut. There's always been a little crack there for the sacred Energy to seep through and surprise me if it wanted to.

Ratu Bagus is highly regarded as one of Asia's top paranormal healers and as a woman who *still* reads the tales from the *True Ghost Stories from Around the World* iPhone app. every night before sleeping (please don't judge me), this fills me with more excitement than you can imagine. It's just a bit scary, being in the heart of it ... in an ashram ... in Bali ... near a sacred mountain ... with no escape ... and no alcohol ... and the cast of *Thriller*.

Occasionally, when things need to be done, Ratu Bagus stops the rain.

'I've seen it happen,' a frail man called Dan told me yesterday as we lounged about on the giant purple sofas, reading. 'Even in the rainy season, when it rains all the time, I've seen him stop the rain for two days straight so that ceremonies can go uninterrupted.'

Dan also told me how just before the recent earthquake, Ratu Bagus helped to summon a very powerful Energy to protect the entire island of Bali. Allegedly, this Energy prevented a tsunami.

'He'd never admit this himself, because he's incredibly humble,' says Dan, 'but everyone knows what he did.'

So there you go. Ratu Bagus, as well as being super nice and smiley, is actually the Balinese Superman. If it wasn't for him we all would have perished back in October at the mercy of a massive wave. I'm not sure anyone would recognise him without his glasses.

I've been a bit anti-social so far, sitting on rooftops and exchanging texts with The Diver, who's become my sane saviour from afar. He tells me how the current is around Gili Trawangan, and how he's planning the Christmas party and how he saw three trumpetfish giving a starfish a spa treatment and I think, *Jesus, what I am doing discussing extra-terrestrial dogs in an ashram?* Seriously, I *actually* had that conversation last night.

But after a lot more studying of my instruction manual and a good 'deep and meaningful' with my roommate, a skinny French girl who's come to heal herself of acne, I decided that I *have* been listening to my ego way too much. *Focus, Becky, focus.*

Instead of standing at the back of the room like I've been doing, worrying about my boobs, I tried my best today to block everything else out this afternoon. I stood at the very front, before the pointy-finger painting and chanted *Om Swastiastu Ratu Bagus, Om Swastiastu Ratu Bagus, Om Swastiastu Ratu Bagus,* over and over again to some very heavy trance music. I felt for the Energy, welcomed it in, imagined light all around me, shooting from my heart.

As people screamed and released their inner demons, Beethoven's fifth symphony mix came on and I threw my hands in the air, feeling, I have to say, like becoming a helicopter (gasp!). Was that it? Was I was feeling it … the Energy?

I felt lighter, like shaking was easier and didn't even require any real effort. But then, the dizziness took over. Ugh.

I stood on the outskirts of the room and walked around, and then whipped out my phone to film the madness. When I played it back later, I saw them; little pink and blue circles floating between Ratu Bagus and PMS, who was wobbling herself into absolute ecstasy with her eyes shut. I also saw a bigger Energy Orb follow Ratu Bagus as he walked away from her. It floated over another guy's dark-blue shorts at a different speed to the camera movements, so you can see it pretty clearly. It kind of looks like a face. A mini Ganesh? Hmm, I'd have to call the experts.

How great is that, though? My very own Orbs on film! The only thing I think that distracted me from getting back into my trance-like state after that was the hacking, which unfortunately is a common occurrence in these parts. I've been meaning to come back to this.

The hacking is a distraction from everything, for me at least. As if the demons weren't enough, it's quite uncomfortable listening to the sounds of all these people ejecting their tobacco on a regular basis, too.

The Sacred Medicine, as it's called, is snorted up the nostrils or swallowed by means of a syringe (never smoked) and is a huge part of daily life at Ratu Bagus's ashram. It's taken prior to a shake, though some people use it more frequently as a means to clear their blocks and connect with the Energy faster. Apparently, this naturally grown tobacco is really very good for you because … wait for it … it has been blessed.

Yes, this special tobacco has been transformed on a molecular level by Ratu Bagus himself. It has been charged with energy, light and power, so it's not addictive at all and it has no negative side effects ... well, aside from the hacking.

All you can hear in every shake is the unholy regurgitation of this miraculous substance.

You take the Sacred Medicine to unblock you if you're sick. You take it if you're *not* sick to unblock you. But inevitably, the tobacco will turn your throat red raw on the inside, help you hurl unceremoniously into a bucket whenever you least expect it and ensure that anyone new (like me) looks at you like you're dying on the spot.

At yesterday's 'group sharing' I expressed my fear of tobacco syringes, only to be told I shouldn't do it unless I was ready, and even then I have to get an experienced shaker to help me. Once someone has physically shot some up my nose on my behalf and I've survived without chucking my guts up, I'm all set and can apply my own whenever I like. Yay! Two people here have told me individually that their eyesight has improved since taking the blessed tobacco.

Anyway, another treat today was the Stick Game, which according to Plane Jane is played quite often (not much else to do, really). You should have seen the joy on everyone's face when this object came out. I don't think there's been quite so much glee over a game involving a stick since the 1800s actually, but what happens here is Ratu Bagus 'charges' this stick and hands it to various people who walk around guided by the Energy inside it. Strangely, even though they're laughing and spinning and performing martial-arts type moves as they're going with the flow, no-one ever bumps into anything or hurts themselves. Even with their eyes closed.

Plane Jane told me afterwards that once when Ratu Bagus handed her the stick, she found herself actually running at full speed in the car park, clutching it in front of her. Milliseconds before she was set to run full throttle into a tree, she was twisted by an unseen force and thrown to the ground, laughing. 'I was protected by the Energy,' she said.

Don't try this at home, folks. Especially if you're on any sort of Sacred Medicine.

When I captured the Orbs on video this afternoon I was tobacco-free and shaking of my own accord. On reflection, though, I can't really say I was plugged in to anything except the music. You're supposed to feel the Energy from within, let's not forget, and I'm pretty sure I was bouncing to Beethoven for the majority.

Getting into the real groove and staying there is tricky, I'm thinking. Maybe my ego is just *too* big to break these barriers. Maybe I *do* need some Sacred Medicine. Or an Energy-infused stick.

It's like being at Hogwarts round here.

05/12

Day 4 at the ashram: It's all part of the Process ...

There is no change for the better without a Process. Process means change and is a sign that the Energy is working well within us ... When we get a Process, the best thing is to say 'thank you', to feel grateful, to understand that it is needed to achieve our goal. To panic, recoil, run or hide does not help the Energy Operation.

— Ratu Bagus Instruction Manual

Today, I ache all over. I effing HURT. My legs, my back, I have a pain in my side. I could barely get out of bed for the 7 a.m. shake. Ouch, ouch, ouch. Obviously it's because I'm not used to doing all this exercise. Shaking for six hours a day is intense.

'You're just Processing,' said Peggy at breakfast this morning as I limped around pathetically with a plate of scrambled eggs. 'You must have had some kind of Energy blocks in your legs and now your body needs to work through those.'

I sat down and took a massive slurp of my own Sacred Medicine — coffee — and thought about it. 'Are you sure it's not just 'cause I've been bouncing barefoot on a tiled floor like Skippy?' I asked.

She shook her head, carefully peeling a banana.

'So, the pain will go away if I keep on bouncing on the tiled floor?'

'Oh definitely,' she said, and everyone else at the table nodded affirmatively. 'Absolutely.'

'Are you sure I won't just collapse?'

'Maybe,' she said. 'But even if you do collapse, that's the Energy's way of helping you Process. You should be grateful for that collapse and say thank you.'

Everyone at the ashram is going through some sort of Process, every single day. And every single one of them is grateful for it. A Process is a form of sickness, which should be thanked, not begrudged, because each one means another block has been cleared.

Basically, when people purge, it's not because they're shoving a watered-down, brown weed up their nostrils and then pulsating to trance music for two hours … it's because they're Processing.

Even without the tobacco, there's a lot of sniffing and sniffling going on around here. People develop colds and other sinus issues a lot and apparently a sore throat is a very common sign that someone's finally discovered the sacred Energy and has started to benefit from its healing properties. Knowing this, I'd almost be grateful for a sore throat. At least I'd know I was getting somewhere.

According to the instruction manual, I need to face these things and not run away to my dorm room every time something starts to hurt. I started to seriously consider the Sacred Medicine. Maybe a tiny bit wouldn't be so terrible?

It was my duty to help with the washing up after breakfast today. Even though it costs $200 a week to stay at the ashram, you're encouraged to help scrub and clean the place because it feels good to be involved and help others. It creates a sense of community. Chatting to my new friends, Matt and Little Al, I tried not to let on that it had been at least four years since I'd cleaned my own plate and pretended I was fine about my manicure peeling off in soapy suds.

Little Al used to watch his parents shaking all over the house back in England but would never join in. He'd never say anything against it, he says, because it made them happy, but it was just never really his thing. He told me how the neighbours would complain about their shaking, too … not because of the music, but because of the constant laughter coming from the house. Imagine! Of all the things to complain about these days, imagine being the neighbour who complains about laughter.

'So, should I take the tobacco?' I asked Matt, as I handed him a plate to dry. Matt's a Brit who shakes topless. He's covered in tattoos. He told me his first and most dramatic Process was throwing up blood as soon as he entered the ashram several years ago. He'd never thrown up blood in his life before that.

'I think you should try it,' he said. 'Try it in your mouth before you take it up the nose.'

'Noooo, it's better up the nose,' PMS interrupted, wobbling dangerously on the spot with her hands full of cutlery.

'Yeah, but she has to start small. She's not ready for it up the nose,' Matt said, stacking his dry plate on the pile. I tried not to look annoyed. How did he know I wasn't ready? I *wasn't* ready, clearly, but I wanted to be the one who said so.

'How bad is it, up the nose?' I asked.

PMS took a deep breath and shot me a sideways smile. 'It burns.'

'It burns like hell,' Matt confirmed. 'But my God, you'll be shaking harder than ever. It opens the door to the light!'

'It's blessed by Ratu!' Little Al chimed in, in case I hadn't heard.

After breakfast, lounging about for lack of anything else to do, I played over in my mind what I'd felt, albeit briefly yesterday, before the Orb sighting. I wanted another glimpse of the Divine, dammit. I wanted it to last longer. But to stand the pain caused by over-zealous shaking already, I would *definitely* need some Sacred Medicine. I'd start small, like Matt advised, and get an experienced shaker to shoot some in my mouth.

Lining up by the row of Sacred Sinks at lunchtime, dressed in leggings and a T-shirt, felt a bit like queuing for heroin in a gym — all the colours of wrong. Matt was grinning next to me, his tattoos looking more menacing than ever before. I panicked a bit. What was I doing? What was really in this stuff? What were all these people seeing? Was Buddha waiting with an arrangement of rainbows and unicorns? Would I orgasm embarrassingly on the floor? Would it open my eyes to a world of Orbs, a world of no return? Should I go back and get my phone?

Before I could voice anything out loud, the syringe was under my tongue and a burning sensation was creeping round my entire mouth, a bit like I'd licked a heap of *wasabi* off a chopstick too quickly. It didn't actually taste too bad, just like wet tobacco minus the nasty chemicals, I suppose, but I've got to say, I started to feel the effects almost instantly. *Shazam!*

It wasn't like a drug … or anything else I've ever experienced. It was more like a stab to the senses. It didn't blur or distort them, but it made everything sharper in a sort of dreamy way, if that makes sense. Hmm, I don't think it does, but I can't really describe it any other way. I could still think in a logical manner, but everything was a bit lighter, a bit simpler, not as important or stressful. The pathway was clear, perhaps?

It could have all been down to the power of suggestion. I mean, my God, I *wanted* it to work. But either way I hobbled into the *Taman* with a new sense of purpose.

OK, Divine Energy, if you're here — reveal yourself! Make my soul whole!

Somewhere in between *Sweet Dreams are Made of These* and *Boom Boom Boom, I Want You In My Room*, I felt the light again, and yes, yes, yes, it was better than before. I shut my eyes and focused on the mantra, while bobbing my head like a trooper. It was almost like it wasn't me shaking again; it felt like a different presence was working my limbs … Pinocchio in the hands of Gepetto. I disappeared for a while into the feeling and although I could still hear the music and the hacking, nothing was as distracting.

And then Ratu Bagus entered the building.

When the mighty Good King put a hand on my lower back, reciting his usual 'electric, electric, electric', I literally felt a jerk. It was like my soul, my pain was snatched by the claw of a giant forklift truck and hoisted into the air, and my physical body was thrown backwards, like trash. It only lasted a second, this splitting of my being, but it stunned me so much that I said 'WOAH!!!'

loudly, lost my footing and stumbled. I opened my eyes to see I'd shouted in his face, straight at that infectious smile. *Holy shit!*

I never thought I'd do that. Was that me, laughing at the front of the room next to Little Al? Was that *me*, one tiny step away from screeching like a monkey? I came back to myself after that ... or perhaps my ego took over. I lost it and headed outside to process what had happened. *Did I just have a spiritual bypass?*

'You have to surrender your soul,' Peggy said when she saw me later in the kitchen. She'd seen me leave the *Taman* in shock. They keep telling me to do this, to surrender. Fuck it. Maybe I should. These little moments of 'enlightenment' are awesome. How blind I've been. How blinkered up till now. Screw you, ego. I belong *here*.

Pass me my purple robe. It's time for my pill.

06/12

Day 5 at the ashram: Soul Control ...

> The mind always wants to understand what is happening so it can stay in control. But the shaking happens at a spiritual level; something which is not there (invisible) is suddenly there (Energy). It's about miracles, the impossible becoming possible. It's about accessing and surrendering to the Divine, which is beyond the mind.
> — Ratu Bagus Instruction Manual

I take it all back. What we witnessed last night at the end of the evening shake was not normal. At least, it was a hundred times more abnormal than anything else I've seen since I've been here. I'm confused all over again.

'They look like they're possessed,' a new girl called Kris whispered in my ear. She actually sounded terrified and her fear rubbed off on me as Ratu Bagus stood there in front of us in the *Taman*, grinning serenely, dressed all in white as usual, a sturdy ship in a sea of thrashing fools.

We were watching two grown men, one of them Matt and the other a stick-thin French man, writhing uncontrollably on the floor. They were laughing so hard they looked like they were about to wet themselves. It was the kind of laughter that hurts, the kind that traps your intestines and halts your breathing. Prior to their squirms and squeals, Ratu Bagus had pointed a microphone at them, which seemed to make them leap up individually like their bums were on fire and dance chaotically among the crowd, waving their arms about in all directions.

As Matt barrelled towards us, Kris shrieked. A look of pure horror flashed across her pretty face. She grabbed my arm and together we ducked as he performed a circus-style roly-poly over our heads.

'This is black magic!' she cried, before clamping a hand over her mouth in case anyone was listening. They wouldn't have heard anyway; they were all too entranced by the show.

'Yeah. They do look like they're being controlled ...'

Just then, both guys began to convulse on the floor like electric shock patients. Matt's tattoos flashed in and out of focus as he flipped about as crazy as a live fish in a frying pan. The crowd was laughing even harder as Ratu swung the mic around.

'Electric, electric, electric!' he chanted. For the first time, the words sounded a bit creepy.

The more experienced shakers in the *Taman* seemed to lose all control completely at that point. When the mic reached them, a couple of English ladies in their mid-sixties started bobbing their heads up and down manically like nodding dogs, and then lay sprawled on the floor in hysterics. Tears were pouring from their eyes.

Big Al was shuddering on the spot, Little Al and his mum were trembling in ecstasy and in typical, over-achieving fashion, a Balinese teen who's grown up on the ashram stood up, stomped around on his feet, ran circles round the entire room and issued a harrowing scream before crashing to the floor beneath the Ganesh statue in convulsions. Other people, mostly the newbies like us, were admittedly looking a bit bewildered.

I watched the scene unfolding, feeling Kris's nails digging into my arm. I guess lots of westerners would be a bit reluctant to let themselves go in this situation. Loads of us are scared of things that threaten to 'open us up', like hypnosis for example (or sound healing, or Ecstatic Dancing). Being in control is something we clearly all value very highly in our everyday lives, right? Else we get mugged on the subway, or charged way too much for a kilo of oranges. The Balinese, however, spend most of their lives surrounded by and being controlled by their parents, ancestors and the supernatural forces they must appease on a regular basis. Surrendering control is not an issue for them and they're naturally more suggestive. Maybe watching them act so openly insane around the ashram has made some of the long-term westerners more willing to surrender themselves. I just don't know.

The young Balinese was still thrashing about, heading in our direction.

'This is not right,' Kris said, standing up and turning on her heel to run outside. No-one watched her go, except me. They were all laughing too hard to notice.

Because of his lithe, toned body we could see every vein poking through the French guy's skin as he twisted scarily into different positions on the floor. For about five minutes he was crouched with one leg behind his head and the other stretched out at an angle that would make most Yobud Pros want to kick his *asana*. He was giggling and snorting the whole time, too, a bit like he was being tickled. I'm a bit reluctant to use the word 'voodoo', but seriously, that's exactly what it looked like to me. Or severe hypnosis.

If all this stuff is to be believed, the people here aren't being controlled by anyone or anything when they find themselves losing it. I spoke to Matt afterwards in the dining room.

'I wasn't thinking with my mind, I was just feeling it with my soul,' he said.

'Feeling what?' I pressed.

'The Energy, through Ratu.' He was grinning. It was almost half an hour afterwards but I could tell he was still on the verge of hysterics.

'But you looked like you were being controlled, like you were possessed,' I said.

Matt laughed again, jabbing his fork into some pineapple. 'It's just for fun. Everything Ratu does is for love and fun. He just wants everyone to laugh!'

'So it's mind control, without the mind part?'

The French contortionist next to him nodded, looking tired but also insanely happy. 'Soul control! You just have to surrender. Once you feel the love in your soul, it's stronger than anything the mind can comprehend. You're not meant to understand, Becky, it just is what it is.'

I gave up. Maybe I never really got there yesterday after all. I mean, surely you need your mind in order to focus on your soul?

If you're not using your mind, how do you know *not* to think about your mind? The more I think, the more I think I shouldn't. The more I think I shouldn't, the more I think I'm going mad.

I am *actually* going mad in this ashram.

The singing was a bit weird, too. I mean, the Ratu Bagus song that everyone sang before leaving the *Taman*, it was something I'd never heard until that point; a special song just for the king, with different verses and its own tune. Everyone joined in. Ratu beamed as their voices filled the room, the proud father of his spiritual rainbow family, soaking it all up in his ever-so-humble fashion. I can't stress it enough, he really is a lovely, lovely man ... even if he's secretly Voldemort's cousin.

I never saw Kris again and neither did anyone else. Rumour has it she fled before anyone had left the *Taman*. Had I seen what she'd seen on *my* first day, I probably would have done the same thing.

'Don't let them steal your soul!' The Diver warned me via SMS when I told him the latest drama. His words and correspondence have been soul food for me this whole time. In fact, it's him who's been filling me with bolts of an Energy I'm starting to doubt I'll ever fully discover again unless I leave.

The minimum amount of time you're 'allowed' to stay at the ashram is five days (unless you run away, obviously), so I'm leaving tomorrow. I guess I could have stayed a full week, but really, I'm not sure it would make any difference at this point. I'm not sure it would make any difference even if I stayed over Christmas, so I guess I'll miss out on seeing Ratu Bagus in his Santa outfit this year. Shame.

Perhaps I'm just not ready for whatever it is this place could teach me, which is a bit sad really. I feel like a spiritual failure; like I've missed the point again. But the next step on my quest for enlightenment within these beautiful walls would be to literally snort the Sacred Medicine ... just to see ... and I'm not sure I want burning tobacco frying my brain cells like it did my mouth. Who knows, perhaps that's the key to unlocking the laughter. Or perhaps I already had the key and just forgot where I put it.

I never seemed to fit in here. I never hacked, or embraced a Process, or ran with a stick with my eyes shut across a car park. I never got a sore throat. I'm a big black hole in their buzzing solar system; the darkened void that will never see the sun but burns all the Energy up while it tries. It's best if I go.

I think I'll be heading back to Gili T for Christmas now. Call me shallow but if I'm going to surrender my soul to anyone, I'd rather it was a hot guy who swims like a merman and shaking between sheets that don't have a wise man's mantra printed on them.

One thing's for sure: Ratu Bagus is a powerhouse. He carries so much energy around with him that I can capture Orbs on my iPhone in broad daylight. ORBS! I'm still excited about those. And if he *is* controlling these people somehow, it's not in a terrible, terrifying, evil, black-magic way. It's in a wonderful way. Plane Jane, PMS, Matt ... they're all testaments to the fact that he's helping the world, one shaky person at a time.

People love this, they revel in it, they travel from far and wide to be near it and they *do* heal. Magic exists. As much as I might fight it, even when it slaps me in the face, it's pretty much undeniable ... especially here in Bali, where magic seems to happen everywhere, all the time. But I can't get my head around it, or my soul, or my ego, apparently. I suppose the French contortionist is right — some things just aren't meant to be understood.

I won't be buying the special pendant before I leave, tempted as I am to get one as a keepsake. It's twenty-four-carat gold and costs about $500, and boasts an embossed Ratu Bagus on the front looking all wise in some heavenly rays of light. Many people wear them proudly on various chains as advertisements for their devotion. Big Al and Co. have all got them and they shake at home while touching them. Of course, each one has been blessed with the sacred Energy.

I currently wear a turtle carved from a coconut around my neck. I'll just have to trust that it carries on working in its own special way.

Om Swastiastu, Ratu Bagus.

10/12

This land is my land, this land is your land ...

You know you're in Bali when you wake up and your neighbour asks: 'So, what are you doing for the full moon?' On this occasion, I was planning to help my friend Paul with his land-blessing ceremony by taking numerous photos, so he can remember it.

These types of ceremony, as we know, are best held on a full moon. It's an extra special one this time too, as there's a lunar eclipse tonight. So, once I'd ridden my new motorbike very, very slowly there, I parked it by the roadside, shook off my shoes and walked barefoot along the banks of the rice fields to join in.

Oh, yes, about the motorbike. Well, I'm a bit embarrassed to tell you it took me so long to get on one, but I was terrified and ... you know, I didn't want to become another statistic. But since Susan flew back to Australia I've missed the thrill and convenience of zooming around on the back of hers. I realised I was really just being a baby. I've been riding my own around

213

Vroom vroom! OK I'm parked, but you get the idea

for the last few days non-stop and I'm loving it now. Plus, it's only $50 a month to rent. FREEDOM! I feel like a proper bikie chick … just in linen instead of leather.

Anyway, I spotted the group easily, thanks to the white of their ceremonial clothing. Paul stood up, waving when he saw me. He had a brown and gold sarong on in place of his usual jeans and it was a bit like approaching a dashing scarecrow as he stood smiling with his arms outstretched, issuing a panoramic gesture to his new land. I felt a rush of pride for him.

This time next year, Paul's personally designed new house will be standing on this very spot. A turquoise swimming pool will be sunken into what's now an emerald rice field (don't leave me, just yet) and the vibrant flora curtaining off his view of the river below will be swept aside, providing a view of the gushing rapids and distant paddies tumbling down a dewy green staircase.

Knowing a lot about real estate, it's taken Paul a while to fend off the cowboys, weed out the bad from the good, and finally find the perfect patch. He's chosen to build the house about three kilometres out of town, past the Bali Botanical Gardens.

'The traffic's better from that direction. It's a nightmare coming in from Penestanan these days,' he reasoned the other week, just before he had to sign on the dotted line.

As the original home of the 'Young Artists' in the 1960s, thanks to a Dutch artist who successfully encouraged young locals to paint, Penestanan has long been a prime spot for expats, set at the top of a slope so steep it's been dubbed Ubud Heights by its residents. Paul lives there now but can't wait to move. He says it's way too developed these days for his taste.

I made it through the squishy mush and grass to their woven mats, which they'd lain on top of hay in the empty paddy, and sat down. I was immediately handed an incense stick and a small *pandan* leaf full of flowers and as everything was prepared I amused myself by taking photos of a cute little chick, which was pecking around in a clump of dry grass.

The priest was there, as well as some of the people from the village and several children. Land blessing ceremonies happen all the time in Bali. No building can be started anywhere without one and this particular ceremony set Paul back the grand sum of $400. They involve, judging by what ensued, the ringing of an excruciatingly loud bell over and over and over again, and some chanting. We also held flowers in our fingertips and raised our hands to our foreheads in honour of the gods. The bell made my head hurt but I tried to concentrate on asking the forces unseen to bless Paul's land and look after the building process of his new home … and tried not to puke when they killed the little chick.

It's a custom, it's a custom, it's a custom … think of Caesar salad. Mmm, yummy chickens …

If it didn't die as a sacrifice for this land, I suppose I might have eaten it myself, covered in croutons. But as I watched its life oozing out all over a wooden block, its blood being mixed with some grated coconut while its head was still bobbing for mercy, the last thing I could think about was Caesar salad. In fact, as happy as I am for my friend, finally scoring the patch that will soon become the Balinese abode of his retirement dreams, I'll admit, I am a little bit torn over the whole thing.

Ibu Kat has taken up the issue of building houses on rice fields on several occasions in her newspaper column *GreenSpeak*. She's been here so long, it's a matter very close to her heart. She writes:

> Every year, Bali's agricultural land bank is reduced by about 1,500 hectares — lost to strip malls, tourism projects and villas, mostly owned by non-Balinese and with profits going offshore. Common sense suggests that it's a bad idea to take farmland out of production on a small, agriculture-based island in a country where food security is an urgent matter. Let me rephrase that. It's not just a bad idea. It's insane.

It does sound a bit silly, but …

> High real estate prices are very tempting to Bali's poor
> farmers. But what could be sadder than a farmer selling
> the family's rice fields because his son wants to buy a car
> or motorcycle? The vehicles will be history within a few
> years, and the money will be long spent and the land gone
> forever.'
>
> — Cat Wheeler, *Bali Advertiser*, 2007

OK, yes. It's hard to argue with that. Hmm …

But we have to consider these cases individually, I suppose. The land Paul has acquired is leased, not bought, so it will definitely stay in the family. And it's hoped by all that the land he's leasing will be far more productive as a villa than a rice paddy as it will require staff to help run it.

Of course, the completion of one more villa could also be viewed as an opening for other farmers to sell their land and turn the whole area into another tempting neighbourhood for westerners. And the poor, who don't have land, don't speak English and can't get jobs in town, or in villas or hotels, will become even poorer if there aren't any fields left for them to work in. A recent visit to Bali's surfers' paradise, Canggu, suggested to me that it's probably the next Kuta, as development creeps along the coast. Farmers still work the land just minutes from the black sand beach in Canggu, but there are two five-star resorts going up and more For Sale signs that I could count.

Even Bali's officials have expressed concern over all this construction. The pessimistic *Time* Magazine article, *Holidays in Hell: Bali's Ongoing Woes* back in April also noted that the governor himself even warned that his lush birthplace might turn

Sari Organik – a healthy eater's dream
in the rice paddies

into a dry land full of concrete buildings. It's happening before our eyes, but he doesn't seem to be stopping it.

There's a popular little cafe just out of Ubud, set far back in the rice fields, called Sari Organik. To reach it, you have to turn right off the main road and walk about twenty minutes. This walk used to take you through glorious greenery, surrounded by men and women working knee-deep in mud with scary-looking ancient tools. It's the kind of walk you'd have felt proud to do with your visiting mum or dad, for example, who up till that point had run away from a few monkeys, been woken up by a few brooms, but hadn't yet seen the *real* Bali.

Sari Organik, a welcome respite at the end of this walk, used to be a smug little secret among the expats. But then it was featured in *Lonely Planet* and put on the itinerary for various tours, and getting there is now a game of dodge-the-noisy-motorbike. What's worse is that in the space of just a year or so (and definitely since I've been here), the walk to the cafe and beyond has become a building site.

The fields used to stretch to infinity before you, but these days you're lucky if you can see more than a hundred metres without your eyeballs hitting concrete. There are now at least three art shops along the route, catering to the tourists plodding through. The other week I noticed some pointy witch's-hat shaped structures going up around a dug-out swimming pool, which are probably about to become huts in a new, exclusive resort.

A few metres away is a gargantuan circular structure with a pizza oven in the middle of it. Once the roof is on, this new pizza restaurant will be amazing, stunning but ... it's kind of not supposed to be there ... in the middle of a walk people used to take to get away from Ubud's mad development. Is there really anything good that can come from this, apart from a tasty Hawaiian Deluxe with extra pineapple and a view that might have been spectacular had some thoughtless swine not chosen to put a witch's hat where your moonlit rice paddy used to be? The moral battle could rage for hours.

As I watched the chick's blood wash away with water onto the hay and the Balinese ladies started to dance around giant piles of offerings, now blazing in flames, I fought the urge to ram my hands over my ears to muffle the bell. I took a nice panoramic shot of the spot that Paul wants to start building on as soon as possible. He plans to shop around for local furniture and employ lots of local people to help with construction, so that's a contribution to the economy, right?

I don't know … I haven't been here long enough and I probably won't be here long enough to know the real consequences of all this development. Sadly, the debate over houses replacing rice fields will rage on long after there are no more fields left around Ubud, I'm sure. Unless, of course, something drastic happens and development is curbed. You never know, I suppose!

I didn't think twice about moving into a villa in the fields when I first got here, before I got to know a bit more about Bali. It's one big, sensitive, emotional issue that bubbles up in conversation every now and then like an angry volcano and everyone's got their own reasons for doing whatever it is that they choose to do.

I'll attend the house party in April and we'll all lean over the edge of the infinity pool and remark how beautiful the view is, and how we can't believe that people are still living all the way up the hill in traffic-clogged Penestanan. And some of us will silently still wonder if the chick that died in honour of another man's dream was just the beginning in a line of sacrifices.

13/12

A modern day Mother Teresa …

For eleven weeks, people in Ubud have been spreading the word about the importance of voting for Robin Lim in the CNN Hero of the Year awards. Posters have been flapping all over town. In fact I can't think of one single person I've met here who hasn't gone out of their way to click in support of Ibu Robin and her amazing work for the non-profit Yayasan Bumi Sehat (Healthy Mother Earth Foundation). When you mention Robin Lim in this place, people smile and sigh and say something like, 'Aaaah, Mother Robin. What an incredible woman.' I suppose you could say that she's an adopted Indonesian Mother Teresa in action — much loved, very much admired and now, deservedly internationally acclaimed. Yes, in a star-studded ceremony in LA on Sunday night, American Robin Lim was named the 2011 winner. Wa-hey!

CNN Heroes is a multi-platform campaign that rewards extraordinary individuals for their work in serving others. Everyone who's worked with Robin is very excited, not just because she totally deserves it, but because the money and the exposure will be a huge boost for the foundation, which has been working since 1995 to bring about 600 new babies safely into the world, every year.

Yayasan Bumi Sehat was originally set up after Robin's younger sister died from pregnancy complications in Hawaii. She moved to Bali with her husband to reinvent her life and make a difference, opening a small clinic in her village home.

Over the next decade, more and more women started flocking to her for help. Eventually, the non-profit foundation was formed to provide general health services, emergency care, prenatal, birth services and breastfeeding support to those in need. Gentle birthing (a concept pretty much unheard of in the west) has always remained at the heart of Bumi Sehat's work.

'Every baby's first breath on Earth could be one of peace and love. Every mother should be healthy and strong. Every birth could be safe and loving. But our world is not there yet,' she said, during the awards.

What Robin Lim has done for mothers and babies here in Indonesia has vastly improved the quality of life for thousands of people, both directly and indirectly. Here, women are a whopping

300 times more likely to die giving birth to a baby or from other pregnancy-related issues, than they are in developed countries. Something to think about ... even for those of us who've never been pregnant.

Miley Cyrus, Chris Colfer and Emma Roberts, all practically embryonic members of Hollywood's glitterati, presented at the awards the other night, as did Jerry Seinfeld, Ice Cube and George Lopez. Miley crooned her triple platinum hit *The Climb* and in spite of over 10,000 submissions from more than a hundred countries, Robin Lim left with everyone knowing her name. The *Bali Advertiser* is practically exploding with positive words about it all.

There are many people in Bali doing lots of amazing things for children, animals and the environment. I've offered my services, to the best of my ability, to the dogs and cats along the way but learning a bit more about Robin Lim's work made me think back to a guy called Pande I met at Bar Luna a few weeks ago.

Pande has set up a foundation called Anak Alam (Nature's Children) high up in the mountains around Kintamani and close to Lake Batur. This is a very poor area of Bali. The kids in the tiny village of Blandingan have practically nothing. They go to school but they also have to work in the rice fields and sell snacks around the village to survive. Pande encourages people to go up there and spend time with them, even if time is all they can give. I've decided to go visit after Christmas; take some books and pens and skipping ropes and toothpaste, at Pande's request. I'll never be a Mother Teresa type, like Robin Lim, but I can do what I can to help. If they've managed to find mobile phones by the time I arrive, of course, I'll be terrified. But who knows, maybe I can even have my Mary Poppins's moment after all?

Plucked chickens and the Poo shop ...

I think I've flashed more genitalia to strangers this week than a pregnant woman does in nine months. And that's not an admission of my sluttiness, by the way; it merely comes down to the obligatory prep for meeting up with a man. I'm heading back to Gili T in a couple of days for Christmas fun and diving with you-know-who, so obviously I needed a bikini wax. But let me tell you, there's a bikini wax ... and then there's a Balinese Brazilian bikini wax.

I'm still not sure if what went down on that 'operating' table yesterday was entirely legal, but over twelve hours later I'm still feeling the pain. I wasn't aware I had stray hairs on the *lining of my womb*, but with her fingers firmly clasping bits of me that have never been touched by a woman, and probably never been reached by a man, the 'technician' prodded and poked and smeared and stripped and ripped me red raw. I look like a plucked chicken.

She wasn't even wearing gloves. I'm serious. At one point I saw the jewel of her wedding ring flash from somewhere within my labial folds and thought, *Holy crap, she's gonna lose that in there and it'll all be my fault* ... but she was smiling a ruby-lipstick smile the whole time, delighting in showing me every single used waxing strip after each excruciating tear. Lovely.

Anyway, like I said, a Balinese Brazilian; it was never going to be run-of-the-mill.

Moving on ... to today's colonic irrigation treatment. As you know, this is actually something I was supposed to do a while back, but not having access to my finances for a while meant that even though I stuck to a week of eating boring raw food in preparation, I had to postpone. I thought about postponing again this morning, but then I thought … The Diver.

You might wonder why I need a colonic irrigation to meet up with a man. Granted, getting old, stodgy poo pumped out of your bum doesn't tend to sneak its way into the usual getting-ready-for-a-date regime, but my friend Sarah told me that when she had hers, she lost up to eight pounds (3.5 kilos), instantly.

I *know*.

Plus, she said her eyes were brighter, her skin was glowing and her stomach was practically concave. What girl heading off to a tropical island to prance about in a bikini with a hot merman wouldn't want that?

It's not like The Diver will ever know, clearly. I very much doubt he'll see me gliding towards him at the bar, give an appreciative nod in the direction of my bowels and then say, 'Hey, nice clean colon you've got there. Bet your poo is looking great, baby,' but you know, *I'll* know. I'm doing this for me and hopefully, when I'm beside him in my bikini, minus eight whole pounds, it'll be worth it.

It was with some trepidation that I made my way to what's affectionately called 'The Poo Shop' in Penastanan, to see a lady called Suki, who's responsible for the purification of pretty much every blocked-up bum in Bali. Alchemy, which is the actual name for the shop, is also an organic store selling fresh juices and raw foods. You get the colonic upstairs in a little room and then when you're done, you can skip, light as a feather, down the stairs to have a nice piece of raw chocolate pie. It's the perfect place, I suppose, to crap your cake and eat it.

The note that came with my confirmation email had asked me to please avoid meat, dairy, sugar, fried foods, carbonated drinks and wheat products prior to my colonic. So I tried not to let on that last night I ate a chicken curry, some banoffee pie and had three margaritas with Paul in Bar Luna. Like I said, I did my week of raw eating before and it was most unpleasant, and Paul said that it shouldn't really matter what I ate last night because it was all about to get sucked out again anyway.

I'm not sure that as a retired real estate agent Paul offers the best advice on colonic irrigation, but at the time it seemed more exciting to believe him and carry on with my curry.

Anyway, what happened? What *happened?*

Well, up in the little white room, which is very Zen by the way, Suki handed me a pastel blue gown and instructed me to remove all my clothes and underwear. I did as I was told, then lay on the spa-style table with my head on two proper, fluffy white pillows. Very nice.

'Turn to your left,' Suki said, and before I'd had a chance to really think about what was going on, a lubed tube was being thrust firmly up my bum. I told Suki that it felt a bit like putting a large tampon in the wrong hole and asked if anyone else had ever said the same thing.

'No,' she replied.

What followed was really rather uneventful, I'm glad to say. There was a bit of tummy massage to release the blockages, and I suppose every now and then I felt an uncontrollable urge to do a poo, right there on the table. Luckily the tube took care of that and as the water flushed through me, what I felt after roughly forty-five minutes was … thinner! It was a miracle! All I had to do was keep my hands on my tummy and feel what must have been … well, let's face it … thirty-two years' worth of crap vacating my system.

My hipbones were protruding once more. The slight bulge that I'd put down to being in my thirties practically disappeared on the spot. I had a slight panic that my boobs might shrink too, which would not have been an improvement, but thankfully they're unchanged.

When it was all over and the tube had been whipped out, I had to go straight to the loo and crouch over it with my feet up on a wooden block. All that came out of me was excess water. I am so happy to say that I am no longer full of shit.

I decided not to have some cake afterwards. Suki handed me a sheet of paper that tells me what I can and can't eat for the next few days and it says that I should please enjoy fresh juices, green salads, vegetables and coconut water. And I should please avoid alcohol, pasta, meat, lentils and heavy meals.

Before, these suggestions would have appalled me but strangely I feel no urge whatsoever to fill my new, cleansed and de-clogged colon with anything terrible. I actually want to eat greens. I drink a lot of coconut water here anyway. It's hard to avoid coconuts in Bali; they practically assault you on every street corner. But the idea of downing a can of Coke or a glass of wine right now seems positively suicidal. After all that work why would I want to go and ruin it?

Suki sees about five or six people most days for the same treatment, so chances are when I'm sitting in a cafe ordering another *kalapa muda*, the person next to me eyeing up the celery juice will also be sitting proudly in possession of a pristine colon. I feel like a member of an exclusive club. And almost three hours later, I feel better than ever.

If you're wondering whether or not to get a colonic yourself, I would highly recommend you take the plunge, so to speak. The Diver may be able to appreciate my new plucked-chicken look when I get back to Gili T in a couple of days. But as a woman prepping herself for a close encounter of the sexy kind, I can tell you now, ladies, it's what's NOT on the inside that counts.

An ocean of emotion ...

I've been listening to some of Alissa's finished *kirtan* CD online ...
you know, the lady who popped into my homestay a while ago
to lend me a guitar tuner? I can report the tracks now sound
amazing and all the more so because I'm not on any of them.

With a new sense of intrigue I went with Paul to the Yoga Barn
to experience a Sunday *kirtan* session first-hand the other night.
When we arrived there were just a few other people sitting on
pillows on the studio floor as a pretty lady called Starr sat tuning
her guitar at the front. A projector screen was flickering behind
her. It looked a bit like a *karaoke* set-up for hippies.

I was a bit disappointed that no-one sang any Karen Carpenter
while we were waiting, but within roughly twenty minutes the
room had filled up and people of all ages were dragging cushions
all over the place and making themselves comfortable. As one
woman in her fifties, with long, grey hair and bright, almost
luminescent orange linen pants grabbed two big pillows and sat
down in front of us, Paul leaned over to whisper in my ear:

'That's the sleeping woman. Watch her.'

'What?' I asked. But he had turned to talk to a dreadlocked
man with B.O. on his other side.

Starr adjusted herself on her pillow and made her
introductions. She now had two more musicians on either side of
her with guitars, mics, a drum and a xylophone. The projector's
green screen flickered into life, revealing Ganesh's smiling eyes
and big long trunk and our first set of *kirtan* lyrics appeared as
a gentle, rhythmic tune sounded out around the room. People
started swaying. A glazed look came over their eyes as they stared
at the screen but it was one of utter contentment and almost on

autopilot I found myself humming a random melody over the soundtrack.

Starr chanted the mantra first, and like a class of kids learning a nursery rhyme we were encouraged to follow her lead until we didn't even need to look at the words.

In unison, we sang:

Ganesh sharanam sharanam Ganesh
Om gang ganapataye namoh namah …

… for about thirty minutes.

As was explained to us at the beginning, this particular mantra is usually chanted at the start of a new endeavour in order to invoke and involve Ganesh, the Hindu god of success. I noticed that almost everyone, Paul included, once they'd gotten the hang of it, had drifted off into another world behind their eyelids roughly ten minutes into the song. It was so peaceful and beautiful; there was definitely an elephant in the room.

I suppose because these ancient Sanskrit lyrics don't involve any familiar words or sayings, it's easier to switch off and empty your mind of everything but the music and the feeling … easier than trying to locate the Divine Energy through the song *I'm a Barbie Girl* in an ashram, anyway.

'We all have to walk through the place where we can get kidnapped by the shadows', Starr informed us in a very meaningful tone as the mantra drew to an end. And slowly but surely, people started opening their eyes again.

Apparently, *kirtan* itself invokes powerful healing energies that can not only help connect us to the 'ever present and eternal being inside us', but can lead us all into a new life of health and wellness. Powerful stuff for a Sunday night.

After a couple of minutes of silent contemplation, the next mantra started.

'I really like this one to involve Shivaya, who helps us see clearly when multiple options or oppositions are clouding our path,' said Starr, gently plucking the strings of her guitar as the man on her right performed a little flurry on the xylophone for emphasis. Her eyelids folded slowly. She leaned into the mic. 'It's like we're sailing on an ocean. An ocean of emotion.'

Everyone nodded in silent understanding (although I'm quite sure they didn't understand that any more than me), before breaking into song. This time I memorised the words much faster and concentrated on the music.

Om namah shivaya, om namah shivaya hari om hari om
Jaya shiva shankara bom bom Hari Hari

Roughly twenty minutes must have passed before Paul prodded me and nodded in the direction of the woman in orange. As predicted, she was indeed sleeping soundly, sprawled out on the floor like a splattered satsuma. Her mouth was now gaping wide, an open invitation for a spider dangling from the ceiling to crawl right in. She was letting out small, muffled snores that seemed, strangely, to be keeping time with the music. Paul rolled his eyes.

'She comes here every week and every bloody week she falls asleep. What's the point?' he said, grumpily.

I couldn't help thinking it might be the only sleep this woman ever gets. I know for a fact that sleep can be tough to catch in these parts at times, what with the geckos and the *gamelan* and the roosters and the sweeping. But in any case, if trading the entire session for some sweet, sweet dreams is how *kirtan* works for this woman, so be it, I suppose.

A lovely little number was up next ... one which made me think back to a certain special yoga fan with a bashed-up foot.

The ocean refuses no river
Om namah shivaya
Ganga ma Ganga ma

This time I lost myself completely in the music and chanting for roughly half an hour! I think that's the deepest I've ever gone in any form of meditation whatsoever, and looking back I'm quite proud of myself for being able to clear my mind completely for so long in a room full of people. I was wide awake, yet I wasn't really *there*. It was quite amazing, really. Plus, I felt quite refreshed afterwards, like I'd taken a little power nap right there on the floor along with the squashed satsuma.

I think I'll do *kirtan* again!

27/12

Ho ho ho, but enough about me ...

We're over thirty, we are both so over playing games, I thought, before I came back to the Gilis. We're excited to see each other, I thought, reading our textual relations again with a stupid smile on my face as I sat on the speedboat over from Bali. The Diver told me he couldn't wait to have a drink with me when I was shaking myself into madness in the ashram. He told me not to let them steal my soul. He told me ... he told me ... he told me ... oh fuck it.

I thought I was different. Tragic, I know. And for reasons I probably shouldn't even try to analyse (although clearly I'm

Me and my mate Dan having a happy Christmas,
Gili Island style

going to) The Diver has now decided that even though I'm eight
pounds lighter, I'm not worth his time after all. I have a sneaking
suspicion he's placed me in the 'scary girl who's followed him to
a tiny circle of land he can't get away from' category ... which is
essentially what I've done, I suppose. But he *told* me ... he told
me ... ugh.

It doesn't take a self-help book to figure out that he's just not
that into me anymore. I think this could well be my *karma* for
ditching the chance at true spiritual enlightenment in favour of
some sexy fun and having a hot man stroke my ego. I can almost
hear Ratu Bagus laughing at me.

I'm now drowning my sorrows at the Pesona Resort with
a lovely new friend called Dan. Dan is also here staring into

231

his computer every day on a work assignment, trying not to think about girls. Working on an island is distracting, as you can imagine. There's a reason people built office blocks in cold countries and made workers wear clothes. I have to face facts that whereas I now get to work in my bikini from a blissful spot gazing out over God's creations with my hair blowing out in the ocean breeze, I've been screwed, without actually being screwed very much at all. Why *is* it that a woman can never truly have it all at the same time?

Everything was fine before Christmas Eve. We had a fun few nights doing dinners, catching up under the covers. I started my Advanced PADI diving course, which means I get tons of time in the twinkly sea and we laughed and held hands like we did before as I slowly got up to scratch with … um … buoyancy control. And then it all went a bit weird.

Oh come on, it's not even New Year's Eve yet, you might be thinking. How do you know you're not just being silly?

Well …

WELL, there's no greater sign that a guy isn't really all that keen on a girl than when he'd rather go to bed alone at 5 p.m. on Christmas Day than watch *Elf* with her. Is there?

'Did you manage to get *Elf*???' he texted excitedly while I was trying to work back in Ubud. And because I'm a woman who doesn't like to disappoint I snapped my laptop shut on responsibility and trawled at least seven highly illegal fake DVD shops to find him a copy. When I got here I even arranged to show it on a giant projector screen with other people around.

I thought we could all laugh together and The Diver and I could look at each other adoringly and maybe bond even further over Will Ferrell being funny and the fact that it was all *our* idea to bring Christmas joy to everyone on the island. Pesona has butter chicken curry and really comfy cushions all around the screen to allow for snuggling, and so it was really going to be the comfiest, funniest, yummiest, snuggliest Christmas ever. No pressure, you know.

Anyway, he may as well have slapped me round the face with a cold mince pie and shot a reindeer because Christmas died right there on the spot when, after a very nice dive, he yawned and stretched and said, 'I'm tired. I don't think I'll be watching *Elf.*'

He even made a slitting motion across his throat as he said it, as if to murder the ridiculous idea in my presence. 'I think I'm going to eat food and then sleep.'

This happened in my head:

'WHAT?!?

SLEEP?!?

WHAT THE FUCK DO YOU MEAN YOU WANT TO SLEEP?!?

WHAT THE FUCK DO YOU MEAN YOU DON'T WANT TO WATCH *ELF* ANYMORE?!?

WHO THE HELL DOESN'T WANT TO WATCH *ELF*?!?

WHO AM I SUPPOSED TO SPEND CHRISTMAS WITH NOW?!?

WE PLANNED THIS.

WE WERE GOING TO SNUGGLE!

MUMMY!!!!'

As my inner child tore through an entire Christmas colouring book, snapped a set of crayons in half and burst into tears, I leaned back in my seat and smiled. I raised my eyebrows, fixing The Diver with a stare that was cool as a sea-cucumber; a calm and couldn't-care-less reaction. Oh yes. I wasn't fazed at all. He could walk away, tuck himself up in bed and take his sexy, salty hair and tanned arms and perfect teeth with him.

Namasté, namasté, namasté …

The Diver never knew how a fairy spontaneously combusted in the distance. A children's stocking exploded. Santa himself was gunned from the sky somewhere over Greenland. A small baby cried, the Grinch's laugh echoed around my eardrums and Christmas vanished. He stole it away, still dripping in his wetsuit. From his little island of birthday joy he'd offered me a Christmas more perfect than if Nigella Lawson herself had sped in on a bright red boat wearing tinsel and offered to cook a private feast for us both on the beach. And then he'd kicked her into the surf, just as she was about to put her apron on.

I wanted to say all sorts of things, you know … if you don't like me anymore, you don't even have to talk. I'd forgive you if you didn't even smile … even at the funny parts … like when Will presses all the buttons in the elevator at once or answers the phone with the greeting, 'Buddy the Elf, what's your favourite colour?'.

I'd forgive you if you slept through it next to me, maybe with one hand on my leg, maybe even with some drool escaping from the corner of your mouth like a toddler tired out from tearing open all his presents, as long as you were physically *there*. But preferring to eat without me and sleep in your bed without me, in the middle of the day, on Christmas Day … I really do happen to think that's the worst insult any man has ever paid me. *And* a guy on magic mushrooms once told me I looked like I had Downs Syndrome.

OK, time for a new list, I think. These things always make me feel better.

Why I could never *realistically* date a diving instructor:
1) He would be more likely to survive a tsunami than the average man, but ultimately less likely to be on land to save me when it happened.

2) Nitrogen is a sleepy gas and lugging heavy equipment around in the hot sun doesn't do much for boosting energy levels either. He would be way too tired to do anything exciting after work (as exhibited).

3) He would be around hot girls in bikinis all day while I was staring at a computer screen, sitting on my arse, getting too big for mine.

4) He would look at me in disappointment every time I ordered fish in a restaurant.

5) I heard about a scary disease that divers get where any cuts that might occur as a result of a coral collision may actually result in coral trying to grow in the skin. No-one wants to date a reef.

He was just another friend who was sent to you for fun. Just a friend, sent to you for fun. Remember. Letting go is good. I reminded myself of the sharing session, of what the girls told me about River and how much it helped.

Kisses aren't contracts and presents aren't promises, presents aren't promises, presents aren't promises … I repeated internally as I wished him a merry Christmas and set off to enjoy mine, all by myself.

But wait. He didn't even get you a present! You bought him a hammock.

YOU BOUGHT HIM A HAMMOCK … AND *ELF*.

You are the biggest idiot in the whole wide world.

As I turned the corner feeling Christmas fall apart, I felt like screaming back over the fence, 'I cleaned my colon for you!!!' but I let it slide. I guess I did romanticise our encounter a bit.

But then … it's not like I wanted to marry him! I thought it was a mutual agreement that a bit of no-strings-attached nookie would be the perfect stocking filler for both of us. I really did.

OK, admittedly I thought we might also take a few sunset strolls along the way. I thought we could do another dive in stupid Santa hats and maybe have a picnic on the coral and look for shooting stars, and maybe spoon every night and gaze into each other's eyes and communicate without saying a word that we're happier than a Mariah Carey music video and all we want for Christmas is each other ... but really, that stuff would have just been a bonus. Like I said, no pressure.

The Diver has clearly decided that everything he told me via text since we left each other after my birthday meant nothing. He has decided, I think, that instead of having fun with me like we planned, he's going to pretend I'm not even here, sitting on the same circular sandbank, wondering what I did wrong (and Googling his family).

Kisses might not be contracts and presents might not be promises, but let me tell you this: the next time I think about plucking myself like a chicken and getting my colon sucked clean by a hosepipe for a man, I'm bloody well going to remember the Christmas nookie that never was, and think again.

Oh, and *Elf* can fuck off, too.

Namasté ...

29/12

A lesson in spitting and swallowing ...

Taking a Maturity Holiday sounds like something your boss might suggest you do when you've tried to hump the photocopier at one too many office parties. In parts of Indonesia, however, nipping off to 'mature' is an important rite of passage and I was quite surprised to discover it doesn't actually involve sitting at home in shame, remembering the look in your colleague's eyes when you showed up drunk and tried to Sellotape his stapler to his head.

There are a few Maturity Holidays in Bali. Perhaps most interesting is the one that girls have to go through when they get their first period. Now, before I explain, I want to you remember (if you're a girl) exactly where you were and what you were doing when you got yours. Seeing as I'm here, I'll share first ... mine was during the ad break of *Home and Away*.

After dismissing the idea that I was dying from an internal disease at just eleven years old, I told Mum, begged her not to tell Dad, watched her do an excited little dance off to the airing cupboard to fetch me some supplies, and, well ... that was it. It was never mentioned again. I'm thirty-two and still don't know if Dad ever found out.

Imagine, though, even attempting to forget the following:

'Mum, can you come here?'

'*Home and Away*'s about to come back on ...'

'But Mum ... I, um, I need you to come to the bathroom.'

'Seriously, *Home and A*— oh, right. Oh, your period? Oh how fantastic! Sod the soaps, we should run through the village and tell everyone! Hurry, get your coat on!'

When a girl in Bali gets her first period, it's a big deal. Not only is she instantly ready to tie the knot, she's shut away inside for three whole days on her own.

During this period of seclusion (literally) she is fed various drinks and spices by her mother, consisting of the six basic tastes: sweet, sour, salty, tart, bitter and burning hot. The consumption of these tastes is a symbolic lesson in striving for the perfect measure of everything in her life, now that it's all extra tempting.

At the end of her spell in seclusion (though admittedly, this isn't done everywhere or as often these days), the girl will then be paraded through the village so everyone she's ever known will know without question that she's ready for mating, and marriage.

And you thought getting your first period was embarrassing?

Let's bear in mind also, that should you fail to keep your legs shut around a man who's not your husband and you fall pregnant, your amorous lover will be forced to marry you or face time in the slammer. In fact, unwanted pregnancy is the most common reason for early marriage in Bali, as most men would prefer a lifetime commitment to a woman than a few miserable years behind bars in some of the world's most appalling conditions. It would probably be a bit different where I'm from:

'Would you prefer to marry your young lover and help raise your unwanted child forever and ever, or spend a few years in prison?'

'Hmm. Does the prison have TV?'

'Some of them do now, yes. They're quite modern, thanks to taxpayers …'

'Does the prison have decent food?'

'Well, these days, most of it's not too bad.'

'Will she be able to visit me lots?'

'To be honest, not really. Only on weekends, for an hour or so.'

'Well then, let's lock me up!'

Another intriguing Maturity Holiday in Bali is centred around filing a person's teeth. Not for the squeamish, the tooth-filing ceremony (known as *matatah*) is the time in a person's life when the six upper canine teeth and incisors are evenly filed off, usually in the presence of a priest.

'The only thing I can remember about my wedding is someone going "swallow, swallow, spit, spit!"' Anna, owner of the Big Bubble dive shop here on Gili Trawangan told me today. Anna, from the UK, met a Balinese man named Ketut back in 1999 and, allegedly, he knew he would marry her when she taught him how to scuba dive (oh, the allure of a diver, dripping with salty water and oozing authority … sigh). Theirs was a love that would last.

In 2006, Anna opted to get her teeth filed in a pre-wedding Hindu ceremony, which involved lying on a mat in the priest's lounge with her feet facing outwards towards the door and her head facing his knees. 'A bunch of rusty tools' including a hammer and file all sat ominously on the side, as did a crowd of onlookers all gawping like goldfish at the tourist about to be chiselled in their presence.

Her mum and dad, who'd flown over to take part in the ceremony, were also in the crowd. I spoke to them too as we sat eating lunch in Anna's gorgeous Gili T home. Instead of the wedding they'd probably envisioned for their child who'd grown up predominantly in England, featuring a church, a white dress, a layered cake and maybe some drunken dancing in a restaurant, they were forced to witness their precious daughter undergoing the worst kind of dental surgery imaginable by a robed man who claimed to be over a hundred years old.

'It was a very interesting day,' Anna's mum told me, clearly still not entirely sure what it was all about.

The grizzly sounding process of filing down your teeth is intended to bring the six human instincts of lust, anger, greed, arrogance, intoxication (either through passion or alcohol) and jealousy, down to a more manageable level. The lower teeth remain as they are, because passion and desire should never be squished completely. Gotta love those loopholes.

As tooth filing is very expensive, it's sometimes postponed and performed on several people in the same day. Presumably a discount is given the more operations take place! It can also, as in the case of Anna and Ketut, take place once a marriage has been sanctified or just before it.

'Every now and then I had to rinse my mouth out and spit into a coconut,' Anna said. 'Spit, swallow, spit, swallow … it only lasted about ten minutes and it wasn't really painful. I think the coconut was sealed and sent out to sea, which is funny because when we got married the next day, he [the priest] cut my hair and Ketut's hair and put that in a coconut, too. There's a lot of stuff sent out to sea in coconuts from Bali!'

Other rituals during and after Anna's teeth filing, and a Hindu birth ceremony included the obligatory showering of holy water, walking three times around a fire in one direction and three times around it in the other, hard eggs being rubbed into bodies and wafting dried flowers over incense.

'I was hoping my sarong wouldn't catch on fire,' she said as we flicked through a mammoth photo album of the events. At one point, Anna had to step outside with a ball of string under one arm and some twigs and flowers under another. She then had to step downwards off a platform onto a dead chicken.

'I could hear its bones crack,' she told me, shuddering at the memory. 'And because I couldn't walk without wobbling from all the stuff I was carrying, I felt like a chicken standing on a chicken!'

Like a Crate and Barrel gift registry screwed up in cyberspace and muddled with a delivery order for a farm, Anna got four chickens as a wedding present. Live ones. Unfortunately, though, she couldn't take them home. They now lay beautiful eggs for her Balinese mother-in-law up in Singaraja.

Anna's full name is Ketut Anna Dharmayanti, which means both peace and beautiful, and one which I think we'd all agree she has earned. And even though she's slightly lesser-of-tooth, she's full of Hindu wisdom and has a very nice husband and one of the most successful dive shops on the island to boot.

I'm still not entirely sure which I'd rather endure — the village parade in celebration of my period, or the filing of my teeth in favour of a balanced life. Either way, taking a Maturity Holiday in Bali isn't all bad, it seems. Just remind yourself during your casual strolls of how that maturity was gained, and try to be respectful of any coconuts you might find washed up on the beach. You never know which ones might have Anna's teeth or hair in them.

31/12

Ghost hunting on Gili T ...

There's as much magic here on Gili T as there is anywhere in Bali. OK, so it hasn't been happening under the covers quite as much as I'd hoped, but that hasn't stopped me making the most of my evenings here in this island paradise. Hell no. With my newfound freedom I've done what any single girl on holiday would do ... I've shunned men completely and taken on the role of paranormal investigator once again, whoo hoo! I'm the Orb-collector after all. And oh boy, what I've uncovered would make anyone lose sleep at night, whether they were being romanced by a diver or not. Hmph.

Anyway, many of the locals here are Sasak people, who've come over from Lombok and brought with them their belief in the existence of spirits and ghosts. And even with the prominence of drugs on Gili T, I've met locals straight as a line who swear they've seen the souls of the dead roaming after dark, particularly in the middle of the island on a hill that should be home to nothing more than a huge radio tower and some goats.

One of my friends who works behind the bar at Pesona Resort was so afraid of what he saw up there one night he could barely relate his story. 'I saw a *leyak*,' he whispered, looking around as he put the final flourish onto my glass of pineapple juice. He looked frightened just saying the word.

Leyaks are witches of the spirit kind and everyone knows about them. If you're keen for visuals, a *leyak* is featured as the villain in the 1981 film, *Mystics in Bali*. Rangda is the most powerful and most feared of them all; the head honcho, if you will, and she ain't no *Wicked* green Elphaba defying gravity on Broadway either. She has very gravitationally influenced droopy boobs and bulging eyes, long, tangled hair on her head and a body that needs some serious all-over waxing. She has sharp, evil fangs and occasionally flames erupt from various orifices that had better go unmentioned. She's pretty messed up. She probably has no friends. And because she's such a freak, she carries a white cloth to put over her face in case anyone suspects who she is as she moves in for attack.

Legend has it that there are ways we humans can spot a *leyak* … and if you're really keen to see one you'll have to go in the dead of night to a magical place such as a crossroads or a cemetery (like the one here on Gili T), remove all your clothes and bend over with your head between your knees.

Off you go then. To the cemetery with you. No, this is not a joke. Have you taken your clothes off yet? Still can't see one? Well, that could be because you're foreign. It doesn't work with foreigners (sorry, I should have said that sooner) because the *leyaks* get all shy and confused when foreigners are about. Apparently, only the Balinese and some of their neighbours are

The staff at the Pesona Resort know how to party!

susceptible to a *leyak*'s power, which has, over the years, virtually made them invisible to tourists.

If you're really keen, you can try and force the issue by partaking in a mushroom shake, or, God forbid, some nice, fresh crystal meth (sadly, this too is available here). Let's face it, one would probably reveal itself if you went to that much effort in pursuit, but there's a reason why the locals live in fear of crossing from one end of the island to the other after dark, while the tourists roam about in the moonlight, fearless.

'I saw the head of a woman, but she had no body and she was hovering above the ground,' my friend at Pesona confided when I pressed him for more information. He handed me my juice

243

nervously and I had to wonder if anyone else had seen the same thing. Turns out they have. And a whole lot more.

On the very first night I got back to Gili T, there was a freak storm. I've never heard thunder and ferocious wind like that in my life. The next morning it was revealed that a tornado had struck, something that rarely happens here even in the rainy season.

But you want to know the weirdest part? The tornado only seemed to strike one tiny patch of the island. It knocked some tiles off the roof of the dive shop next door, yanked their tree out of the ground and used it to completely flatten a new structure erected by Pesona Resort. They'd been building this structure for a few weeks but as owners Sumeena and Sandesh told me before, they had yet to get around to blessing it. As we know from Paul's new land purchase, every time you build something new in these parts it must be blessed in order to gain permission and protection from the gods and spirits.

As I type, the structure at Pesona has been re-built on the beachfront and I attended the blessing ceremony myself the day it was finished.

The tiles were put back on the roof of the dive shop pretty much as soon as it happened, too, but no-one really knows what they did to deserve such collateral damage.

But the dive shop's had problems before, I found out. One staff member told me how the swimming pool turned green and sludgy overnight, soon after it was filled. They called in the experts, poured in the chlorine, tried to clean it for days but to no avail. No-one knew where the sludge had come from but it rendered their pool unusable, which was clearly no good for business.

Eventually, someone who knew someone who knew something about this sort of thing was summoned to perform a ceremony on the land, which should have been done before.

The *balian* (traditional healer) chanted and wafted the all-essential incense. As if by magic, witnesses sitting around the pool saw the water dip as though being sucked by a giant vacuum before being blasted back out again. What was an unsavoury green turned crystal clear before their eyes and the next day the pool was back to normal!

The same *balian*, without ever setting foot behind the dive shop, also remarked on a clothesline hanging back there above an important underground waterway. He said it was disrespectful to the dwelling water spirits for the dive staff to hang their laundry there and he advised them to move it. Sure enough, there *was* a clothesline there, which was quickly relocated. There haven't been any problems since.

The Balinese attribute certain happenings, illnesses or deaths to *leyaks*. A *balian* will conduct a *séance* using witchcraft to identify who is responsible for whatever's gone wrong.

I heard a story like this regarding another local business. I don't think I should reveal which one because I'm still a teeny bit scared of being black-magicked; this one also involves powerful magic … and three thieves.

The manager of the business had his suspicions about which of his staff was stealing, but on consulting the wise *balian*, he was warned not to do anything about it. 'I can help you and I can tell you who it is, but only if you let me handle it and say nothing.'

The manager was annoyed at this; it was obviously going to be hard to act like he didn't know anything once he'd learned of the culprit. But he agreed to let the *balian* deal with it.

'Two of these people will leave of their own accord,' the *balian* said. 'And it's up to you whether you fire the other one or not.'

As soon as he got back to work, one of his guilt-ridden staff members admitted to stealing money from the tip box. On seeing how sorry he was and surprised at how suddenly this magic seemed to be working, the manager decided to let him keep his job. But in the course of the next few days, after weeks of deceit and without anyone saying a word, the other two suspects quit with no explanation and left the island.

In Balinese folklore, a *leyak* is said to fly about in search of a pregnant woman in order to feed on a newborn child. Some people even think that *leyaks* are humans who've become so involved in practising black magic that they've gone a bit mental and started exhibiting cannibalistic behaviour. The ugly, hairy Rangda plays a prominent role in public rituals and demons are said to follow her, their mistress. These demons can change themselves into pigs and other animals, and fly.

One bloke I met here the other day, told me he saw a giant sea turtle spin from the sea across the sky and into the clouds. At the time I thought he was 'shrooming (he *was* actually the one who also told me I looked like I had Downs Syndrome) ... but my new knowledge of demons in disguise throws a whole new light on his observation.

Another local I met at a reggae bar called Sama Sama offered to take me to his house in the middle of the village where allegedly the spirit of a young girl (who drowned after falling from a neighbour's boat) likes to swing in the hammock all night, humming. Eek. I didn't go, because after careful consideration and observing his swaying form after more than a few Bintangs I wasn't too sure he could be trusted, and everyone else was too scared to come with me!

Eager for a personal encounter all the same (or maybe just another one of the Orb kind), I hired a bike last night, downloaded the flashlight app. for my iPhone (genius!) and set off for the graveyard at sunset. I didn't feel quite as brave as I'm making out. Actually, I was shitting myself. As I pedalled as hard as I could through the sand, trying not to skid and fall off and break my neck, the fear kept growing, and growing, and growing.

All the stories I've been hearing freaked me out so much that in the end I didn't even make it to the graveyard. I stopped, parked my bike at a posh spot called Hotel Villa Julius and sat down among the people. Strangely, as I was sipping my drink on a cushion on the darkened beach, I received an email about an upcoming workshop with Galactica Blanco, my favourite psychic and spiritual woman in Ubud. It's a course coming up in February exploring the 'Seven Levels of Consciousness'. It even promises a bit of astral travelling, which I've wanted to try for ages. Maybe I can come back here after that and travel astrally in search of some spirits …

For now, though, when it comes to the weird and wonderful on Gili T, it turns out that for all my talk I much prefer my wonderful in the form of a nice, cold vodka and Coke. And who knows, maybe a few of those 'shrooms …

03/01

If it ain't broke, don't bring it here …

In another futile attempt at cleaning myself on an island with no fresh water, I stood under my shower just now, looked down and saw tiny red maggots slithering about on my skin. Jesus! I jumped back and screamed and almost fell over on the bathroom tiles just as the water turned brown.

Sumeena at Pesona (where I can't afford to stay long-term) says the landlord at the shady homestay I have stupidly paid for up-front (for the *entire* time I'm here — error) needs to clean his water tank. The little red maggots are actually mosquito larvae. Yes, the mozzies have been laying their eggs in the open tank and they're now whooshing to their early demise through my showerhead. And the brown stuff? Oh, don't worry, that's just dirty rainwater.

I also have bedbugs. I'm pretty sure they're bedbugs because I keep waking up all itchy. Only when I turn the light on I can't see anything at all. Ugh. At night it's like my feet are on fire. I feel like I've regressed to the days of enduring hovels and I feel even sillier because it's my fault.

As a result of the squished idealistic notion that I'd be getting romanced on a nightly basis in a blur of bed sheets and kisses, and The Diver's heavy workload and general lack of enthusiasm about my existence, I have actually rendered myself the lone resident of a living hellhole full of evil critters. That'll teach me.

Everything is breaking here. I won't say my heart because I'm not that pathetic (ahem). And actually, just before New Year's Eve I did meet a really amazing man, like a gift from the ocean itself. American S (ooh, yes, he has the initial 'S') and I met smoking *shisha* on the cushions at Pesona that have become my second home. He's tall, funny, curly haired, highly cultured, well travelled and handsome. And while I won't make the mistake again of counting my chickens before they hatch into cocks, suffice to say he has cheered me up and given me hope. All it takes is a glimmer sometimes and the whole world gets brighter, right? Gotta love being a girl. Especially on a Gili island. As long as there's a sea we will always find more fish in it.

When I say that everything's breaking here, I mean that literally. The salty air kills things. I'm surprised my computer hasn't snapped in half (touch wood). The pink plastic casing

I bought for it in Bangkok has chaffed around the edges. I keep finding pink shards in my laptop bag. The case on my phone, featuring a rather tropical blue dolphin hologram (from Singapore's Chinatown, baby — one of the few treats I afforded myself when I was poor), is destroyed too. Oh, and the soles on my relatively new sandals have split down the middle.

That's not all. Everything that was white is now yellowy brown. My hair resembles a bale of hay, my nails are as brittle as a butterfly's wing, even my bikinis are thinner where the chlorine, salt and sand have eaten away at the fabric. A leather wallet that was brown when I arrived is now grey thanks to a fine coating of mould that seems to have sprung up overnight in my damp room. It's a harsh environment in so many ways here and I'm really starting to think I'd happily sacrifice my island of sun and sin for the monsoon season in Bali right about now. At least my accommodation there is clean and dry. Maybe it's time the party stopped.

But I still haven't done all my dives and I still haven't captured a *leyak*, either. Maybe I can sleep on a sun-lounger and shower larvae-free at another hotel. Hmm … there *has* to be a way to come out of all this a winner.

04/01

Biorocks and eco-efforts …

In the daytime, the waters surrounding Gili Trawangan are more inviting than a hug from Oprah Winfrey, but for some reason, the ocean at night has always scared me. Entering its watery clutches with the sun switched off seemed like one of the most terrifying prospects in the world, even without a heavy tank of nitrogen strapped to my back. With this in mind, the thought of my very first night dive and the end to my Advanced PADI diving course was something that caused waves of fear to rush over me all day.

As a human, I'm not supposed to be here, I thought, pulling the straps tight on my BCD (buoyancy-control device) and adjusting my weight belt around my waist as our boat rocked on the waves above the reef. But voicing any of my concerns about doing a night dive seemed pointless, not least because I was still trying to look blasé in front of The Diver (and because I managed to fall off a moving dive boat in front of him on my last dive — *stupid*). Perching my bum on the edge of the boat I shoved the regulator into my mouth, took a gulp of air and went for the backwards roll. I'm so glad I did!

In 1998, an agreement was made between the local people on the Gili islands to protect their coral reefs. Thanks to dynamite and cyanide fishing, these reefs were in pretty bad shape. In 2000, the local, non-government-funded organisation, Gili Eco Trust jumped onboard and in 2004 introduced the Biorocks, which is one of the reasons why diving in the Gilis is so good again.

Biorocks are as cool as they sound. They're super-planetary contraptions that utilise electrolysis to enable the development of hard and soft coral and sponges to grow up to *six* times faster than they do in normal conditions. Over sixty Biorock structures are now regenerating the reefs all around the Gilis, providing a brand new home for all kinds of marine life and, of course, making our dives much more exciting.

They're incredible things, these Biorocks, made from crisscrossed gridwork and each being fed a low-voltage current of 1.2 volts that's harmless to swimmers (and fish). Dan and I took turns to sit on the frame of an old motorbike the other day, about three metres off the beach! Other sculptures are shaped like fish and turtles.

My very first night dive was a journey round the Manta Ray Biorock reef, which used to be shaped like a giant dome until a boat threw its anchor on it. It's still the most impressive thing I've ever come across with a torch. Groupers and sweetlips, crabs and shrimp, scorpionfish, frogfish and ghost pipefish all swam through my light beam, and we saw huge nudibranchs (colourful ocean slugs) up to fifty centimetres long. It wasn't scary at all when I was down there, probably because I was too busy trying to take it all in. In the daytime all the colours are distorted, but in the clean white light of a torch at night you can see the *real* underwater Gili world. Everything seems more alive and yet surreal; the shades of reds and pinks in particular are the most vibrant your imagination can design.

The Gili Eco Trust, as well as helping the turtle population and regenerating the reefs, is also working to improve waste management. Trash is a huge problem on the Gili islands, as it is in most of Indonesia. In fact, you could write an entire book on the topic of waste management issues in Bali alone. It's something that causes everyone endless concern and the longer I spend here the more upset I get too. Next time you're here, stand on any bridge and look down. Chances are you'll see the trash before you see the trees.

I took a trip to the less debauched Gili Air for a couple of days and although the outskirts of the smaller island will beckon you with sandy carpets and interchanging patchwork blue waters, inland you'll find more of a war movie feel, especially at night. To get back to my homestay I had to navigate my way around blazing piles of rubbish in the blackness. And the smell of burning plastic bottles is one that stays with you long after you're back at sea.

It lingers in your nostrils, festers at the back of your throat and accompanies you off the island, where unfortunately people in Bali and Lombok are doing the same thing.

Bali produces an unbelievable 5,000 tonnes of garbage per day. Most of this is organic waste but the plastic waste generated is estimated at roughly 600–750 tonnes per day in Bali alone, which equates to a whopping 167 truckloads. The constant burning releases all manner of toxic chemicals into the air … the clean, holiday island air that tourists flock to from their various polluted cities *en masse*, just to breathe. Gili Air in particular should probably be called 'Gili No-Air' most of the time. Luckily, there *are* efforts being made to change things.

In Ubud, the Say NO to Plastic organisation (SNTP) was established in 2007. Along with like-minded groups Bali Fokus, the GUS Foundation and EcoBali, their HyperGreen campaign got people shopping with reusable bags. EcoBali works hard to raise awareness of waste management problems and create sustainable solutions. Along with local waste recovery facilities, they currently collect over fifteen tonnes of non-organic waste every month, of which up to ten tonnes is recycled at facilities in east Java. The rest is sent to government landfills.

EcoBali provides onsite composting solutions for businesses, as well as the opportunity for people to 'adopt a school'. This means that anyone wanting to contribute can finance the cost of training students and teachers in waste management. Thousands of kids in schools in Canggu and Kerobokan have already been involved.

The Gili Eco Trust works with the waste collection and treatment company on Gili Trawangan to collect rubbish every day. They're also raising awareness of the dangers involved in burning trash, and slowly but surely the message is sinking in. Over a thousand recycling containers have been placed around the island (although my friend says some of these have been nicked for personal use because they're good-quality bins). Children from the local school, as well as visitors and volunteers, all take part in a big clean-up on the first Friday of every month. Free dives are sometimes offered as an incentive to help — good for the backpackers on a budget.

Some hotels in Bali, like the Alila Manggis that I visited back in June, are conducting projects to encourage locals to start taking more care of their environment. They run an ongoing, eco-friendly initiative called The Green Bank, whereby the kids are rewarded for bringing in their litter for recycling. They even paint bags made from old hotel bed sheets for their parent's shopping, so less plastic is brought into their villages.

All of these efforts are truly admirable and having some positive imapcts. Bali, if it pulled its act together quickly enough and continued its development with such things in mind, *could* become one of the most environmentally friendly tourist destinations on the planet ... as could anywhere, I suppose.

But Desa Seni, a fairytale style eco-friendly 'village' resort in Canggu serves nothing in plastic, dedicates 40 per cent of its land to organic farming (the produce is served in their restaurant), composts and recycles and even offers guests reusable bamboo drinking straws. But sadly, while some people are busy making 'green' improvements, even more are carrying on regardless of the environmental impacts of careless waste disposal.

I had a tour of one of the poshest five-star hotels currently in operation in Canggu, out of interest. It has one of the hugest information packs I've ever seen, with full colour brochures and CDs and literally hundreds of pages detailing various luxurious, wallet-crippling menus and spa packages. For twenty minutes, the ins and outs of their intricately crafted cooking schools and breakfast-in-bed-on-the-beach packages were all passionately explained. When I asked the marketing manager where the hotel waste went, she said she didn't really know.

I spoke to a few surfers who, as a group, are becoming increasingly concerned about the development in the area, not just because this welcoming, quiet haven of rice paddies and black sand beaches is set to become an ugly extension of Seminyak, but because of the decline in the water quality.

'The reef around Uluwatu is all dead,' one guy told me, 'and they're building all these new places up the coast without a plan to put the waste anywhere. Well, some say they've got tanks but where does it go when they empty the tanks? Canggu is just gonna turn into a sewer.'

Sipping my Bali *kopi* surreptitiously in another surfers' cafe (surfers' gossip is the best!), I also overheard that a staff member from a very popular tourist restaurant on the beach had to be taken to hospital a few months back because she'd been struck by typhoid. In fact, they were saying that several tourists have also been admitted to hospital quite recently with the disease. Typhoid is contracted because of inadequate toilet hygiene (the Balinese aren't really used to using toilet paper and soap, let's put it that way). Flying insects that feed on faeces also spread the disease. And what helps breed flies? Duh ... all that discarded trash.

Anyway, I digress ... hard not to get sidetracked when it comes to stuff like this ... so yes, we were underwater with torches and in that moment, at least, everything was stupendous. My fear had subsided and had my tank not limited me to forty minutes, I could have spent all night down there in the deep. These amazing Biorocks look like mini, twisted shipwrecks with new surprises round every corner. I half expected a giant octopus to swim out from behind the mesh and do a little dance, waving a top hat.

At one point, The Diver, as professional and sexy as ever (damn him) instructed us all to grab a rope attached to what looked like a huge wooden wheel, made sure we all had our lights strapped tightly to our wrists and then gave the signal to turn them off. As we were plunged into darkness, his silhouette swept through a galaxy of stars as the current and his bubbles forced the bioluminescence into a swishing, neon frenzy. We were space-travellers floating light-years away from Earth in a world we did and didn't belong in at the same time. Amazing. I'll never fear the ocean at night, or night diving again. At least, maybe just not as much as before.

Now I really want to do the shipwreck dives in Bali's Amed too. I emailed Jen who managed not to relocate naked to the jungle after her retreat, and she's up for coming with me. I'm getting seriously addicted to diving. Or maybe I'm just addicted to divers. Hmm. Either way, I think I've probably exhausted all my options in the Gilis. It's time to head back to Bali.

08/01

Monsoon blues ...

It hasn't stopped raining since I got back to Ubud. The roads are like rivers. Last night torrential rain hammered on my new pointed roof like a thousand mini fists intent on puncturing the ceiling. I wondered where the animals had gone and whether they were all OK. I half expected a sodden gecko to tap me on the shoulder and beg to be let under the covers.

After handing absolutely every item of clothing I own, bar my dive shop T-shirt and a sarong to my new landlady to be hot-washed and de-Gili'd, I just slipped and fell on wet marble tiles, flat on my arse. So I'm now holed up in a coffee shop, soaking wet, tragically dressed and quite honestly wondering if it would be totally wrong to catch the next boat back. I know, I know, the grass is always greener.

The streets are bare outside the windows, but every now and then a tourist will emerge from a doorway, cloaked like a wet wizard in a bright blue plastic rain mac, looking all lost and miserable. I've watched a few of them trying to unfold soggy maps. It's quite amusing, but I wish the blimmin' sun would come out so we can enjoy Bali as it's *supposed* to be, dammit. Dan introduced me to the term 'White Whine' the other day. I think this is one of them. After our dodgy bus broke down in the town centre yesterday, I considered wheeling a very sandy Winnie the Pooh back to Putu and Mai Malu thinking my little, cosy, bedbug-free bedroom would still be available. But then I thought it might be quite nice to try something different, so I let myself be accosted by an army of men all wanting to help with Winnie and show me their homestays.

I've settled on a Balinese-style house with a huge patio, table for four and a sun-bed/rain-bed just off Monkey Forest Road. It has two scary gargoyles guarding the front door. The tiny windows along the top of the walls are triangles. The room itself has two four-poster double beds in it and the bathroom is even bigger than the bedroom. It's quirky and cheap. It'll do for now.

Gili T has stolen a little piece of my soul. It feels like a dream as I sit here, back in a wetter version of where it all started ... like I've travelled 'round in a weird, emotional circle and maybe, if I'm honest, taken a few steps backwards in my 'spiritual' journey. Oops.

After spending so long in a hedonistic blur of Irish pubs, dancing non-Ecstatically, not eating raw, oh, and trying not to chase a man who doesn't really like me, I've come back to the town that tried its best to teach me a lesson in my soul's *true* value, the meaning of life, soul nourishment and inner beauty. Oh, how I loved my new life here in Ubud. I even started to appreciate the word *namasté*. And my colon was fabulous.

Now my colon is only marginally cleaner than my conscience, because what did I do? I stuck a dagger through this island, flicked it the bird and hightailed it back to my old life (or the closest thing to it).

I'm trying to think why. Rain makes me all thinky … it wasn't just for The Diver, was it? No, it wasn't just for him. Now that I think about it, all this spirituality makes me nervous. And I think it makes me nervous because no matter how hard I try, I don't always understand it. And who likes being around things they don't understand? It makes you feel all out of whack and stupid and vulnerable … like I did at the ashram.

I keep thinking about Peggy's words; what she told me when I found myself in all that pain from shaking: 'Even if you do collapse, that's the Energy's way of helping you Process. You should be grateful for that collapse and say thank you.'

I collapsed 'spiritually' perhaps over a man. Again. How lame. But she's right. This is all a big Process. It may not be as deep and meaningful as any of *their* Processes, but it's a Process all the same, and I suppose I *should* be thanking The Diver, really. If it wasn't for him I wouldn't have been in the Gilis for Christmas and made so many great new friends. If it wasn't for him I wouldn't have been so enthused about learning to dive in the first place … well, I would have been *excited* obviously, but he made it even better.

And also because of him I found myself alone on those cushions by the beach, which is when the tall, funny, curly-haired, highly cultured, well-travelled and handsome American S sat down beside me.

'American S' and I have been speaking every single day since we met, even though he's in Australia. See, lots of things to be thankful for! But I think I should be breaking this pattern now, right? I mean, I don't want my soul to be 'Processing' another spiritual collapse over him, too. No thanks. Not again. I'm seeing him as *a friend who was sent to me for fun* … for now … (sigh).

You know, I'm discovering happiness is everywhere if you choose to see it. But then, so is loneliness really. In truth, I don't know what I feel anymore. Sorry to be all morbid and silly. Like I said, I'm just tired. Maybe my healing will help.

Tomorrow I'm starting what's called a 'Healer's Intensive'. This special time of all-things-'healing' is set to change my life by introducing me to a whole new side of Bali. It's to be led by an intriguing friend of a friend called Made Surya who has promised Jen and me a set of one-on-one encounters with some of the island's most wonderful people, including some *balians* and an introduction to my four spiritual siblings (whoever they may be). This should clear up some of those questions.

Well, would you look at that. It has *finally* stopped raining. Ooh, it's like a scene change in a movie. Better make a dash for it before it starts again …

10/01

Pure intensity …

I'm so pure right now, I swear a white dove could fly from my arse at any minute. I needed the purification ritual I just undertook at

Tirta Empul — one of the most sacred places on the Island of the Gods and consequently one of Bali's biggest tourist attractions.

When Made Surya suggested Jen and I take a trip to be purified this afternoon, I wondered what he was seeing in my aura that needed cleansing.

Anyway, my hair is still dripping from the baths of Tirta Empul but I feel sublime, blessed and healed and I can happily report that my bikini, only just back from the laundry, is now free from sin, too. I mean, it's so clean it can probably hardly remember the times I tossed it on The Diver's floor and then stood on it, naked.

I'd like to think being there with Made Surya, our knowledgeable guru and friend, meant Jen and I were becoming even purer than the other tourists dipping tentative fingers into the gushing fountains for giggles; not just because we immersed ourselves in the freezing water in bathing suits and sarongs (that's commitment) but because we understood *why* we were doing it … sort of.

Jen didn't need as much purifying. She's just back from her five-week Ayurvedic retreat with Arshia. Suffice to say that while I've been riding the waves of both the sea and a few cones of magic mushrooms … oh, and throwing whatever modicum of purity I may have had to the wind, Jen has lost weight, regained her glossy hair and learned an impressive amount about Tantra. Hmph. Ah well, each to their own.

The rectangular pool of water at the mighty Tirta Empul is sanctified by the Hindu society in Bali who believe in its power to heal all sorts of illnesses. For more than a thousand years the Balinese have come to bathe here hoping that the sacred waters will bring them luck and help them to mend.

Surya spent the morning and most of yesterday when we were rained into the Ubud cafe Tutmak, explaining, among other things, the meaning of the purification ritual. In fact, my brain is struggling to keep up with all this new stuff. He's a goldmine of information, this awesome guy from Denpasar with a Master's degree in marketing and a travel resumé spanning much of the globe. He speaks fluent English and does so much for the Balinese community including sponsoring children from poor families so they too can go to school. Surya was also senior researcher for the Society of Study of the Afterdeath, in Bali. How cool is that? He worked on the very first book to be written in English about traditional healing practices in Bali and he knows all sorts of wacky stuff about dancing and masks and black magic. Every minute's an adventure in his life!

Back to Tirta Empul. Before wading through what looked like a giant fishpond complete with colourful koi the size of cats, Surya explained how to purify ourselves beneath the nine fountains, or nine gates. These correspond with the nine different openings in our bodies, being the two eyes, two nostrils, two ears, the mouth, the umbilical cord and the ... um ... anus.

There are actually twelve gates in the pool but some are used only for special ceremonial purposes and it's not polite to stand beneath them.

So with my bikini wondering what I was doing stepping into a body of fluid with no salt, chlorine or mosquito larvae in it, and a pink sarong wrapped tightly round my waist, I waded towards the first fountain. Following Surya's lead I put my hands to my third eye (hoping it would be able to see any approaching koi before I stepped on them) and splashed the water over my head three times. Then I drank a small amount, stuck my head fully under, washed my whole body in the continuous flow and asked if I could please be pure from my head to my heart. I was aware it might take some time ...

Moving to the next fountain I asked to be open to love and to be able to give it, too. Moving on, I asked for forgiveness for thinking any impure thoughts towards anyone who's upset me, and for pure strength and pure courage to handle any obstacles in the future.

On and on we moved with our parts getting purer until we reached the last two gates, representing the chance to beat the 'evil eye' and any bad-mouthing that might be going on behind our backs. Apparently the waters at Tirta Empul are so pure that they can banish any bad energy before it has the chance to take effect. Take *that*, evil sabotage! If only I'd known all this sooner.

At Surya's instruction, I thanked the gods and goddesses at Tirta Empul for helping me cleanse my spirit and my soul and my secret place … which is … you know ladies, your *secret* place. Apparently, all ladies should purify their secret place regularly, just for good measure.

On the way out of the water I saw a giant silvery eel. I saw loads of eels diving in the Gilis; huge yellow-and-black-spotted morays that appeared at random like snapping jack-in-the-boxes from rocky crevices. But this one was swimming around people's feet.

'How did that get in here?' I asked Surya, hurriedly wading over the stony floor and climbing the mossy steps to wring my sarong out on the side of the pool.

'It's always here, it just appeared one day,' he said matter-of-factly, like giant eels just *appear* in pools all over the world, every day, without anyone putting them there. 'It symbolises that nature is watching us, in a good way!'

I watched it slither towards a man still bathing in the fifth fountain and thanked the gods for not revealing it to me before. I may have said or done something most impure.

There are a few rules for entering the sacred waters at Tirta Empul. These are stated very clearly at the entrance on a stone that was erected last September, although you'd be forgiven if you broke one, as they're only written in Balinese and Indonesian.

'The most important rule is that you wear a sarong while you're in the water', Surya translated as we stood before the sign. He then explained that if you enter without a sarong, you must sacrifice a chicken. Now ... a chicken might be cheaper, judging by what the touts will try to charge for a sarong, but that doesn't mean you should be disrespectful, so please keep that in mind if you're heading over.

Thinking about it, I don't know if the *Lonely Planet* warns tourists of these things or not, but if it doesn't, you're also not allowed to use any toothpaste or shampoo in the water. And if you decide to do your laundry in the holy flow you're expected to sacrifice not one, but *five* chickens, so you'd better have a good bird supplier if you're wandering over sarong-free with a backpack full of dirty clothes.

Another no-no, and this goes for all sacred places and temples in Bali, girls, is entering when you've got your period. The reason for this rule was always a mystery to me, until today. When menstruating, the general belief is that women are going through their own ritual. And as the wise (and totally unfazed) Surya said today, not only does blood attract evil spirits but the time when a woman has her period is also when she's most emotionally unstable.

Basically, because the Balinese build these sacred places to try and maintain balance and purity, the last thing they need is an over-emotional woman shifting that balance and attracting negative energies. I think it's a good rule. Those who've experienced my rage know I'm not fit for any holy places at the best of times, let alone when I've got my period. Oh, and before you explain the function of that slim-line saviour we call Tampax, let's remember that these rules date back to the days when women only had cloths to keep the blood at bay and these cloths weren't exactly the triple-padded winged warriors we wear in our panties today.

Another little interesting nugget I think is that those who indulge in Tantra use the time on their periods to do their most intense practice, because that's when they can use this excess of emotion for *good* and explore their own instabilities on a deeper level. It's all very logical when you think about it.

Naturally, I wanted to know what might happen if I dared to enter the temple with my period. Surya was only too happy to share. He's seen the results with his own eyes on three separate occasions; once with a woman from Ohio and twice with women from Java. All three fainted inside various temples and only when they were dragged outside and splashed with holy water by a priest did they come round and admit that yes, they were menstruating and yes, they had indeed felt strangely overcome by the energies inside these temples.

This Healer's Intensive is proving extremely interesting so far in many ways. Now, if you'll excuse me, I'm off to polish my halo.

12/01

Mending hearts and other motors ...

'I came here because of *Eat, Pray, Love*,' said the woman in the purple tracksuit, wiping beads of sweat from her brow and sitting up on the mat. 'A friend of mine told me he was the best in Bali and I've had back pains for years, so I thought why not?'

She was alternating a brave smile with winces of pain as she spoke and I suddenly thought how odd it was that Jen and I were kneeling opposite this makeshift 'operating table' on a healing man's floor, dressed in sarongs, nodding our heads and scribbling down notes on paper.

Mrs Purple didn't seem to mind the audience, however. She was just happy to be there, finally getting her back sorted out by the highly regarded Cokorda Rai (pronounced *cha-korda rye*).

There are fifty traditional healers in each district in Bali, compared to ten medical doctors. As an esteemed *balian*, Cokorda Rai has developed a rather unique way of diagnosis and treatment for illnesses. Jen and I got to witness a session today on a raised platform in his compound surrounded by trees. In describing what I saw it's important to note that I really can't explain what I saw. Not scientifically anyway. Same goes for all the healers here, really.

'You can damage their work and reputations by trying to explain how they do things,' Surya warned. I shut my notebook. Even having seen and heard the things I've seen and heard in Bali, this still goes beyond my realm of understanding and I really do think it would even if I spent a lifetime trying to wrap my head around it. That's probably because it's magic. And as we know by now, most of Bali's magic isn't meant to be understood.

Cokorda Rai is honoured in Bali as a direct channel of divine knowledge, a practice he learned from what's written in a series of wooden holy books called Lontar. Lontar are written in Sanskrit, Old Javanese and Balinese and hold a series of mantras, incantations (spells of sorts) and some drawings. These mystical books — each one long, hard and slim like a pile of stacked rulers bound with two threads — have been in his family for generations. He's not the only one who has them but not everyone can use them for healing. In order to summon the powers necessary to do the work required a person must have a gift to begin with. Normally it's inherited.

We got to see some of these magical books and although we couldn't understand anything in them, Jen and I lapped up this knowledge like students at a school for witches, spellbound!

After Mrs Purple tottered off with her bag of helpful healing herbs, a young girl in her twenties sat down and from his seat behind her in a chair, Cokorda Rai started to rub her temples. I noticed he did this at the start of everyone's treatment and Surya explained that this is how he connects with the patient's twelve main meridians and determines what their problem is. Mid rub, his phone rang and we all waited with bated breath as he finished a conversation with someone loud on the other end.

The girl (from Russia it emerged) was then instructed to lie down and Cokorda Rai got out a short stick, which he used to poke the insides of her toes. He wasn't doing it gently either … he was jabbing that tool hard into her flesh with intent. Most of these pokes rendered no reaction, apart from one which caused her to bolt upright and scream bloody murder. As if he'd been given all the proof he needed of her problem, a black marker pen was whipped out and Cokorda Rai started drawing a series of mystical looking symbols on her body just as his phone rang again.

The pen hovered over her as he jabbered away in Indonesian with the mobile pressed to his face. The girl sat up to look in bewilderment at the cosmic symbols on her stomach. It looked like a series of alien artworks, the kind of mural you might expect to be drawn before some fanciful cosmetic surgery on a spaceship. Eventually he hung up, pushed her backwards again and recommenced the scribbling.

'He's drawing a new organ,' Surya whispered. We later learned that the girl had had surgery on her fallopian tubes and was worried she wouldn't be able to have children.

'All fix,' Cokorda Rai announced moments later. And after a few more drawings, a bit of massage and rubbing some leaves into her body (and answering yet another call), he prodded the same area on her foot that had caused her to scream before. This time, she had no reaction at all. She did, however, mention that she'd also suffered vertigo for years, at which point she keeled over into semi-consciousness on the wicker mat. It was like an episode of *E.R.* from the eighteen hundreds.

Without hesitation, Cokorda Rai was up and furiously chopping spices with a giant knife on a makeshift table in the corner. The ingredients seemed to appear from nowhere but within minutes he had popped them into his mouth and chewed together a fresh, potent mixture of *galangal* (similar to ginger), sandalwood and nutmeg, which he spat without warning through his teeth onto her face. The girl was soon sitting up again saying she felt much better. Smiling, he instructed her to lean against a post and smeared his chewed-up mess onto her face until it felt completely numb. Only then would her vertigo be completely cured.

Next, her friend, a beautiful Russian blonde in a white T-shirt and shorts got up to get her temples massaged.

'I came to you before, do you remember, for my knee, last year?'

Cokorda Rai shook his head, looking down at her blankly. His phone rang again.

'Don't you remember me?' she said imploringly, as he fiddled with the buttons to stop the call. 'This time I brought my friends.'

He shook his head once more, popping the phone into his bumbag and zipping it up as if to silence it for good. The girl looked crushed and almost immediately started crying. I could sense her self-esteem was already at an all-time low and his failure to remember her wasn't helping. Whimpering she lay on the mat and sniffled miserably as Cokorda Rai jumped up with an agility that defied his years and stood on her feet.

Surya was shaking his head empathetically. 'Broken heart,' he whispered to us. The English guy sitting behind in the audience was half smiling. He's been coming to see Cokorda Rai for three months with his autistic son (who's doing much, much better as a result) and has seen hundreds of people healed by his magic hands. Ninety per cent he says come to him with a broken heart. Unsurprisingly perhaps, most are women.

'A broken heart is just an energy block,' Surya told us. 'Most of it is in your mind and Cokorda Rai helps to shift it so the pain starts to fade. Sometimes it's instant. Just watch ...'

I had flashbacks to the French man, Matt and Peggy in the ashram. Energy blocks. All in your mind. Of course. I should be an expert in all this. Clearly, I'm still just Processing it all.

Anyway, perhaps just as fascinating as watching eighty-two year old Cokorda Rai in action, for me at least, is how he came to be a healer in the first place. I often wonder about this. How does it happen that you bypass the regular career paths and decide to fix human beings using magic and spirits and spells? If learning hocus-pocus had been an option for me in the west instead of sitting in my English teacher's cupboard hiding from my maths teacher (that woman was the human embodiment of everything that still terrifies me about numbers and finance), I'm sure I'd be living in a tower by now, boiling up stuff in cauldrons. My good friend Ewan and I often talked about starting a shop called BitchCraft and selling love potions and breeding black cats and starting a line of pretty-patterned brooms for bored housewives … but life got in the way, as it so often does.

As a young man working as a car mechanic in Denpasar, Cokorda Rai started to suffer from insomnia. For eighteen months he couldn't sleep and even though he visited many healers himself, nothing seemed to solve the problem. At one point, in a fleeting moment of unconsciousness, he received a vision of a certain type of leaf that would help to cure his insomnia, but thinking it was a trick being played on him by his tired mind, he ignored it.

A couple of weeks later, Cokorda Rai was helping to clean the family temple before a ceremony when he managed to fall asleep, right there on the floor. When he finally woke up eleven hours later he was holding a Lontar (one of the sacred books made of sandalwood and palm leaves) on the topic of medicine. He recognised the palm leaf from his vision!

To find out more, Cokorda Rai went to a channeller who told him there was no doubt about it — he needed to continue the traditions of the family and study the Lontar to help people. Both his father and his grandfather had been healers too, so this was his destiny.

He fought it at first: 'I fix cars, not humans!' but almost instantly, queues of people started showing up at his house, desperate to be healed.

Scared of the attention, Cokorda ran away from Bali to Jakarta but a crippling and constant headache made him pack his bags once more and head back to face his fate. He read more Lontar books from the family library and soon it emerged that although his father or grandfather had never really shown him anything about their practice, it was what the spirits wanted for him and his power for healing came naturally.

These days Cokorda Rai is highly sought-out for his talents, specifically in treating those with schizophrenia and other mental illnesses. He has also helped many people who've come to him with problems conceiving. For a couple of hours at least today we watched various patients, the majority of them western, show up with serious problems and leave looking considerably less pained.

Watching the Russians walk away, one with herbs and spices still splattered all over her face and the other looking far less broken hearted, I found myself in awe of yet another old and smiley, white-clad magic man. I can only conclude that whatever skills he has, combined with a very active mobile phone, what happens at Cokorda Rai's home on a daily basis is much, much more than spells and BitchCraft.

14/01

Condiments and my long lost family ...

In the incredibly complex world of the Balinese, to help us make our way through the macrocosm and microcosm (greater world and smaller world within it), we each have four siblings as our closest guides. We all have the same ones, mind you. It's not like I've got Jamie, Jenny, Jemima and Maurice and you've got Russell, Marilyn, Peregrine and Hercules ... they're each as much a part of us as we are a part of them, and they don't really have names.

According to Surya today, as our Healer's Intensive course continued, we are all the product of our own ego and its interaction with these four siblings, and when a *balian* does his or her stuff, they are literally striving to rebalance these siblings. Their work is more than physically mending something; they're bringing our broken selves back into alignment and restoring peace and harmony to our souls.

I also learned today that some people call their Higher Self 'My Sibling', because when they finally get to that esteemed level of spirituality — the level at which they're so pure that even Archangel Gabriel would feel the need to scrub himself down with a wire brush before an encounter — that this Higher Self will literally appear in their image. This is something that hurts to even think about because it involves going all third person on yourself, which is always annoying. It's like me going, 'The spiritual, higher Becky walked a heavenly road with her invisible brother Maurice today, but the lesser, lower and not-as-advanced Becky wasn't allowed to go because Maurice said she wasn't ready. Oh, lesser Becky, when will you see the light? You should be at one with yourself, but still, you are two. United we stand, divided you fall.'

See? Annoying.

Anyway, while every *balian* operates differently according to their gifts and instructions from the spirits, every one of them operates with these four siblings in mind. For example, having soothed the Russian girl's broken heart and cleaned her friend's fallopian tubes, Cokorda Rai offered gifts to her four siblings when they left, to thank them for their presence and encouragement during his work. And as we arrived at channeller Jero Nesa's home in Sanur today, she too was paying homage to this invisible family by burning incense and issuing mantras. A very visible family sat before her, sobbing and mourning the loss of a loved one. They seemed to be receiving a message.

Ah, Jero Nesa. Here's an incredible woman. When she was in school she saw things that no-one else could see; things that scared the hell out of her friends and family. It was a long time before anyone would believe she was seeing anything different at all but even a girl with an overactive imagination shouldn't really be sitting in cemeteries at night, insisting she's just spending time with her 'friends'.

People would talk to Jero Nesa. People who were dead. Spirits who had never even had bodies would summon her at all hours. These spirits would want to take her places and show her things, so much so that concentrating on anything else seemed virtually impossible. Her parents wanted to take her to a psychiatrist, though she insisted she wasn't sick. Eventually it was a channeller who cleared everything up by announcing that Jero Nesa had indeed been chosen by the spirits to help bridge these two worlds.

Naturally her parents wanted to postpone this calling.

'Can't she at least finish school before she gives it all up for the dead? We promise we'll let her do whatever she wants to do after that!'

Appeased, the spirits chose to leave Jero Nesa alone for a while, freeing her up to concentrate on her studies. But once her schooling was done, her wary mum and dad were reluctant to let her back on the path she had seemed to put behind her. With their promise to them broken, the spirits weren't happy at all and poor Jero Nesa went back to running off in the night at the whim of her ghostly visitors, acting crazy and talking to spirits in trees. In fact, just like how my friend Budhi refused to become a *Mangku* at first and got sick, and the same with Cokorda Rai, Jero Nesa too, wasn't well.

Realising they were never going to stop their daughter from acting on her true calling, her parents surrendered and Jero Nesa was finally able to go through the purification ritual essential for her official induction into the world of channelling.

Surya first met Jero Nesa when a baby was born into his family, or should we say, reincarnated into his family. They wanted to know which ancestor had come back in the form of this newborn, a riddle usually given to channellers like Jero Nesa to solve. Surya himself, they discovered, is actually the reincarnation of one of the first king's messengers, which Jen and I now think is why he's so dutifully informative and excited to relay all this fascinating, secret information to people in Bali. It's in his blood.

Now in her sixties and married into the Brahma (high priest) clan, the priestess Jero Nesa has lines of people waiting for a connection on a daily basis. She performs her spiritual duties on a little wooden chair on a raised platform just outside the family temple. As we watched, this rotund woman in white was chanting almost under her breath and speaking most intently in an octave that should have been far too low for her throat to handle (eek!). On a table next to her were towers of offerings and two condiment bottles which looked to be ketchup and mustard.

With the sobbing family gone, it was my turn and I sat cross-legged on the mat in front of her. She lit her incense and performed another chant and started explaining what the spirits were saying via Surya, who helpfully translated. I harboured a small hope that I might receive a message from a long-dead ancestor perhaps to confirm I am, indeed, the reincarnation of Joan of Arc.

'You are on a clear path,' Jero Nesa told me, her warm eyes shining through the language barrier. 'The spirits have chosen this path for you and it is very clear.'

Good to know! Um … which path is that?

'You should stay in Bali. The spirits want you here.'

Really? Why? How long for?

'You need to relax. The spirits say you work too hard, too stressed all the time. Always thinking,'

Hmm. Is this working hard? Perhaps you mean in my last life? Which ancestors are telling you this? Are my siblings here?

Before I could voice my many questions out loud, the cap was whipped off one of the condiment bottles. Instead of ketchup, I was coated in holy water, leaving my fringe a wet mess of sweet-smelling sunshine and frangipanis. No wonder England isn't very spiritual. There just aren't enough frangipanis there to satisfy everyone in the spirit world who'd want to talk to us. Not that many people seemed to be talking to me. I don't think I'm Joan of Arc.

'You should stay in Bali. Good place for you,' Jero Nesa told me again, causing a mild panic to surge through me. *Forever? I'm not sure about that. Do you think you could maybe see if granddad's around? See what he thinks? He's up there somewhere, doing crosswords ...*

Alas, my time was up. It was Jen's turn next. Her reading was pretty much the same, except she wasn't told to stay in Bali. She had no specific spirit visitors either. Apparently both of us are quite balanced already, if a little stressed at times. Jen was told she should be working with her hands, which is hardly groundbreaking information. But she *has* been considering doing a massage course in Thailand recently. Hmm.

Perhaps you need to be Balinese, with a real desire to contact a recently dead relative, to *really* experience Jero Nesa's special gift? Having a translator kind of takes you out of the moment, too. It wouldn't be right to feel disappointed for having most things (except for the direction of our entire lives) relatively in order, and everyone we know currently alive, but I suppose Jen and I got a tiny taster ... a few channels from the channeller. We just got the fuzzy ones, you know? The ones you see when the TV's not tuned properly. *Balians* like Jero Nesa are required to help everyone who shows up bearing an offering. The 'proper' *balians* never work for the money, Surya told us. Every 210 days, on

Saraswati Day, which is the day of knowledge, the people who've been helped will return to the healer with a bigger offering and *this* is when they can pay with money if they like. If not, their gift is normally something grandiose, like some flags to adorn the home, or a suckling pig.

Not having a suckling pig to hand, we took our invisible brothers and sisters and waved goodbye to the channeller.

Love in the land of Amed ...

After our intense healing time with Surya, Jen and I decided it was well within our rights to take some time out with our spiritual siblings by the sea. This seemed especially needful after a rather surprising incident with a young tracksuit-clad *balian* who flicked Jen's head until her veins practically popped in an attempt to cure her eye of a twitch. It seems to have healed her, so far. Mind you, she's got sunglasses on so I can't really tell. We're staying at a place called the Baliku Dive Resort in Amed on the east coast of Bali, and it is gorgeous!

Amed, while having built a considerable reputation for great diving, is still essentially a fishing village. The first hotel was only built in 1989 and parts of it only got electricity in 2001. Mackerel, mahi mahi, tuna and barracuda are brought in here from as far out as five kilometres (never from the reefs, of course) and then distributed mainly to the markets in Klungkung and up north in Singaraja.

Surprisingly, according to one local hotel owner we met from the gorgeous Bali Moon Villas (just down the road from Baliku

Dive Resort), there are more German tourists in Amed than any other nationality. Perhaps they're inquisitive by nature and prefer exploring further afield than the usual tourist spots. Perhaps they like quiet beaches, where no-one else can laugh at their Speedos?

Being monsoon season, meaning things are even quieter than usual, Jen and I negotiated for a two-bedroom villa that's so plush it even has those comfy corner bathtubs in each en-suite. Ooh la la! And the living area is outdoors on a sort of balcony set-up, so when we watched three movies in a row yesterday from the king-sized daybed, we weren't sure whether to look at the TV or the sea or the clouds clenching their wispy fists over the mountaintop in the background. Bali, your most eastern point is delightful. I can't believe it's taken us this long to meet!

I should say, though, that there's really not much to do in Amed. Loved-up couples will get all the privacy, peace and black sand tanning time they desire, but Amed for tourists is basically all about nature and a long strip of dive shops and *warungs* offering grilled fish and terrible music. Take a book.

Jen and I had an awesome time on our two shipwreck dives, both of which were close to shore. This means we literally walked into the sea and sank slowly until we were face to face with a small Japanese wreck and then, further along the coast, the more impressive USAT *Liberty* wreck. This one had been sitting on the beach ever since it was blasted in World War Two until the 1970s when a storm blew it out to where it now lies just twenty metres from the shore.

Both of these dives were even more magical than in the Gilis; visibility was better and the coral was far healthier. Our instructors, Murray and Niko, even helped us make a video so we could capture it all. (It's on YouTube, if you're interested.) If you're new to diving in Bali I would highly recommend starting

Getting ready for a shore dive to see a shipwreck

out here in Amed where it's quieter. You'll get better reefs, more one-on-one time with your instructor plus you don't have to backwards-roll off a boat to reach your destination. When you're good, *then* go to the Gilis!

The diving instructors here are also of a very high calibre indeed. In fact, watching one of them do his work-out laps in the swimming pool right in front of us with one lean, bronzed arm whipping up above the other with each masculine stroke, Jen and I have just had the Island Debate. We have this quite a lot in Bali. The Island Debate always starts with the question: 'If we were stuck on an island would we fall in love?'

You can't deny you've thought about this, too. It's just you and a guy you've maybe met once or twice, and you're stranded as a result of a sudden accident (usually involving a plane crash or a shipwreck, you know, something romantic) and you have no choice but to be together, forever. Would you wind up as an item in love or would you rather die?

Personally I think I'd fall in love with any diver if stranded with him on an island even though I *was* ... and we *didn't* ... and ... oh fuck it. I can still dream. They're strong and tough and skilled and they hold your hand protectively when there's a strong current in a way that almost makes you yearn for a freak tsunami.

As Jen has just reminded me (because I do tend to linger most obsessively on this topic) the Island Debate can be had about any man. He doesn't have to be that attractive, either. On your island, it could be a gradual descent into love and perhaps you wouldn't even see it coming. Perhaps for a while you'd recoil from one another in disgust and denial, adamant that there must be something else, someone else, some way off this goddam island. But after a few months of hacking coconuts from trees, bonding over finally lighting that handmade match or fashioning blankets from buffalo skins, your hormones would inevitably take over and that would be it. When you're stuck on an island, you see, anything is possible, with anyone. Or is it? Debate and discuss.

Speaking of love, I've managed to get myself involved in two upcoming Valentine's Day events in Ubud. One is an afternoon charity event at the Lobong Cafe for the blind, deaf and disabled kids of Bali. With a group of others I've met while scribbling in various coffee shops and cafes over the last few months, we are organising raffle prizes, sponsors from local restaurants, hotels and spas, plus a host of musical performances from local bands. The blind kids will be performing with their own band, and the deaf kids will be performing their special *Legong* dances. At least we hope it's that way around.

The other event is at Bar Luna, where myself, Bob and a few others are going to show some clips from romantic movies and read some poems and stories on the theme of 'How We Got Together'. I was thinking of doing a bit of a reading/dramatic performance of *Romeo and Juliet* with a willing male hero as my Romeo. Ironically, I've not met him yet. Maybe I can convince one of these Amed divers …?

20/01

An interesting Twitter account …

Before Christmas I met a guy called Alan who's in Bali doing some volunteer work for an organisation called the Friends of the National Parks Foundation (FNPF). Yes, people, you can be friends with a park. Alan and his team, as part of an extraordinary conservation project, have managed against all odds to establish a bird sanctuary on Nusa Penida, a little island considered extremely holy by the Balinese, just fifteen kilometres southeast of Bali.

Surya told us there are a lot of myths associated with this island and some holy underground caves. So when Alan invited me over there to witness the release of a new flock of birds, I hopped most enthusiastically onto the speedboat with his bunch of eco-warriors dressed in my *kabaya* and sarong.

The FNPF's project is one that has succeeded against all odds. In other parts of Bali — in particular West Bali National Park — hundreds of cage-bred birds have been released only to be nabbed and sold by poachers. The Bali starling, an exquisite white bird with a blue neck of feathers, is so rare that each one can fetch up to $1,000 on the black market. For many impoverished Balinese the temptation to steal them is usually too great to resist.

When we arrived on Nusa Penida I met the man behind the cause, an inspirational Indonesian conservationist called Bayu Wirayudha. As a qualified vet who'd been breeding the rare Bali starlings in captivity for more than ten years, Bayu realised that the population of the birds in the wild was still dwindling rapidly. Desperate to do something, he set about travelling back and forth to Nusa Penida, a quiet, less-populated paradise in which he was certain the endangered birds would thrive. Over the course of two years, Bayu spoke with the island's forty one chiefs about the issue (yes, forty one chiefs on the tiniest island ever!). His idea was that everyone living on Nusa Penida would protect the birds in exchange for the foundation's support in a variety of other social and environmental projects. Apparently, there was some scepticism at the start:

'What's that? You want to release hundreds of reeeeeeally valuable birds on an island where the people have NOTHING else?'

'Yes'

'And instead of capturing them and making ten million rupiah on each one, you expect them to look at them all and go, "oooh aren't they pretty?"'

'Er, yes.'

[Cue laughter]

Much to Bayu's relief, however, it was agreed by all that any birds released on Nusa Penida by the FNPF would be fully protected by the temple, and thus all villagers, under the traditional law of ... wait for it ... *awig-awig*. I love this. Sounds like something Lady Gaga might shout to her slacker wardrobe assistant before she goes on stage: 'Awig-Awig! Where the hell is my wig?!'

Under this magnificent wiggy law not one bird released on Nusa Penida has been swiped for sale since the project started. Numbers of Bali starlings are rising and now the law has been extended to cover *every* type of bird. More than a hundred Bali starlings, lesser sulphur-crested cockatoos and Mitchell's lorikeets (all of which are listed as endangered in Indonesia), live undisturbed on Nusa Penida. How good is that? I admit, with this profusion of birdlife I was quietly afraid of getting shat on as I walked about with Alan today.

Among the foundation's contributions to island life as part of the exchange agreement is a scholarship which pays for one child from every village to go to school. It also pays for two students to attend university in Denpasar. On top of all this assistance, the army of 'voluntourists' who flock here to help all year round are teaching English at the local schools and helping to grow and plant all the trees that are needed to host the hundreds of birds. Forest cover of at least 30 per cent is required on Nusa Penida for a hospitable micro-climate. Behind the foundation's headquarters is a nursery nurturing row after row of baby trees. I saw them there, all lined up and waiting to do their bit like tiny coconut soldiers on call.

The FNPF centre covers a hectare of land right across the road from a yellow sand beach. According to one volunteer I spoke to, every evening the locals come over with their guitars and hang out with the westerners and everyone has a great time.

With a growing international interest in bird-watching the Nusa Penida Bird Sanctuary may well become a destination in its own right, although Alan and Bayu will tell anyone that the island will never be marketed as a tourist attraction. It's still a sacred place for the locals (though I didn't get to see the holy caves on this visit), a place for spirituality, to get back to nature and to witness perhaps the world's most shining example of how a tight-knit community can make a huge difference to their environment.

Whereas other parts of Bali have sold out and allowed mass tourism to swipe the land of forested and agricultural ground, Nusa Penida remains pretty much the same as it was thirty years ago. There are no sky-rise resorts here, no flashy restaurants, no bars and no clubs. And if all goes to plan there never will be. Any development that goes against the island's cultural values is a no-no. For lunch and dinner there are only *warungs* serving traditional Indonesian food and people who visit are encouraged to stay with the local villagers in homestays.

Perhaps a major contribution to the success of the FNPF's Nusa Penida Bird Sanctuary is that it works in harmony with the Hindu concept of *Tri Hita Kerena*. I'd never heard of it before. *Tri Hita Kerena* is the acknowledgement of the unity between the natural world, God and mankind.

Before each bird release, volunteers and local villagers join as one in the temple to offer prayers asking the gods to recognise the bird's right to remain safe and protected once released. As I stood there sweating profusely once again in my princess outfit, the snapping of the media's cameras was the only sound. Hands were held together as the priest said his piece and all around us the birds, who'd already been freed, chirped along to the scene; a real life Twitter account in action, singing their thanks to their followers.

I found myself thinking that I hope Nusa Penida always stays like this — thirty years behind. May it never sell out and may the evil hands of greed never spoil what these people have worked so hard to achieve, because it really is amazing.

I like the concept of *Tri Hita Kerena*. As humans we live with nature all around us, but how often do we really acknowledge it? How often are we really grateful for it? I think of all the time I spend glued to a computer screen, zoning out or buzzing around and I can't help it, right? That's my job and that's my life. That's most of our lives these days. As adulthood crept up on me I ignored the birdsong, didn't stop to smell the flowers. My experience on Nusa Penida reminded me of that loss.

Failing to acknowledge nature is an alien concept to the Balinese. Life itself is an unshakable, harmonious conglomeration of humans, God and the natural world we've all been blessed to share. Our equality, our necessity as a cog in this ever-revolving wheel is as clear as the ocean that licks the sand, the invisible breeze that runs its fingers lovingly through the palm leaves, the rain that hurtles mercilessly from the sky and then surrenders with a sigh to the Bali sunshine. We are one in a truly divine world. And that, right there, is *namasté*.

Whatever our religion, I could tell our combined good wishes were accepted and sent out across the island today and up into the sky. They were carried on the wind along with the Bali starlings who finally flew from their cages fully protected by the unseen forces of human goodwill. The governor of Bali himself was beaming as he witnessed the event and I saw Bayu looking up at the birds settling for the first time on the roof of the temple, smiling in a quiet moment of silent satisfaction.

I think I'm going to come back for longer next time and plant some trees. It might be too late for some of Bali, but how nice it'll be to help make sure it's never too late for Nusa Penida and the Bali starlings.

Jamu or not to Jamu ...

'Of all the healers in this magical land, there is still no man who can cure the common cold,' I sniffled to my friend Dave today. Dave owns a coffee shop in Ubud called Seniman which stands out from the rest by way of his science-lab style of making coffee using various funnels and Bunsen burners and tubes. It's Japanese apparently. It's very good. But for once, coffee was not what I needed. I blew my nose again on a napkin.

'I can cure you,' Dave said. 'What you need is *Jamu!*'

He's not the first person to have told me this. *Jamu* is a traditional medicine in Indonesia. It's kind of like the Panadol of the east in that it cures absolutely everything from hangovers to period pains to toothache. Unlike Panadol, *Jamu* is predominantly herbal, except when they chuck in a bit of animal matter, like goat bile or alligator spit, just for good measure.

Some people use *Jamu* to enhance their sexual pleasure. A bit of research informs me that certain special blends can increase a man's stamina, or if you're a woman, tighten your vagina. Wikipedia says the latter come with names like *Sari Rapat* ('Essence of Tightness'), *Rapat Wangi* ('Tight and Fragrant'), and even *Empot Ayam* ('Tight as a Chicken's Anus'). Wikipedia should come with a warning for parents and guardians, clearly, but if you're out shopping in the Indonesian pharmacy for a nice gift, be warned that the pretty perfume box behind the counter with the fancy name might not be all it seems. It might, however, get you more than you haggled for when you get back to the bedroom. On second thoughts, maybe you should stock up!

Anyway, Dave promised his version of *Jamu* would have no goat bile in it or anything else that might make me tighter than a chicken's anus. What he presented was in fact, a 'modern' blend of innocent turmeric, spicy ginger, lemon and honey the colour of an egg yolk. It stung my tongue, turned my mouth bright yellow and made me feel a whole lot better. In fact the effect was so strong I have no doubt that a few of those each day would kick anything back into action if you were feeling a bit slack ... so to speak. My cold isn't gone but my nose isn't as runny, my head isn't as cloudy. Feels like I took a Panadol, actually.

I'm told I can also get sachets of *Jamu* in Circle K that I should mix with hot water like an Indonesian Lemsip. Genius. What coffee can't fix this herbal miracle in a cup definitely can. Let me know if you want any posted to your house. This is one Bali drug I could get away with smuggling.

01/02

Happy Galungan ...

Today is a special day in Bali and I'm currently dressed to the nines in my finest attire, which I always love, apart from the sweating it induces (sorry to go on about this but I've asked my friends and I'm not the only one who has difficulties — ugh!).

Anyway, *Galungan* is great. It's sort of like a Bank Holiday or Australia Day, only whereas in England and Australia we might choose to celebrate the birthday of an old woman we've never met, or the ancient arrival of a fleet of ships to justify a day off work, the Balinese celebrate on *Galangan* because this highly auspicious day marks the almighty victory of good over evil.

As Jen and I walked to the Pura in Peliatan, another little village just outside of Ubud, her lovely neighbour and friend

These things are much heavier than they look

Wayan chattered happily about the meaning of the celebrations and let us take turns carrying the huge *banten* on our heads.

The local ladies make carrying these huge *banten* look easy. They smile those dazzling smiles as they walk with them on their heads and you never see *them* tripping over any gaping holes in the streets. Sometimes they walk miles. But when it was my turn to have a go I could barely move one inch without grabbing the base of it with my hands and steadying myself to a worried little 'eek' from Jen. It was probably heavier than Winnie the Pooh has ever been and I've never ever tried carrying him on my head.

Galungan is celebrated every 210 days, ending ten days later with another special day called *Kuningan*. Saraswati Day (the day of knowledge) happens every 210 days too, as the Balinese calendar (Pawukon) is actually only 210 days long. The series of Hindu religious ceremonies taking place during this particular ten-day period are generally considered to be the most important ones in Bali. It's during this time that the followers of the Balinese Hindu religion stop to think even more about the importance of living their lives based on *Dharma*, versus a life dominated by the ego.

Dharma, in case you're not familiar with it like I am (ahem), is the 'law of being' and technically, without it, nothing can exist. It's a sort of spiritual discipline that, combined with moral law, holds the people of the world together. Well, Bali at least. *Galungan* means 'When the *Dharma* is winning'.

There's an excitable energy in the air right now and two men wearing a wooden and hair-covered dragon costume just wiggled past at the front of a jangling procession on Jl Hanoman. If the explanations I've been given are correct, the Balinese gods visited the Earth today to say hi, and they're still here. They're not due to leave until ten days from now and they're clearly very important visitors, hence all this entertainment. Everyone seems to be involved on quite a spiritual level; all the shops are shut and everyone's paying their respects by hanging out with their loved ones and generally being very happy, especially the Chinese tourists, three of whom I just witnessed standing next to the dragon, shouting at each other to film at close range with an iPad.

Wayan and her daughter Ayu plus a number of other women from their village have spent the last four days preparing for today. They've been sitting for hours at a time on their marble and stone floors creating beautiful items woven from young coconut fronds, and they've also been cooking. Their husbands have been busy too, constructing the *penjor*, which are long bamboo poles that bend over in the middle and sway in the breeze when they're placed outside, like natural lamp posts with bulbs too heavy to support.

You can see these *penjor* dangling in the entrances to each family compound and pretty much every construction has got something similar, so the result is a maze of strikingly decorated streets that you can't help but feel honoured to walk through, considering the effort that's gone into it all. It's what Christmas would look like in the west if we all decided to shun places like Marks & Spencer, banish tinsel and weave our own decorations from household items and the bark from our garden trees.

Wayan's husband was up extra early this morning to help slaughter a pig, which they'll all be enjoying by now. *Babi guling* is pig roasted on a spit and served covered in herbs and spices with heaps of hot white rice. I'm slightly jealous. My own Wayan from the homestay has offered me dinner with the family tonight though, so I'm trying not to pig out on too much pig.

Much of the food used in these beautiful *banten* has been 'offered' by noon, taken home again and tucked into, along with various other hot items. It's thought that the act of offering itself is enough to appease the gods and spirits, so giving these treats and then taking them all away again to eat is normal. I don't know about you but I always find it quite fortuitous that the gods, demons and humans of Bali all like to eat *exactly* the same things. I mean, obviously I don't know for sure but I can imagine there must have been some light bargaining or bribery involved somewhere, way back when:

'Do you have the entrails from that delicious looking thirteen-year-old dog we saw yesterday?'

'*Er, no. But I made you a cake!*'

'A *cake*? I'm a demon. Demons feed on death and destruction. Fetch me a decaying snake at once.'

'*I don't have any snakes. I've got some Ritz biscuits.*'

'Right. GUYS! They forgot the snakes. Let's take their children ...'

'*NO! Wait, I also have some Rice Krispies. They're pink.*'

'Hmm. Well I do like pink ...'

'*And a chicken!*'

'Ooh, yes, chicken is good. Is it raw and as it was when you strangled it, or is it still screaming for mercy?'

'*No, sorry. But it has been marinating in a fine mix of ginger, garlic and onions for a day and my wife is currently cooking it on the ...*'

'FINE. Fine. We'll take the chicken as it comes. And the Rice Krispies, as long as they're pink. Your children are free to live.'

In the *Pura* we all knelt down and performed the *Galungan* ceremony. It took place in a sea of all-in-white males and beautifully dressed, rainbow-clad females with the priest speaking on a microphone between each part of the ceremony. Same as always, we raised the flowers from Wayan's smaller offerings to our foreheads and placed them in our hair, and a collection of women performed the duty of sprinkling everyone in turn with holy water.

There were hundreds of people packed into the *Pura* grounds; so many in fact that I was practically sitting on an old woman next to me as I made my offerings. And there was absolute silence as the ceremony took place, which is rare, because usually there's at least some light chatter, or the ring of a phone, or a child jabbering somewhere. As we left, another crowd of people piled in and Wayan told us this would go on all morning, until everyone who wanted to perform the ceremony had been given their turn.

During the *Galungan* period, each family's deified ancestors descend to their former homes. They come expecting to be entertained, welcomed and prayed to. I did think for a moment that my beloved grandma and granddad might be paying me a visit today too from beyond their English graves, so I've decided to play them a special version of my newly modified Facebook Stalker song on Dave's guitar when I get home, just to make them smile. I don't have any official offerings but I do have some leftover chocolate on my nightstand that I could give to them, I suppose … and then take back and eat myself. Happy *Galungan*!

05/02

Nature's Children …

The other day I overheard three girls talking about their planned trip to Anak Alam (Nature's Children), the foundation based high up in the mountains around Kintamani. I thought it was weird because I'd been planning a visit anyway. Bali's magic moves in mysterious ways. Or perhaps I'm just a nosey eavesdropper?

Either way I sidled up to their table and the very next day, loaded up with Bintang supermarket's entire stash of colouring books and crayons (plus Dave's guitar) we all wound our way for three hours through the emerald countryside with Wayan Number 9.

Pande — the guy I met back in mid-December at Bar Luna — lives in a village called Sonang, a short drive away from Blandingan, the much poorer village where the kids live that his foundation supports. He is basically working to bring these kids, aged from around two to fourteen, a bit of extra happiness in whatever way he can. Bringing gifts and donations to the village also helps, although Pande was clear when we met at Bar Luna that he doesn't want hordes of tourists heading up there and creating the impression that white people do nothing but dole out presents.

Staying a couple of days at least and getting involved in activities with them though is encouraged, which is how we found ourselves crammed into a double bedroom in his parent's house at the bottom of the mountain.

Pande wasn't there on our visit. During the week he works at an art gallery in Ubud in order to support his real passion, which is helping these kids. What a guy! His mum, who runs a laundry business, and dad Pak Mantri, the highly revered local doctor, seemed more than happy to host us in his absence and welcomed us in with cups of steaming tea and spicy *nasi goreng*.

They don't speak a word of English so out came the phrase books and notes from my lessons with Fivi. Once again we established the weather; that it was colder up in the mountains than in Ubud, our names and the fact that *nasi goreng* is delicious. We were unable, however, to ask where the poor children were or when we'd actually get to meet them. We all sat politely around the table for about two hours smiling at each other … and then we visitors excused ourselves to go for a walk.

On the streets of Sonang the girls and I were instantly surrounded by about thirty kids. These children were bright-eyed and runny-nosed, aged between three and eight, shrieking, beaming, chattering and whizzing round and round on motorbikes, four to each bike, wearing no helmets. That night we were so wiped out it was all we could do not to fall asleep as Ibu Mantri and her granddaughter showed us how to weave palm frond offerings on their living room floor. Children. Are. Exhausting.

The next morning after a yummy breakfast of fried coconut dough balls and hot Bali *kopi* we were assigned some teenage guides to walk us up to Blandingan. Yes, *walk*. With Wayan Number 9 long gone, there was no other option at the time. So there we were, four white girls, three large Nikon cameras plus equipment, two Balinese teenagers playing Kuta rock music out loud on their mobile phones and sackloads of books, crayons, colouring pencils, toothbrushes, toothpaste, hair bands, skipping ropes and paper … and a guitar … all heading at snail's pace up a mountain.

It wasn't easy. It took ninety minutes. One of my thongs broke. We had no water. But once we reached the village, the smiles we were greeted with made it all worthwhile. You could tell we were the highlight of their week.

Some of these kids are orphans adopted unofficially by other families and Pande says they often get sinus illnesses and suffer skin irritations because their surroundings are so filthy. Living in tiny concrete and bamboo houses, they run about in bare feet with the dogs and chickens and we saw numerous children, no more than nine years old, carrying their tiny brothers and sisters around their middles in slings. Other kids were carrying baskets of building materials down the street on their heads. None of them had mobile camera-phones.

In a curl of chilly fog creeping down from the mountain top I watched three adults walk up to a deep well that was no more than a drain full of rain water and litter. One of the women dropped a bucket with a rope tied to the handle. Leaves and rotten flowers slopped in the water as she heaved it all up again.

'What will they use that for?' I asked our teenage guide.

'Cooking,' he replied.

The Bali Advertiser tells me (and not in a chirpy tone at all) that Indonesia should be ashamed of its failure to reduce poverty. Allegedly, the combined wealth of Indonesia's forty richest people is equivalent to that of roughly 60 million of its poorest citizens. The economy here continues to be dominated and manipulated by a group of super-duper rich people, which angers absolutely everyone you talk to, from taxi drivers, to teachers, to *balians*, to policemen ... even the corrupt ones pocketing cash from various daily pay-offs. They've all got something to say about it, as you can imagine.

Over the last three years, the number of 'poor' Indonesians has risen to 43.1 million and poverty here is *worse* than in Cambodia and Laos, so says the trusty *Bali Advertiser*. Those countries actually managed to lower their numbers of 'poor' people in the same time period in spite of a challenging lack of natural resources. With all the riches being generated from tourism alone in Bali these days, there probably shouldn't be women cooking with dirty rainwater on the same, 112-kilometre-long island. But then, there shouldn't be more trash than sand on Kuta Beach either.

On a slightly happier note in another project called '1 Camera, 1000 Smiles', the kids of Blandingan are being donated old, unwanted digital cameras and other equipment so they can learn how to take photographs. I absolutely love this idea, not least because I love photography myself and I could see these kids light up the way I first did when I could see a photo I'd taken on a digital screen. I handed over my SLR and watched one girl run around with it in a blur of excitement as she snapped over 200 photos of her friend's eyeballs at close range.

This project is now linked with a sister school in Australia so the kids can learn from each other's photos about the differences in their lives. The school in Melbourne helps the kids in Bali by organising fundraising events. How many of us have replaced digital camera after digital camera for one reason or another without even thinking that someone else might absolutely love our older models? I urge you all right now to have a rummage in your drawers and old boxes to see what you can rustle up and donate. And please delete the memory cards first, especially if you're a bit naughty. Think of the children.

My three new friends plus the teens who'd accompanied us up the mountain spent two days playing games with the Blandingan kids of Anak Alam and yes, I even got to be Mary Poppins … for a bit. I wasn't sitting under a palm tree as we taught each other 'head, shoulders, knees and toes' in our respective languages but a dirty floor in a community hall. At one point a toddler peed in the dust and the other kids, so used to running around in filth, actually stood and sat in it.

It was an eye-opening visit.

How would you like your eggs?

'Hi ladies, sorry to interrupt you, but I'm from New York. Well, it's Jew York where I come from! Anyway, I'm holding a charity event and all the money raised will be matched by a local entrepreneur. You're looking at him. It's me!'

My friend Hanna and I looked at him blankly over our coffees, this overweight, sweaty man in a football shirt. But he pulled out a chair and continued to talk about himself.

'I'm going to Maui next. You know, in Hawaii? I'm planning to tie-dye jeans and sell my marijuana swim shorts. They go for $200 a pair. Oh, and I've also got a range of pet clothing I'm designing called Doggy Style ...'

He paused so we could laugh. We didn't.

'Anyway, I'm *really* going to Maui to sell the black bamboo you can buy here in Bali. The Balinese use it for building? Only *I'm* not going to use it for building, if you know what I mean!'

He paused again and made a giant bong-smoking gesture with his arms and mouth. When neither of us laughed with him, he stood up and looked a bit embarrassed.

'Sorry, but I think you should go back to Kuta,' I said. Hanna nodded. And with that, he was gone. But not before tarnishing our pure little eco-friendly, raw-chocolate-cake-selling Ubud cafe with his presence.

It was an unfortunate interruption indeed, not least because my new friend from Sweden and I were *trying* to have a sensible conversation about vaginal smoking and the benefits of yoni egg insertions. You know, finding respite from people like this in Bali's spiritual centre is getting harder as the days go by ...

I digress. I have recently become quite fascinated with vaginal treatments. The fascination began when I saw this tempting advertisement on a board outside a spa:

LOTUS TREATMENT

Lotus is a special treatment for women famous in Balinese tradition. For cleansing and health, herbs and spices using a 'smoking' method are directed into the woman's area.

1 hour: Rp. 100,000

I started scouting around for similar treatments for the 'area' and found that vaginal smoking is actually a Javanese pre-wedding ritual intended to cleanse the area ready for … well … you know. Several spas here offer the treatment and I've since learned that it's also becoming quite trendy in L.A. Allegedly, people will pay up to $50 over there to steam and smoke their vaginas, and even more interestingly, they're all probably pretending to know why.

As if by magic — or quite naturally, this being Bali — shortly after beginning my research, my friend Bob pulled up beside me on his motorbike as I was walking down the street and handed me a card. 'I thought you might be interested in this,' he said.

The card was advertising Hanna's services and read: 'Vaginal Releasing — Intimate Acupressure for Women'. I called her at once.

Intimate acupressure, which leads to vaginal releasing, goes one step *further* than vaginal smoking. Literally. Hanna is in Bali to see how she can help women who may be experiencing blocks in their private areas; blocks that might be preventing them from living up to their full sexual potential. This is a skill she honed in Sweden while hanging out with various spiritual communities.

At the moment she works in a supermarket while she figures out how to go about implementing her methods on a more permanent basis here in Bali.

Shortly before the drug lord's intervention, Hanna showed me her yoni eggs, the tools she uses for her vaginal releasing work. She unwrapped each one carefully from its little green mesh bag like a gypsy unveiling her crystal balls and worked the hard, shiny marble eggs around in her fingers. She explained how they're inserted and 'hugged' in order to strengthen the muscles.

'Why is one bigger than the other?' I asked, noticing that they were different sizes.

'Because sometimes if a lady has had a few children, the smaller one will just fall out,' she said. She held them out to me.

I didn't touch them.

Each egg has a hole drilled carefully through the top which Hanna threads with a piece of disposable dental floss at the start of each session. This then hangs from the vagina in case of the other scenario, which is of course the scenario in which the egg gets stuck.

Hanna isn't really offering her treatments here yet; she's just testing the waters to see who might be interested. She said she's had quite a lot of calls as a result of her business cards and in fact, since she's been in Ubud she's been getting invites to take her yoni eggs to a host of spiritual health conventions in different countries.

It's easy to kick yourself, isn't it? Why didn't *I* think of this? They're just little marble eggs of the sort you might find at an Easter market. Harmless, worthless little marble eggs that granny might put on the mantelpiece. Drill a couple of holes in them, however, pick up some dental floss and HOLY SHIT, you're the *only* one in God's given galaxy with a magical cure for sexual blocks and everyone wants to fly you across the world, for *free*.

Hanna is a genius. I told her so. And in honour of our new friendship we decided to go and get a Lotus Treatment together.

Turns out that a Lotus Treatment is a bit like sitting on the toilet without doing anything at all, for forty-five minutes. It's not so much a toilet, though; it's more a pretty wooden box with a padded hole in the top and some burning coals, herbs and incense underneath your 'area'. But either way, it's not a very eventful process. Naked but for matching brown sarongs we sat there on our little boxes, strangers being steamed. Occasionally droplets would form and free themselves, at which point the coals would sizzle, releasing even more steam and causing us to squeal, but the novelty soon wore off and we were just a bit bored really.

It was a strange experience that felt a bit like I'd imagine crouching naked over a campfire might feel once the flames have died and everyone else has gone to bed, in that you're not really sure why you're doing it but it doesn't feel too bad, so you might as well carry on.

As we chatted and played with our phones and read magazines Hanna and I were allegedly getting purer, and purer, and purer by the second. When our time was up, we were instructed to climb into individual bathtubs filled with clumpy, boiled herbs and spices, poured in from giant cooking pots. These mixtures made the water turn the colour of fresh blood. Cheap curtains were drawn around the tubs and we were told to wash, which we thought was a bit weird because weren't we supposed to be cleansed 'down there' already?

As we dressed and prepared to leave, however, the lovely Balinese lady who'd set up the Lotus Treatments threw in a surprise bonus: 'You virgins again!'

What?

'You beautiful virgins!' she beamed.

The boiled clumps in the tub! They must have sealed us up again. Incredible. The promise of my restored virginity wasn't on the board outside in the description but I assume they've just left this off because they don't want everyone pouring in … you know … like what happened to Ketut after *Eat, Pray, Love.*

Hanna and I have promised not to tell anyone where this particular virginity-restoring spa is because we plan to enjoy being the purest girls in Ubud (for a while, at least).

Anyway, you do make friends in the strangest ways in this town, but needless to say Hanna and her yoni eggs are both extraordinary and she and I have already made plans to have another Lotus Treatment together soon, just in case our virtue gets lost again.

Oh, and if a bamboo-bong-creating drug lord tries to interrupt us next time I'll show him some new smoking tricks that'll have him crying all the way back to Kuta.

10/02

Sharks and other players in Candi Dasa …

Did you know that Indonesia has been the number one shark-fin exporter in the world since the 1970s, and that they're still slashing their fins off today?

No? I didn't know either until my diving instructor in Candi Dasa told me.

'Oh yes,' he said, looking out to sea from our table at the well-manicured, impeccably operated Candi Beach Cottages on the coast. 'During the "season", September to October, they still catch between sixty and eighty sharks every day around Indonesia's islands.' He pointed a finger in the direction of the hazy island in the distance where just a short time ago I stood watching the caring villagers releasing a flock of lucky, protected birds into the sky. 'And all around Nusa Penida over there is a prime fishing spot,' he said, sadly.

If only Bali starlings could talk, eh?

As Jen and I signed the papers for two dives off Bali's sleepy eastern coastal town of Candi Dasa yesterday, our Dutch dive instructor told us that finning, while outlawed in many countries, is still very much legal in Indonesia. He said that twenty years ago he couldn't do a night dive in Candi Dasa without seeing at least twenty sharks. Now, he says, he's lucky if he sees one.

In the early 1990s, demand for shark fins in Indonesia grew thanks to the countless luxury hotels and Chinese restaurants sprouting up in its major cities. These days it's still very much a lucrative trade for some Indonesian fisherman, who can make up to $100 for each fin. Shark fishing also occurs around Seraya Secrets, a diving hot-spot in Amed not too far from the USAT *Liberty* wreck where Jen and I explored not so long ago.

They don't keep the whole sharks when they catch them, either. These fishermen have small boats with no refrigeration facilities, plus, shark meat isn't worth anything anyway as it contains very high levels of mercury. Instead, the fisherman slash the fins off, store them on ice and chuck the sharks back into the sea, where they're left to die a slow, agonising death. Shark populations are dwindling to practically nothing around here because these unfortunate creatures can take more than seven years to mature and even then they can only raise one or two pups every year. They're being murdered before they've even had a chance to breed.

What makes all this even worse, perhaps, is that shark fin is basically tasteless. It's just used to bulk up soups, like an evil, gelatinous alternative to croutons. Pointless. Makes you want to watch *Jaws* again, doesn't it? Maybe there was a motive we missed somewhere? Maybe he'd just swum from Bali and was pissed off.

'But how can they get away with this?' we asked at our lunch table, as the waves crashed beneath us on the tiny beach. 'How can this still be happening when so much of Indonesia is being plugged as prime diving territory … and when so many tourists are coming here, just to dive the reefs?'

Our dive instructor told us that every now and then, to appease the protesters who might find out and try to make a fuss, and to show the media that they're doing something about the issue, the Indonesian government will take action and reprimand the fisherman. But the sick finning trade continues and no-one in charge cares enough, or has enough foresight to think too much about the consequences.

Jen and I were so sad listening to all this, we couldn't even bring ourselves to have the Island Debate when he wasn't listening. We almost didn't even want to dive. I can't believe The Diver never told me this in the Gilis, or that the guys in Amed never said anything. Is it possible that they don't even know? Have they been told not to say anything? I haven't seen anything at all about this issue on any of the dive shop websites. I emailed The Diver to ask. He said people know, it's not *exactly* a secret, but no-one really makes a fuss about it either.

When Susan and I wanted to come to Candi Dasa months ago, we were put off by the thought that it would be boring and full of old people and we went to Lovina instead. Candi Dasa is not full of old people, it's full of Germans, like Amed. But what Susan and I didn't know back then was that the reason there's nothing much for anyone to do is because it has been more or less destroyed by greed and environmental decline.

Candi Dasa used to have a beach that was bigger and even more beautiful than Sanur or Kuta (I mean how Kuta beach was before it became a rubbish dump). Several large, expensive hotels ruled the roost along Candi Dasa's beach, where the well-to-do came to relax, recline and be pampered. But, seeing the coral and lime as ideal construction materials for building even more touristy hotspots, the locals began blasting the reefs that protected their alluring beach.

With no natural protection or barriers offshore, the waves just carried on crashing towards the land. Beach erosion happened quickly and all the happy sunbathers in their lovely hotels soon had no sand left to sunbathe on. But wait. The Balinese had an idea. They would make a block themselves to stop the waves! They would fix the pesky problem they created by building a GIANT CONCRETE WALL all along the shore. Yes! Great idea. Because in the end, no-one really comes to a quiet piece of Balinese paradise to revel in the rolling blanket of blue, blue sea, do they? And if they do want to see the sea, well, they still can. They just have to look over the wall.

So, now, what do we have in Candi Dasa? Well, we have dead coral around the shoreline, a giant concrete wall blocking the Bali sunset and no natural beach. Oh, and no sharks to attract what could have been global interest from keen divers probably more than willing to pay $100 (the price of a fisherman's shark fin) for the chance to dive with up to twenty sharks at once. Error. Multiple errors.

Jen and I did our two dives around Candi Dasa's tiny islands of Gili Tepekong and Gili Mimpang. And while knowing a bit more about the horrifying effects of shark finning and what's been lost in quick pursuit of the tourist dollar put a dampener on things, there was one underwater surprise that brightened our time. As we swam around a coral wall and towards a mushroom-shaped rock, we noticed a lengthy sliver of silver grey moving at lightning speed, back and forth, back and forth in a hollow crevice beneath us. We stopped and waited for it to slow down.

There in the deep, as if King Triton himself had been listening and decided to grant a small oceanic miracle, was a shark — a one-and-a-half metre long white tip shark trying his best not to be noticed.

'It's a miracle!' our instructor cried, when we climbed back onto the dive boat. 'We hardly ever see sharks anymore, maybe he heard us talking?'

Maybe he did. But I think he probably also said a small sharky prayer as he saw us, in the hope that we wouldn't slice his fin off in the name of a chewy bowl of soup.

12/02

Not so spiritually minded ...

So I was really quite excited about my four-day 'Seven Levels of Consciousness' course with Galactica Blanco. I emailed to let her know my PayPal account was being stupid and please could I just pay in cash and she said that was fine, although worryingly, some three days before the event I'd still received no information about where exactly it was set to take place. I emailed to ask, after which she informed me she had just posted details on her website.

I looked and they were indeed there, right at the bottom. I'd never have seen them, but anyway, not to be deterred by lacklustre marketing or communication processes (there are more important things in the world you know, tut!), I withdrew the considerable amount of US$300 in high hopes of experiencing everything promised on her eye-bogglingly large-fonted musical website.

These things included 'working with meditations and exercises to experience cosmic, Nirvanic, astral, and spiritual levels of consciousness', as well as being 'guided through dimensional shifts to your highest vibrational energy, doing special crystal meditations, contacting the Akashic Records, working in conjunction with a transformational Spiritual Healer, Oriba (an Indonesian sacred movement system), Dance of the Soul, finding spirit guides from Seven Dimensions, astral travelling, chakra healing, group healings, sacred mantras, sacred mudras, sacred yantras and much more.'

How good does that sound? I mean ... what the 'much more' might entail I can only imagine ... maybe we'll fly over her rice field at the end of it all on a magical woven banana-leaf carpet, waving at Dewi Sri, who we'd now be able to see with our own eyes thanks to being shifted through those various celestial dimensions, vibrating with energy, clutching crystals in a splendiferous journey towards the soteriological goal of Nirvana ...?

I will never know. Because she cancelled it.

And she cancelled it the night before we were due to start.

I'm so disappointed. How will I reach the seven levels of consciousness now?

Apparently, the lady she was working with to host the course is feeling 'under the weather' and Galactica Blanco hadn't prepared enough material to do it on her own ... which is a real shame. I maintain that she could have just made us all lie down for an extra long amount of time with crystals on our bellies, chanting *om*. We wouldn't have known any better. Some people at the Yoga Barn make us lie down for so long that they might as well call it a sleepover. Sometimes, we might as well just be paying to lie on a wooden floor, in other people's sweat, with our eyes shut. Oh, but it's nice, though. No-one ever complains because as I've learned by being in Ubud, paying a lot to do not very much sometimes is all part of the healing or growth experience.

I'm quite sure Galactica Blanco could have just made us shake on the spot for three more hours each day and told us that this was the only way to reach our highest vibrational energy. We wouldn't have questioned that either. Well, it works for Ratu Bagus ...

I couldn't help but feel a bit annoyed that I'd received a cancellation the night before, especially because her cancellation email offered the chance to join a 'Shamanic Retreat' in a few weeks, or an upcoming channelling session without so much as a discount. Call me spoilt but I do believe there's such a thing as customer service no matter what dimension you're operating on.

Feeling a bit PMS-y, I'll admit, I sent Galactica Blanco an email to say I was disappointed. I probably wouldn't have done this had she not turned up thirty minutes late to my last one-on-one appointment at her house, leaving me standing outside in the frazzling sun before pulling up in her car. Perhaps making phone calls are too mundane a chore for a psychic mind.

Anyway, I got rather an angry email back (the longest one Galactica Blanco has ever sent me), telling me I should try to be more kind and respectful. Hmm. She also told me that the people who had paid their deposit had received details on where the course would be taking place ... so it was obviously just me who'd been left in the dark. This was in spite of her telling me that it was OK to pay the deposit and the full US$300 (donation) in cash on the day. It seems she forgot.

I'm not being funny but, for a psychic, forward planning should probably come a bit more naturally.

I think I'm mostly disappointed because Galactica Blanco did give me a few accurate predictions when I first went to see her back in September and I hate to think that they may have just been … gasp … *coincidences*. Galactica Blanco is always fully booked; she says herself how busy she is. She's the single most sought-after person at the annual Bali Spirit Festival and in spite of the odd mishap she's always been very nice in person. I still really like her. I have a suspicion she's just taken too much on and as a result is losing a bit of her charm. Must be hard work, reaching into people's psyche every day while still operating physically on this mundane plane; running a house and getting your kids to school and grocery shopping in Bali Buddha.

Anyway, maybe I shouldn't have been so quick to hand my money over to psychics. There are far more deserving causes in Bali. That money could sponsor a kid to go to school … which is exactly what I'm going to do with it. Hmph. I've been thinking about this more and more and more since Blandingan.

I guess I'll never get to learn how to astral travel, though. Good thing AirAsia's still cheap.

20/02

A Valentine farewell …

'Hey, are you coming to kirtan on Sunday at Yoga Barn? I have got to tell you about my upcoming two-day reiki course and noni-berry diet!'

— Me

I offered to help with the copy but somehow the invitation to our Valentine's Day children's charity event in Ubud still went out promising 'Blind children band. Deaf children dance.' Hmm.

Either way, you can't fault the good intention behind what was one of the best events I've been to in this town. It was a night of absolute loveliness even though I spent the majority of it on my motorbike zooming from the Lobong Cafe, where the disadvantaged kids were performing, to Bar Luna.

One minute I was taking money at the door as an inspirational group of deaf children danced a perfectly choreographed *Legong* dance in their fuchsia pink and yellow costumes. The next I was reciting Shakespeare and paying tribute to Whitney Houston with the gut-wrenching final scene from *The Bodyguard*. (Oh, this bit I played from YouTube, obviously. Even with the success of my recent 'head, shoulders, knees and toes' endeavour in Blandingan I would still never attempt *I Will Always Love You* in a crowded room.)

The 'How We Got Together' night went well. Romeo turned out to be my friend Trevor, who's a very dashing Englishman. Bob read a romantic scene from the novel *Shantaram* and then we got the audience involved by letting them read various dialogues from famous movies. The deli scene from *When Harry Met Sally* went down a treat, thanks to Paul and a nubile young yoga instructor he's been trying his luck with.

The bar was packed. We even had special aphrodisiac cocktails on the menu. When I first started coming to Bar Luna just six months ago it was a quiet backstreet spot that was relatively unheard of. These days you're lucky if you can get a seat.

Back at Lobong, we raised a lot of money for the kids (I'm told over 70 million rupiah in the end!). I did my little bit by helping to source prizes for the raffle, including a lovely stay on Gili

Trawangan with Sumeena and Sandesh at the Pesona Resort. I managed to avoid the dodgy drug lord on the dance floor (the one who interrupted our yoni egg chat) and everyone bopped away till midnight, which trust me is extremely late in these parts. When I got home, I had a nice chatty email waiting for me from 'American S' in Sydney, wishing me a happy Valentine's Day. Aww. Such a great night.

In the end, though, Bali is my Valentine. Cheesy, but true. It's nights like this, dancing ecstatically *and* like a fairy, sober on the dance floor with my fifty- and sixty-year-old expat friends that I realise how much love this little island has shown me over the last six months and how much love I'm probably projecting now as a result of being happy. It's a good feeling. And actually, being single on Valentine's Day didn't really cross my mind ... honest! I had too much else to organise for other people, too many friends to call, which is just the way it should be, I suppose. I'm *not* single, as some of my more esoterically aware acquaintances here would say. But I'm not half of anything. I'm whole.

I'm coming to the end of my time in Bali now. In fact, the other day I realised I accidentally overstayed my current visa by twenty-four days, which meant a nasty expense of 200,000 Rp per day in fines and almost $500 in total. Ugh. Don't ask me how I managed that. But still, this opportunity has been worth it.

I've decided to learn reiki before I go and finally try and harness some of this positive energy for good, like a last attempt at white magic perhaps (sshh). It kind of feels like I'm in a protective little bubble ... like Bali has cast such a spell on me that I'll fall apart the moment I try and leave its cushiony warmth. But I can't stay here forever. My fashion options have become limited to a crumpled heap of what smells mouldy and what doesn't in the bottom of my damp homestay wardrobe. I haven't seen my friends or family in ages. I now wash my hair out of necessity instead of for style. Maybe I just have to trust that Bali's made me better in other ways and that I'll be all right wherever I go next.

I thought maybe I'd be enlightened by now with my chakras all aligned, stick-thin and eating raw food, practising tantra with my *kundalini* busting out all over the place. I definitely thought Gaby would have smacked me for smelling of hemp. But the truth is that none of that stuff in its individual parts has really stuck. Those soul, and spirit-building endeavours have all been interesting in their own ways but they're all just pixels in a much bigger picture of Bali.

I'm calmer now, though. I can walk at a slower pace and not feel uneasy for having nowhere in particular to be. I think I listen more. I'm more open-minded. I'm not afraid to ride a motorbike, or backwards-roll into an ocean at night, or even dance ecstatically anymore without any wine inside me. I don't hear the sweeping as much. The roosters don't wake me up but I hear the birds when I stop what I'm doing and listen. I beep loudly at scary dogs and make them eat my dust. I can say the word *namasté* without frowning ... just. I can tolerate the Yobud Pros as they continue to reign supreme at headstands. But I still don't know why people would want to milk nuts.

So what do I *know* that I didn't know before? Well, I know how to speak Indonesian badly. I know how it feels to shake for two hours staring at a holy man's bottom. I know what a community can pull together in spite of an unlawfully corrupt government, but also what it can destroy. I know not to trust a psychic, but I believe in magic.

I know what it's like to get my colon sucked dry by a hose and my senses blurred by a man in a wetsuit. I know how to sing for Ganesh, how to chant to a pack of frozen peas, how to spot a wicked witch on an island of magic mushrooms and what a teenage boy looks like when he's possessed by a monkey. I know how children can still light up at the sight of a single smile, even when they're carrying bricks on their heads. And I know now that this mental ride we all climb aboard unprepared for is not just about a career, or finding a man to be our eternal Valentine. Western society may try to tell us that these are the important things in life, but I think I can vouch for the fact that they're not, even though we might look and act the fool at times in our ongoing quest to prove otherwise.

This mad ride is more about making *yourself* a better person so that you attract the right people into your life. Ultimately, you're a candle adjusting your flame so the right moths flutter into your light. It's about being good and thinking of others. It doesn't necessarily mean being a hippy or not wearing deodorant, or holding raw food parties and telling your guests they're nothing but illusions … although of course, those things might happen on the way if you're not careful. You're a firework waiting to make a crowd go 'ooooh', but before you can really jazz up the world you have to go back to the source. You have to find what inspires you to shine the brightest, so even more people can be warmed by your light.

I came here thinking mostly about CK, and how I needed *Someone Like Him*. Now we barely even speak. Inspiration has come in other forms, all of which have carried me away without him. Kisses will never be contracts, but if you can see the wrong guys as fun previews for a greater coming attraction, you'll keep your head screwed on and your heart will always be open. Plus, if you do things that scare you, or do things your ego tells you you can't, whatever happens, chances are you'll come out the other side being glad you gave it a shot. Feeling awesome, actually.

Sure, it's nice having someone at the end of the phone, someone to spoon at night, to hold your hand when you're exploring new realms underwater, or on land … (really nice, dammit, I still want those things!). But then … would I have had all of these adventures if any one person had wanted to stick to my side the whole time, like superglue? Of course not. I would have chucked it all in, in favour of what I *thought* I was missing. And then I would have missed out.

I'm grateful for the Process, for the shaking up that Bali in general has given me. I've learned that it's OK not to rush. Life and loves just happen as they're meant to. Sometimes I think the biggest rush can happen just by standing still.

I don't know if I've 'found myself'. I'd have snorted a Bintang back out through my nose at the mere suggestion of ever being 'one of those people' not so long ago. But perhaps somewhere along the line I found something *else* in myself without even really noticing. This something was there all along, huddled underneath my ego and my fear, asking politely to come out as I blathered on in a blur of Big City madness. I'll go back to those cities and do the same thing, probably, but I know I'll appreciate far more moments in my life going forward, and press the pause button a lot more.

I've found a new kind of freedom here, to empower and inspire. The expats and locals around me, the people doing amazing things for themselves and other people, like helping children and animals, fighting to save the reefs and the rare birds and the rice paddies; they have all embraced and run with this new, Bali-inspired motivation. And so have I.

We're putty in the hands of the Balinese with their ceremonies and rituals, unfailing belief in the gods and the spirits and nature. We hate that their land is being usurped and there's a long way to go when it comes to saving this island from the devastating effects of its growing tourism but still we want nothing more than to be here. In the moment.

In spite of the poverty they still endure, I guess we know that the Balinese are rich with what really matters; they have love and family, thriving traditions and hope, all the things that loads of us have either lost, or take for granted.

In Bali, it feels as though everyone's teaching someone something; sharing the love and magic, paying it forward however they can. Many people here do this selflessly, without even realising what they're doing. And it's because of *all* of them that I've discovered a difference in myself. A glimmer of a life you never even knew you could lead? That's enlightenment.

So yes. Bali is my Valentine. It's the cheesy Hallmark card on my mantelpiece with a musical chip that plays the *gamelan*. It's made me sweat, cry, laugh and fall head over heels (surprisingly, not through a gap in the pavement, thank God). But as for the future? For the first time in my life, I think I'm actually OK with having no plans.

Namasté.

How to help Bali...

There are so many worthwhile causes that need our support in Bali. If you're interested in finding out more about any of the organisations mentioned in this book, or making a donation, here's a good place to start:

1 Camera, 1000 Smiles
www.1camera1000smiles.com

Anak Alam (Nature's Children)
www.anakalam.org

Bali Animal Welfare Association (BAWA)
www.bawabali.com

Bumi Sehat Foundation International (Healthy Mother Earth Foundation)
www.bumisehatbali.org

EcoBali
www.eco-bali.com

Friends of the National Parks Foundation (FNPF)
www.fnpf.org

Gili Eco Trust
www.giliecotrust.com
www.facebook.com/Giliecotrust

Jodie O'Shea Orphanage
www.careforkidsbali.com

Mule Jewels
www.yinjewelryforthesoul.com
email askjo@yinjewelryforthesoul.com

Say NO to Plastic Organisation (SNTP) Bali Cantik Tanpa Plastik Campaign
www.facebook.com/groups/44297661289/

Villa Kitty
www.villakitty.com

References

Attman, Rebekah, 'Bringing Paradise to Earth: a dissection and reuniting of worlds through Balinese offerings — A case study', (university paper), Ubud, 1996.

Hobart, Angela, Ramseyer, Urs and Leemann, Albert, *The People's of Bali*, Wiley-Blackwell, 2001.

Powell, Hickman, *The Last Paradise: An American's Discovery of Bali in the 1920s*, Oxford University Press, New York, 1930.

Wheeler, Cat, *Bali Daze*, Tokay Press, Stockton, 2011.

Also by Becky Wicks ...

Another suitcase in another hall ...

It's almost 6 a.m. and I've been awake for hours. My mouth tastes weird thanks to a Caesar salad dinner and I think it might be a chewing gum day. There are too many things in my head right now — mostly mundane things, like making sure my council tax is definitely cancelled and wondering whether it's safe to pack the Marmite. I've heard funny things about Dubai customs. There are so many random objects you're not allowed to take in, and far too many rules to abide by once you actually make it through, by the sounds of it. I shook all my clothes for traces of marijuana before Mum got here, of course, but I can't help but wonder if I'm a liability.

Mum and Dad have kindly brought more bags to the flat so I can decide which one to take to Dubai. I've realised I've got way too many clothes. In spite of promising not to buy anything else since I landed the job, I bought a new dress from TopShop yesterday. But *awwww*. It's my new 'I'm off to glamorous Dubai so I really, really need a nice dress' dress. It's red.

I'm meeting Stacey at Heathrow once I'm all packed. Stacey and I have been hired by the same company to be 'deputy travel editors' at a publishing company. I met her for the first time the other day at a pub in Covent Garden, after another British employee already in Dubai, called Heidi, hooked us up on Facebook. We're very excited about our new titles in Dubai and both agree that had we decided to stay in London, neither of us would be 'deputy' anythings. Stacey's from Manchester and she's just finished university, but even though I'm a few years older and possibly, maybe, a rung or two further up the career ladder than her, she's skipped effortlessly to my level thanks to Dubai's unprecedented need for decent English writers. Either that or I'm just rubbish for my age and recent positioning in the realm of employment ... but you know what, at this point, I don't really care.

It's all happened so quickly. To think I met the head honcho of the publishing company just a month ago at the London Book Fair and now I'm sitting here surrounded by the remnants of my London life crammed into bin-bags. Stacey admitted the other day that she didn't even know the job she was applying for was based in Dubai at first. She was just so happy to have a 'deputy editor' interview that she didn't double-check the details when the call came through. She said she sat there before her potential employer, wondering why the strange blonde lady was talking so much about the Middle East!

Lucy'll wake up soon. I'll have to say goodbye to my flatmate of two years. I almost hope she doesn't wake up, you know — I think I might cry. I'm not very good with goodbyes. I do believe my lovely workmates were slightly miffed that the floodgates didn't open until my emotions had been inebriated with five shots of whisky last night. But on the whole I prefer to be happy about this decision. I like to stay strong. Because if I don't, I'll just think too much about what the hell I'm doing, moving to the Middle East.

Lucy reminded me the other day of how, about a year ago, she'd thought about applying for a job in Dubai and I'd scoffed at her; told her she'd be known as 'Letterbox' and would have to cover herself from head to toe in black if she did it. Clearly, I was a selfish moron who didn't want her to leave me, but she didn't go anyway. And now I'm going instead, whether I can fit my life into one of these bags or not.

13/06

Travelling at the speed of Dubai ...

The first thing I'll say is that the Internet here is *soooooo bloody slow*! It appears to be powered by plodding camels, even in the office. Some pages won't load and some flash a giant BLOCKED message across the screen, so huge and sudden that I can practically feel an authority figure smacking me about the eyeballs in disgust. I'm not trying to look at anything naughty. I'm actually trying to log in to the blog I've been diligently keeping for two years. I don't know if it's my company or the country that's rendering this impossible, but I'll be very unimpressed if my blogging days are over just as my life gets vaguely exciting.

Other than that, my first week in Dubai is actually going relatively smoothly, bar an hour-long journey to work every day, ninety per cent of which is spent twiddling our thumbs in a cab stuck in traffic, and ten per cent of which is spent explaining to the driver where exactly it is he needs to go, even though we don't quite know ourselves.

Stacey and I have discovered very quickly that the roads in Dubai change so frequently that many drivers have no idea whatsoever if the route they took yesterday will still be in existence the next day. Every trip is an adventure. There's no GPS. Google Earth reveals from above what looks a little like a children's sandcastle after it's been battered by a loon with a pile of metal rods. From the ground it's not much different.

It's hot outside, too. And by hot I mean the kind of hot you might experience if you installed your household oven in your wardrobe, turned the heat up to 300 degrees and sat with your face in the open door, wearing a balaclava while drinking soup. It's so humid that when Stacey and I step outside the office block, our glasses steam up instantly. We fumble about, praying we won't get hit by a car, begging for a breeze. And when a breeze does actually blow, it's like someone pointing a hairdryer at our faces.

We're told that this is something that'll get even worse, which is difficult to think about right now. Temperatures are set to soar into the high 40s and maybe even reach the 50s in July, August and September. I can't help but feel like a bit of a sucker, if I'm honest. Clearly, I was too busy buying hot red dresses and worrying about which yeasty extracts to pack to actually check the weather in Dubai from London, but it appears we've been shuttled in at the worst possible time. And there I was, dressing like a Londoner in my leggings and slouch boots, ready for a day at the office as the fashionable import from the East End's Mile End to the Middle East's middle of … well, a little hamlet called Karama. I've never sweated so much in my life.

Justifiably, people here seem to be afraid of going outside. We offered to attempt to walk to work on our first morning, which judging by the map should have taken roughly twenty minutes, but we were met with puzzled looks and a shaking of the head so severe I thought the lady downstairs at our hotel apartment block was going to have a seizure. 'You don't walk anywhere in Dubai' was her warning. It seems she was right. Instead, you shut yourself in an air-conditioned car and sit in traffic for what feels like all eternity before literally turning the corner and getting out again. Occasionally, says Heidi, you're stared at long and hard by the person in the car next to you, causing colossal paranoia and an urge to cry, until you realise it's because you're showing your knees under the dashboard.

The apartment in the hotel is nice — Stacey and I were given one each, but seeing as mine was three times the size of the flat I've just left behind with Lucy, we moved all our stuff into one so we wouldn't get lonely. I've really never been the type to get homesick, but having one relatively close friend means everything at a time like this. Saying goodbye to Lucy was tough, as predicted. I'm not even sure when I'll see her again, and even though she's only a few hours away by time zone and we can chat in real time with the aid of modern technology (if any of it ever starts to work properly), this place couldn't be more different. It doesn't seem all that modern, either. I was expecting something rather glamorous and special. What little I'd heard about Dubai from other people before I got here was all extravagant and glitzy, but then, we haven't been to many places yet. Perhaps Karama isn't the *real* Dubai.

Everyone's tanned here, though. Heidi met us at the hotel on our first day, when jetlagged and bleary we stood with our bags at our feet, looking out at the cab drivers inching in and out of the lanes outside trying desperately to move through stationary traffic. In the light of day, Heidi is the kind of russet brown, just verging on orange, that manages to look healthy in spite of a little voice in your head screaming *Premature Ageing and Wrinkles!!!* whenever you comment on the colour.

It was nice to meet Heidi after writing for weeks via Facebook. She lives in a mammoth villa in Satwa, which is an older area in the city, some of which actually has pavements for pedestrians and roads with less than six lanes. When we arrived at her place, the maid was leaving. Heidi proudly exhibited her washed, ironed and hung-up clothing collection and announced she hadn't done any of the above since she moved in. Stacey's jaw dropped only marginally faster than my own. I imagined my room at the flat I shared with Lucy, the mess spilling over the laundry bin to the point where it was so much a part of the furniture I didn't even notice it till I ran out of knickers.

Stacey and I have decided to embark on the flat hunt on our own, once our company-sponsored hotel stay has expired. The price of rent here is shocking, though. Probably more than sharing in central London. We're hoping to share a room for a while if we can, which will make things cheaper.

As I'm writing, someone's just told me that I might not blog again. Ever. I'm feeling a little sick at the thought. Apparently, along with porn and dating sites, anyone with an opinion that might not be appreciated in Dubai is banned from expressing it via TypePad and other popular blog hosts. Facebook is allowed, however, so for now I must turn to writing notes on my favourite blue-and-white buddy. I can tell you now, it's going to take some getting used to, travelling at the speed of Dubai.

17/06

Wanted: One Bacardi with Mexican hat

It's becoming glaringly apparent that Stacey and I have indeed landed ourselves in Dubai's black hole — the quiet, older part of town that's still semi-stuck in the nineteenth century. The glitzy, glamorous hotels and dazzling nightlife we read about before arriving lie slightly out of reach at the end of an enormous highway. Having thrown ourselves almost immediately into a routine involving our hotel apartment, an office and a deliriously heated walk home, we haven't seen much of it yet.

Tonight, I would have killed for a nice cold beer back at the hotel, but there isn't even a bar. You can't buy alcohol in Dubai unless it's in a licensed establishment, and there aren't really any hotels anywhere nearby that we've seen. The days of skipping over to the off-licence for a bargain bottle of cheap merlot, or a cool, inviting can of Stella are over. Stacey and I already both admit we took them for granted.

Sitting at our computers and emailing each other all day, which has quickly become as routine as complaining about the job we moved here to do (to be honest, it's dull, monotonous and disappointingly doesn't appear to involve any proper deputy-type tasks at all), Stacey and I started dreaming of the mini Bacardi I smuggled into the country in my make-up bag. It's been sitting on one windowsill or another in its little Mexican hat since 2004, and when it came to packing, I couldn't bear to part with it.

The time had come, I thought, to tuck in. We'd mix it with some orange juice and break the fast with a nice rummy nightcap. But — and you won't believe this — on getting back to our apartment, mini Bacardi was missing. He'd gone AWOL. I saw him this morning, I swear. I'd placed him lovingly by the telly opposite the beds, next to a disgusting German aniseed concoction Lucy once brought me back from Hamburg. But when I reached for him, he'd gone.

The maid must have nicked him. It's the only explanation. She obviously left the German crap behind because she thought it was some sort of evil medicine, but my beautiful Bacardi baby … she swiped it for herself, to drink, no doubt, in a darkened doorway, or to exchange for a few thousand dirhams in a land where my blessed Mexican rum child is as precious as a newborn baby on the black market. I'm gutted!

At least he's gone to a good home, I suppose. At least he's been enjoyed and appreciated instead of glugged in a last-minute attempt at prolonging a night of inebriated joy. Stacey and I face another night sober, but I suppose I shouldn't be too annoyed, really. She could have taken my laptop.

22/06

Where everybody knows your name …

Last night, Stacey and I cabbed it to a far more salubrious part of town, right near the Dubai Marina. It's currently a bit of a crane-filled construction site that happens to overlook a pool of water; a rich man's yacht-filled extension of the sea surrounded by apartment blocks. According to our guidebooks, behind a beachfront hotel called Le Méridien Mina Seyahi, hid a cocktail-lovers' paradise. We clambered out of the cab in awe of the glistening fairy lights and tottered down the sparkly path towards what was essentially a welcoming Garden of Eden to two Brits in dire need of some sweet intoxication.

The Barasti bar occupies the space between the hotel and the beach. It sprawls around swimming pools, palm trees, the sandy shore and a host of beds on well-tended grasslands that you're free to lounge upon at your leisure. In the cooler winter months it's heaving, apparently, although last night we couldn't even stand outside without dripping into a Dove-deodorised pool of our own bodily fluids.

En route to the loo, we kept passing two businessmen who were (quite stupidly) sitting outside at the bar, and with every little trip these guys looked wetter and wetter and wetter. By the end of the night, not only were they slumped in a drunken heap across the bar, one of them was sweating so profusely he looked as though he'd just taken a running jump into the nearby swimming pool. Like a couple of Homer's slurring friends from *The Simpsons*, they were getting more and more leery with every journey, and consequently less and less attractive, if that was even possible.

We met M&M* inside the bar. He's a great guy with a big smile. A friend of a colleague of mine in London introduced him to me. M&M in turn introduced us to his equally lovely work colleagues, buying us a couple of Coronas each in quick succession as we all chatted underneath the fans. Trying to ignore the beads of sweat sliding down my back beneath my new red TopShop dress, I did my best to focus on the novelty of being bought drinks without having to hint, or buy any first. This kind of thing never happens in London; certainly not in my social circles, at least! To get a drink from a male you barely know, he's either drunk, or it's happy hour and your nasty beer only cost him a quid.

There was no happy hour in Barasti last night. I instantly warmed to this man of apparent power and generosity; so different to me yet clearly thriving in a world I know absolutely nothing about. He chatted with ease and regaled us with tales of his working week that made us laugh out loud (he's funny too!). In turn, Stacey and I told the group about our experiences

---

* *Looking back, this was my very first encounter with M&M, whom you'll definitely hear more about later. I changed his name. You'll know why soon enough (sigh).*

in Dubai so far. 'You haven't seen anything yet,' was the general consensus.

I must mention that last night we also had our first encounter with a bunch of Dubai dickheads — a group of male expats who can't hold a conversation without interspersing it with how much money they're making. To top off their charms, they purchased two very expensive bottles of wine 'to share in their rooftop hot tub' and took great offence when Stacey and I refused to leave with them and enjoy it. In fact, the way they exited the bar can be described in no other way than in an 'angry strop'.

M&M seemed amused. I thought again what a gentleman he was as he saw us into a cab and promised we'd hang out again soon. I hope he means it. Thank Christ there are decent guys here, too. If we hadn't met M&M in Barasti, I would have been left with a totally different impression of the local talent.

As it was, it was an awesome night! And as we got our first glimpse of the mighty Burj Al Arab in its nightly display of changing colours, I suddenly felt excited to be in Dubai. It's been a long time coming but I actually do feel as though I'm going to love this place now!

Coming in 2013, olé!

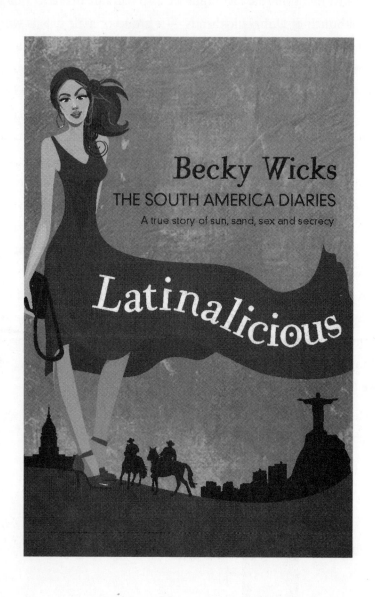